Politics Without Politicians

THESIS

Politics Without Politicians

THE CASE FOR CITIZEN RULE

Hélène Landemore

T

THESIS

Thesis
An imprint of Penguin Random House LLC
1745 Broadway, New York, NY 10019
penguinrandomhouse.com

Most Thesis books are available at a discount when purchased in quantity for sales promotions or corporate use. Special editions, which include personalized covers, excerpts, and corporate imprints, can be created when purchased in large quantities. For more information, please call (212) 572-2232 or e-mail specialmarkets@penguinrandomhouse.com. Your local bookstore can also assist with discounted bulk purchases using the Penguin Random House corporate Business-to-Business program. For assistance in locating a participating retailer, e-mail B2B@penguinrandomhouse.com.

Book design by Alissa Rose Theodor

LIBRARY OF CONGRESS CONTROL NUMBER: 2025036452

ISBN 9780593713983 (hardcover)
ISBN 9780593713990 (ebook)

Printed in the United States of America
1st Printing

The authorized representative in the EU for product safety and compliance is Penguin Random House Ireland, Morrison Chambers, 32 Nassau Street, Dublin D02 YH68, Ireland, https://eu-contact.penguin.ie.

To my younger self, and all the other
shy people out there

Contents

Politics Without Politicians

ONE

Fixing a Broken System

I've got both good and bad news. The bad news: Electoral politics is beyond repair. The good news: Democracy isn't. We can fix it.

The rest of this book is about the good news. But to get there, we first need to start with the failure of electoral politics. Believe me, it gives me no pleasure to see myself converging on a conclusion associated with the populists of the left and the right. Yet the populists have a point: A system based on electoral representation is no longer—if it ever was—capable of delivering either democratic or good governance.

Consider that the United States Congress currently holds a 15 percent approval rating and has consistently hovered well below 50 percent, on average, for decades. Is it because voters can never be satisfied or because Congress consistently does a subpar job?[1]

Consider that in three of the world's so-called most advanced democracies—the United States, the United Kingdom, and France—over two thirds of the population think their governing elites are corrupt. (In my native country of France, this figure reached 74 percent in 2025!) In both the United States and France, large majorities think their political system needs drastic changes.[2] Sixty-three percent of Americans express little confidence in the future of the US political system,[3] and 56 percent of the French want a Sixth Republic.

Consider that in recent high-stakes elections, the 2016 Brexit vote in the UK and the 2016 and 2024 presidential elections in the United States, voters seem to be rejecting the status quo as much as choosing outcomes.

Consider that when the media cover politics they talk only about the horse race, the scandals, the strategizing, the posturing, and rarely—at best superficially—the substance of issues. Consider that when political scientists crunch the numbers, they find that the preferences of rich people shape policy outcomes and law substantially more than those of the majority do.[4]

We could blame these problems on external factors and forces, such as globalization, capitalism, and the fast-paced changes brought by new technologies, foreign threats, or immigration—all of which undeniably make the job of governing at the scale of a nation-state quite difficult. And politicians are naturally the first to place the blame for their failed policies and the persistent "crisis of democracy" on these external factors.

But excuses can go only so far. Chronic underperformance and widespread dissatisfaction with the system—along with a growing retreat from it—should make one thing clear: There's a fundamental problem with the system itself. While electoral representation may have made sense two centuries ago, in a vastly different context and for very different populations, it's no longer up to the task, especially in modern societies of educated citizens with access to information.

I've reached this conclusion after a decade or more of resisting it. Like many people, I initially blamed empirical, external factors for the increasingly glaring inefficiencies and injustices of the system. My thinking was remedial: How can we improve the system without fundamentally changing it? For example, what if we got rid of money in politics or at least engaged in campaign finance reforms that leveled the playing field? What if we reached out more aggressively to minorities, women, and those on low incomes so they are given greater opportunities to run for elections, in the hope that we then have a greater diversity of profiles in government? What if we introduced strict term limits to prevent power entrenchment and expand further the pool of decision-makers? Or what if we did more to educate voters? For if they were better informed, they would care more, and democracy would yield better and more legitimate results. Surely, my thinking was, we have the politicians we deserve. The problem must be us, not them.

But this line of thinking, as it turns out, is flawed. Worse, it shifts the blame onto the victims—the ordinary citizens, especially those who've given up on a failing system. The next step down that slippery slope is often something like this: How about, as the political philosopher Jason Brennan suggests, we disenfranchise those who can't be bothered to learn the basics of politics, or "correct" their votes to better align with the preferences of the educated? What's so wrong with disenfranchising, say, 5 percent of the population, i.e., those who can't pass a basic civics test? Or how about "10 percent less democracy" and that much more of a role for experts, as the economist Garett Jones has recently argued?[5] From these "solutions," it's a short hop and a skip to dictatorship of the (supposedly) knowledgeable.

A question arises: Why do most of us continue to adhere blindly to democracy as we know it and struggle to envision alternatives? The answer is quite simple. It's inherently challenging to imagine a future that diverges from our current reality and to move from what *is* to what *should be*. In my experience teaching political philosophy to undergraduates, I've observed that many struggle with the distinction between descriptive statements (what is) and normative statements (what ought to be). People often assume the future both will and should resemble the past, partly because the present is heavily influenced by it. Yet, as the philosopher David Hume famously argued, moral conclusions cannot be derived from purely factual statements or observations. In other words, you cannot derive an "ought" from an "is."

Additionally, the people currently in power are seemingly incapable of seeing the problems and the need for reform in a system that has worked so well for them. Not unlike many among the "boomer generation," who blame their kids and grandkids for failing to have a stable job, a house, and a couple of kids by age thirty, as they themselves so successfully did, our current elites (also mostly boomers) do not for a minute suspect that they might be part of the problem. And so, when people complain, they try to shame the rest of us into thinking that it's our fault because we don't vote often or well enough. Meanwhile, young people have figured it out. They no longer expect much from periodic elections and party competition. For them, life-changing politics—of climate, social justice, and other topics of urgent importance—happens elsewhere. Unfortunately, they are largely right, and this book is mostly for them.

If you picked up this book, young or not, chances are you already agree—at least in part—with its diagnosis. But the title might have you scratching your head. *Politics without politicians?* What does that even mean? Sure, politicians are often bad—but aren't they a necessary evil? Politics is a job, after all. In large, complex industrial societies, surely we need professionals to run the show? If not politicians, then who? And isn't politics itself what creates politicians? Even if we got rid of all the shady characters we grudgingly vote for every few years, wouldn't their replacements—whether ordinary citizens or experts—inevitably become politicians too? You can remove politicians from politics, but politics, by its nature, seems destined to turn anyone with power into a politician.

And anyway, what do we even mean by "politician"?

I try to answer these questions and more in this book. But the gist of it can be summarized by a famous quip by the American conservative author and journalist William F. Buckley Jr. In a 1961 *Esquire* magazine interview, Buckley said: "I would rather be governed by the first 2,000 people in the telephone directory than by the Harvard University faculty."

On the surface, this quote seems like a lighthearted jab at Harvard elites—an easy target, especially coming from someone who went to Yale. Most people read Buckley's remark ironically: Surely, the idea of preferring governance by a random group of citizens over Harvard's faculty is too absurd to be taken seriously. But there's another way to interpret it—a literal one—and I suspect that's what Buckley truly meant. A large, random sample of the population might not be such a bad mix of people. In fact, it could be both more democratic and more effective to be governed by them than by a group of Harvard academics.

If the first two thousand names in the phone book are a better choice than Harvard's faculty, then why wouldn't they also be a better bet than the few hundred elected officials who actually govern us? Especially when so many of those officials come from Ivy League schools themselves. Today, there are compelling historical and social scientific arguments to support this provocative, seemingly counterintuitive claim. My first book, *Democratic Reason*, explored many of these arguments, and I'll revisit them later in this book. At their core, they relate to the collective wisdom of ordinary people and the unique way a true, deliberative democracy can harness and channel that wisdom.

Bringing the Shy People Out

Another crucial element of my answer, however, is something I have come to appreciate only recently, and which I elaborate for the first time in this book: the importance of designing institutions from the perspective of and for the people least likely to seek or want power—those I will call, for lack of a better term, "the shy." I was inspired by a striking quote from the early-twentieth-century British essayist G. K. Chesterton, a figure with both conservative and radical leanings, who, though not otherwise a major influence on this book, offers this brilliant definition of democracy: "All real democracy is an attempt (like that of a jolly hostess) to bring the shy people out."[6] I first encountered this quote in Maurice Pope's posthumously published *The Keys to Democracy*, a visionary work defending lot-based democracy in the 1980s, when few believed such an idea was practicable. Given my small role in helping Pope find readers for his book,[7] I take the liberty of lifting this incredible quote, hoping to do more with it than he had the chance to.

It is a strange and unusual definition. It's also an "ought" type of definition, of course, not an empirically accurate or descriptive one. It says something about the nature or essence of democracy as a normative ideal, which reality typically fails to measure up to. According to it, democracy is not primarily about counting votes, elite competition, choosing one's rulers every few years, or "kicking out the rascals." It is about creating the conditions under which all of us, even the shy, feel comfortable enough to speak up and participate in public life.

The content of Chesterton's parenthesis in the above quote—"like that of a jolly hostess"—is also important. There is certainly something dated about the term "jolly hostess." The noun refers to a role that women at the time of Chesterton's writings did not necessarily choose, and the adjective comes across as somewhat paternalistic, if not downright sexist. But there is also something powerful and even feminist that we can reclaim for modern times in the idea of an inviting, joyful female figure who seeks to make everyone feel included and good about themselves as a metaphor for democracy.

This quote also suggests that if the test of a real democracy is whether it can make room for and listen to its shiest people, we should therefore conceive of it not merely as a set of impersonal rules, procedures, and institutions. Instead, we should envision democracy as a certain way of being and of treating people. Chesterton, for his part, suggests that democracy ought to emulate a party hostess who at least *attempts* to make all feel welcome and valued. For him, a real democratic system encourages and prods the people who least want power and lack the self-confidence to speak up to find their inner voice and make it heard. How about that for a radical vision of politics?

Contrast this with the definitions of democracy we are more familiar with. They are often exalted and vague on the specifics, such as "rule of, for, and by the people." Or they are utterly uninspiring and even downright cynical, like this one, supposedly from Churchill, that declares democracy "the worst form of government except for all the others."

Occasionally, definitions of democracy are both specific *and* uninspiring, like the one I was first exposed to as a graduate student and which, I came to realize, still completely dominates political scientists' understanding of democracy. Democracy, in that view, is simply a method, specifically "that institutional arrangement for arriving at political decisions in which individuals acquire the power to decide by means of a competitive struggle for the people's vote."

This definition was formulated by an Austrian economist named Joseph Schumpeter, who was no friend of democracy. It is minimalist and premised on the worst-possible assumptions about citizen competence and agency. Yet somehow it is now the official definition used by influential think tanks like Freedom House, not just to define democracy but also to measure it around the world. Freedom House thus defines democracy as a political system "whose leaders are elected in competitive multi-party and multi-candidate processes in which opposition parties have a legitimate chance of attaining . . . or participating in power."

What is striking about both the original Schumpeterian definition and the derivative version by Freedom House is its exclusive focus on elites competing for power and on the role of leaders, parties, and electoral candidates. Ordinary citizens—those who actually do the electing and for whom the whole system is supposed to be functioning—are nowhere to be found. Such an oversight is a good illustration of the problems with existing representative systems. Ordinary citizens are peripheral to them, convened now and again for the purpose of selecting representatives but kept at bay most of the time. When they are consulted on the substance of issues, in the occasional referendum, it is to express a simple yes or no, not the nuanced and rich opinions they often hold.

Another issue with this common definition of democracy is its narrow focus on vote counting and majority rule. In this view, the winning party gains the right to implement policies simply because it received more votes than the losing minority. While counting votes and majority rule are undeniably important—essential, even—they are not the whole story. Democracy can and should deploy mechanisms that make minorities feel valued and heard, not just outvoted. The problem with focusing purely on voting and competition, as seen in Schumpeterian models of democracy, is that it overlooks the importance of deliberation and listening—that is, the giving and receiving of reasons for the policies and laws that are ultimately imposed on all. This perspective reduces democracy to a numbers game, ignoring the potential for a more constructive process where diverse voices contribute to shaping decisions.

In this book, I pursue an "ought" definition and vision of politics, one that is constrained but not determined by what is. It consists, first, in imagining politics without professional politicians—that is, people for whom politics is a job—and envisioning instead a system run by ordinary citizens, who exercise politics as both a right and a duty. It consists, second, of a vision of politics centering deliberative processes—ordinary people talking to one another with the goal of coming to a joint decision that works for most, rather than elites and interest groups bargaining with one another, or just aggregative procedures tallying up votes. It consists, third, in paying particular attention to the perspectives of what Chesterton called "the shy." Chesterton probably had in mind the natural introverts. As I use the term in this book, however, "the shy" refers more broadly to the many among us who are shy not so much by virtue of a natural predisposition as by structural forces that create in them a sense of inadequacy, inferiority, or lack of worth. Class,

gender, race, age, and sexual orientation are among the many possible sources of this constructed shyness, which prevents many people from speaking for themselves and sometimes causes them to
retreat from politics altogether.

And it is a fact that the shy are not well represented in electoral
politics. Elections thrive on the ability of individuals to stand out
and compete. They oversample and empower the extroverted, the
confident, and the downright arrogant and entitled. They turn off
the self-effacing and easily intimidated, as well as those who de-
spise aggressive tactics and self-promotion.

You might rightly ask: Why is that a problem? Maybe politicians bring qualities to the table that more than make up for
their flaws. Perhaps the people who are missing are absent for a
reason—maybe they have nothing to say or contribute. On the flip
side, what's the real benefit of "bringing the shy people out"? Might
there be a good reason why talented orators and speakers should
take, and hog, the floor in politics?

It's natural to hold tight to what's familiar, but this book aims
to loosen your grip. It proposes a different vision of politics, one in
which confidence is not the responsibility of those who want to
participate but that of the system itself, which seeks to make everyone comfortable enough that they want and are able to participate.

An Alternative System

Let me first paint with a broad brush a picture of the alternative
system I have in mind. Imagine hundreds of everyday people from
all around the country, from every age and walk of life, all selected

by a national lottery. They come together for extended periods of time in a parliament-like institution to deliberate and decide ways to address the housing crisis or the opioid crisis, or how to do something about gun regulation. They are paid for their time and all their expenses are covered. Their deliberations are enriched by input from the larger population and by the support of experts and civil servants. Their recommendations either feed into the legislative process, are sent to a referendum, or become law. When they are done after a few months, they go home and return to their regular lives, though many may now be friends and keep in touch. As generations of people rotate in and out of this parliament, and its equivalents at the local level, the quality of laws and policies improves all around.

In previous works, I called the core elements of this vision "open democracy," emphasizing that it is a system in which power is accessible to all. Here, I call it "politics without politicians," partly as a provocation, and partly because it more clearly suggests making room for regular people.

Regular people, ordinary citizens, or everyday people—whatever we want to call them—are different from politicians in that, for them, politics is not a career or a business or even a vocation. In my vision of politics without politicians, politics is neither a job nor a chore. It is instead a civic duty and an occasional, albeit momentous, responsibility.

We will see in later chapters what politics with ordinary citizens and without politicians could mean in terms of preferred institutional design. As a preview, my own vision (which is by no means the only possible one) centers on deliberative assemblies of citizens appointed through civic lotteries—large juries, if you will—

and combines those with regular moments of mass voting on salient issues or issues put to a referendum by citizens' initiatives, as
well as other forms of direct participatory mechanisms building
on local practices and customs. Please keep in mind that this vision is not complete. It's not extremely detailed. It's not going to
answer all your questions. But it's a vision that can hopefully guide
a different kind of politics, whether we take it in a more radical
direction or a more reformist one.

Some of you may balk at some of these ideas, in particular the
idea of replacing elected politicians with citizens chosen by lot.
Such an alternative goes by several other names—random selection, sortition, lottocracy, minipublics, or citizens' assemblies—yet
the underlying ideal is the same. Support for it is no longer fringe.
In France, where only 44 percent of the population still supports
democracy in its current electoral form, 37 percent would rather
move to a system based on lottery and mass referenda.[8] There is
also a long and growing list of established academics and prominent activists who are pushing a sortitionist agenda and who will
make appearances in this book.

The idea of a citizen parliament has, for example, been endorsed publicly by Kofi Annan, Nobel Peace Prize laureate and
former secretary-general of the United Nations. Reflecting on the
crisis of democracy on the occasion of the 2017 Athens Democracy
Forum, Annan said:

> We need to make our democracies more inclusive . . . to
> bring in the young, the poor and minorities. An interesting
> idea . . . would be to reintroduce the ancient Greek prac-
> tice of selecting parliaments by lot instead of election. In
> other words, parliamentarians would no longer be nomi-

nated by political parties, but chosen at random for a limited term, in the way many jury systems work. This would prevent the formation of self-serving and self-perpetuating political classes disconnected from their electorates.[9]

Annan was building on ideas from my fellow sortitionist David Van Reybrouck, author of the international bestseller *Against Elections*. Despite its provocative title, Van Reybrouck's book does not explicitly call for replacing parliaments with citizen juries. Annan leaned into the more radical interpretation of his work, but the more realistic and likely approach—a hybrid democracy that blends bodies selected by lot with existing elected assemblies—would still be transformative. Such a system could bring significant change if it shifted enough power from politicians to citizens' assemblies, giving ordinary people a real voice in decision-making.

Whether you believe in it or not, a new form of democracy based on random selection is already emerging, albeit in limited form. Around the world, efforts are underway to enhance political systems with democratic innovations, including jury-like bodies often referred to as "minipublics." These minipublics are experiencing a revival not seen since ancient Athens. In this book, I'll share examples of minipublics I've studied—one of which I've even co-governed. But these are just the beginning. A report by the Organization for Economic Cooperation and Development (OECD), subtitled "Catching the Deliberative Wave," documented 733 such minipublics (as of 2023) across thirty-four countries,[10] including Canada, Ireland, France, Japan, Korea, and Australia, as well as Argentina, Brazil, China, and Mongolia. Expanding the scope to non-government-sponsored projects—such as most deliberative polls conducted by Stanford University's Deliberative Democracy Lab—brings the total to over fifty countries, with examples in Uganda, Kenya, India, Morocco, Egypt, and Saudi Arabia.[11]

Over the last thirty years, minipublics have proven adaptable across cultures and contexts, even in deeply divided societies. These randomly selected bodies are used to generate ideas, policy recommendations, and, in some cases, legislative proposals. They consistently demonstrate that, under the right conditions, ordinary citizens are capable of informed deliberation, reasoned judgment, and even competent lawmaking. In fact, evidence shows they perform as well as, or better than, professional politicians in many respects.

Minipublics also tend to produce trans-partisan recommendations, reflecting the dominant ideological leanings of their populations while remaining inclusive of minority views and responsive to their concerns. They have shown a capacity for bold, innovative solutions—whether tackling moral issues, like abortion or assisted dying; technical ones, like electoral reform; or systemic and multidimensional problems, like climate justice. These assemblies prove that ordinary citizens, when empowered and equipped, can rise to the demands of governance in ways that both complement and challenge traditional political institutions.

After decades of global experimentation, some cities and states are now institutionalizing citizen-led decision-making. In 2019, Belgium's German-speaking region became the first to establish a permanent citizen jury—twenty-four randomly selected citizens tasked with setting the local parliament's agenda and convening fifty-person citizen assemblies to propose policies.[12] In November 2022, Brussels announced the creation of a permanent citizens' assembly on climate, with one hundred randomly selected citizens meant to rotate in and out of it for the indefinite future to help figure out the path to climate justice.[13] In November 2023, Paris created its own permanent, all-purpose, one-hundred-person-strong assembly of randomly selected Parisians. In 2024, the second co-hort of this assembly produced its first citizen-written bill, con-taining twenty measures on homelessness, in collaboration with the city council.[14] The question is no longer *if* other cities, states, and international bodies will follow, but *when*. Even UN officials are now contemplating a permanent global citizens' assembly to com-plement their governance processes.

Meanwhile, various nongovernmental actors and organizations are also looking into this way of including citizens' voices in impor-tant decision processes. In fall 2022, after some initial trial phases at the national level, Meta gathered six thousand randomly selected people from its global user base to deliberate, broken up into smaller groups, on how to regulate cyberbullying in the Metaverse. They followed up in 2023 and 2024 with similar, albeit smaller-scale processes on generative AI. Although the impact of these ef-forts on Meta's internal decision process is largely unknown, they arguably created a precedent for a different way of including the company's stakeholders. In a more modest vein but with the ambi-tious goal of reforming corporate governance, in 2023, an invest-ment fund in the Netherlands piloted a deliberative assembly of fifty randomly selected investors—a process it called a "member dialogue"—to help determine its investment strategy going for-ward.[15] Similarly, Norwegian NGOs recently piloted a citizens' assembly to give ordinary citizens a say over the way Norway's $1.8 trillion wealth fund should invest its money going forward. This assembly presented its recommendations to the Norwegian parliament in May 2025.[16] In both public and private sectors, at both collective and individual levels, the old logic of closed, elite decision-making seems to be giving way—if only for PR purposes in some cases—to a more inclusive approach that invites ordinary people into the conversation. As I write, the analyses of these experiments are just beginning to emerge.

Confessions of a Shy "Aristocrat"

At this point, you might be intrigued, if not quite convinced. I hope the next chapters will bring you fully on board. But before I dive deeper into arguments and examples, let me say a few words about where I'm speaking from. I grew up thinking an author should be self-effacing. But I've come to appreciate that every point of view comes from somewhere, and I owe it to my reader to share a bit about how my life experiences have shaped my current convictions. Also, it is hard not to anticipate the perfectly legitimate question on some readers' minds: What does a white professor of European descent teaching at an American Ivy League institution have to contribute to debates about democracy in the twenty-first century?

In my world, there is a long-running joke that academics write about the opposite of what they fundamentally are. From that perspective, given that my career has consisted of writing about democracy, I should be an aristocrat. And that rings partly true. After all, I teach at Yale University and live a comfortable, privileged life. I like nice things. Plus, I sing opera (not very well).

I'm not an actual aristocrat, of course. My father taught biology at the University of Caen, in Normandy, and my mother was a preschool teacher. Both my parents came from families of peasants, and I spent part of my youth on their small farms. My parents gave my siblings and me a solidly middle-class childhood and instilled in us the knowledge that money does not grow on trees.

But despite this relatively ordinary background, I cannot say I ever imbibed democratic beliefs from my upbringing or school education. I was brought up instead to respect and be extremely deferential to all forms of authority—from my parents and grandparents to my teachers and doctors to essentially anyone else with status when I had none. Politicians like François Mitterrand and then Jacques Chirac, who governed France for much of my youth, modeled a form of republican paternalism that seemed inescapable. As a girl, I modeled my external behavior after that of my mom and many of the other French women around me: self-effacing and constantly seeking to please. I was also reserved and self-conscious, a fair-skinned, bespectacled child prone to turning tomato red when put in the spotlight.

At age twelve, however, I suddenly became popular and was elected class delegate. In this new role, I experienced the corrupting effect of power on myself and others, specifically when it is acquired through what is essentially a likability contest. I lost friends, gained a bunch of fake ones, was suspected of dating the other class delegate (which ruined my friendship with him too), became a little arrogant and condescending in the process, and got co-opted by the teachers and some parents. It was awful. And a good lesson.

At eighteen, because I was a good student, I got to escape to Paris, where I entered the cliquish and elitist world of *classes préparatoires* at Henry IV, then one of the top two schools preparing students to enter the even more rarefied world of *grandes écoles*, specialized "elite" colleges in France akin to the American Ivy League. Even though I had no idea what that meant at the time, I was determined to go there. After two grueling years—of constant academic humiliation but also great learning and self-discovery—I took the national exam and, to my ecstasy, was admitted to the École Normale Supérieure ("Superior Normal School").

As the name suggests, and despite the confusing reference to "normality," this school is not for ordinary people, but for "superior" ones. And it was there, for the first time, that I started to think of myself as belonging to some kind of elite group meant to occupy the top positions in the country. Everybody treated me that way—well, except for my parents, who, to their credit, rightly thought this was going to my head. Professors addressed us as future leaders, while at the same time confusingly made us feel inadequate in plenty of ways. And philosophy, the discipline I chose to study at the École Normale, was telling me, via Plato, that the republic needed to be put in the hands of philosopher-kings. This might seem incredible, but I actually believed that to be the right view, at the time.

I continued on to Sciences Po, where future *énarques* (top civil servants who run the French state) are trained. There, I witnessed entitlement and bratty behavior on a scale I had never seen before. It made me uncomfortable, and I ended up making almost no friends. But I probably came across as just as aloof and entitled. Students from the École Normale Supérieure mostly kept to themselves, and while I like to think I was a bit more open-minded than my peers, I had absorbed both the Parisian hauteur and the *grandes écoles*' air of superiority.

But then things came crashing down. For one, the arrogance that is nurtured by this kind of educational system always comes with great ego fragility and is in itself an obstacle to actual learning. Though I was good at pretending, like everyone else, most of the time I felt like a fraud. I would never admit I did not know something; I would never ask a genuine question in seminars or lectures. When my ignorance was inadvertently revealed, the resulting judging look or comment burned my cheeks red. The norm among *normaliens* was to act as if one were infallible.

Perhaps partly as a result, at twenty-five I failed the philosophy *aggregation*, an exam that is supposed to anoint the top teachers of the republic but mostly opens the academic path to research, which was what I wanted to pursue as the most prestigious option. I failed that exam not once, not twice—which is not uncommon— but three times. The third time, the humiliation was too much. It nearly broke me. I had to decide: Was the problem me, or the system? I decided to leave France and go and prove myself in a completely different environment.

That new environment was Harvard—another elite school. I went for what was supposed to be just a one-year exchange program, but I did everything I could to stay. I managed to do so, in part, on the strength of my then just-published book on the concept of probability in David Hume's moral philosophy. (I may have failed that damn exam, but I *was* a good researcher.) The American experience, however, ended up changing my life completely and is really what put me on the path to becoming an actual democrat.

Harvard University was not, to say the least, a place where much faith was placed in ordinary folks or even democracy as a political system. At the time, in the early 2000s, it was still the cradle of liberals in politics (including those who sided with the conservatives to take us on the disastrous path to the Iraq War) and neoliberals in economics ("globalization lifts all boats" and "there is no alternative," as I idiotically repeated to my skeptical Communist uncle and aunt back in Normandy). It was a place where experts were revered and ordinary people distrusted. Joseph Schumpeter's view of democracy as a competition between elites for popular votes, for example, dominated the government department. Drawn as I was to the literature on collective intelligence in psychology, and deliberative and participatory democracy in political theory, I found myself intellectually quite alone there—except for the wonderful Jane Mansbridge, who was teaching over at the Kennedy School of Government.

However, there was something different about Harvard compared to the elite French schools I came from. The seminar model was welcoming of all views and levels of competency, without judgment. Professors did not lecture from on high, modeling omniscient authority; they practiced the Socratic method of teasing answers out of us. Students listened to one another with respect and disagreed with passion, never contempt. When they did not understand something, they asked, and—*gasp*—no one judged them for it. It took me a long time to stop blushing in embarrassment for students who revealed their ignorance, though. As a student who had never spoken, or really thought, in class before, I blossomed. I also learned to tame my own strongly judgmental French instincts (not completely successfully, though, as my husband can assure you).

Additionally, life on campus taught me another lesson. For all the differences between people, there was a norm of equal respect toward others—regardless of origin, wealth, gender, race, etc.—which, however frequently violated in practice, was nonetheless very much assumed to be right. It is the same norm that struck

Alexis de Tocqueville, another, more famous Norman visitor to America, when he spoke of the "equality of conditions" in the United States.

Only on that background did it start to dawn on me how sexist, paternalist, and even classist, among other things, my French environment had been. I started adjusting my own behavior accordingly. I started lowering my guard and opening up to people I would not have thought of talking to back in France. I started really paying attention and listening to others. All of this internal change, incidentally, did not come without a price, both to my identity and my private life. No changes do, and it is a good thing to keep in mind for the reader of a book pushing forward some rather radical ideas.

Today, I'm a full professor of political science at a prestigious Ivy League university in the United States. That title comes with privilege—and blind spots. I'm hardly the ideal spokesperson for ordinary citizens. Yet, despite the confidence I've built over time, my naturally reserved disposition and a personal history of failure and rejection have led me to question educational and political systems that reward only the bold and ambitious. From my position in US academia, I've had the rare luxury of time—something most people don't—to think deeply about our political regimes, their history, and the philosophical foundations that shape them.

I have spent the last fifteen years writing about what democracy means and how we can do it better. I have researched concrete cases of democratic innovations, like the 2010–2013 Icelandic crowdsourced constitutional process and the 2019 French Citizens' Convention for Climate. I have advised the governments of Finland, Belgium, Argentina, Chile, and France on ways to make their processes more inclusive and participatory. Most recently, I even co-governed the second citizens' convention in France, on the topic of end-of-life issues. This last experience, in particular, gave me access to the engine room of a citizens' assembly. It also gave me a better understanding of the institutional power players who may facilitate or oppose political change.

Meanwhile, at my own academic institution, Yale University, I sat on the Faculty of Arts and Sciences Senate for two years—another mostly disillusioning experience with another electoral politics of sorts. All of this has made me, if anything, more of a radical democrat. I'm convinced that the last thing we need at the top of government is people like me or people chosen through a popularity contest. Like Buckley, I, too, would rather be governed by the first two thousand names in a telephone book than clones of myself or my colleagues, or the latest rotating cast of elected politicians.

Reclaiming Populism

Before I launch into my critique of politicians, let me address a suspicion that may already be forming in your mind. Am I some radical populist plotting to dismantle decent government and replace it with socialist totalitarianism under the banner of "real democracy"? And doesn't it concern me that my book's thesis could be twisted into a justification for anti-parliamentarianism—even violence against elected officials?

I'm not going to dignify the first question with an answer. One should be able to question an existing system without being immediately suspected of the worst possible intentions. But I do worry about the second point. My goal is definitely not to increase cynicism and revolutionary rage against elected authorities. And nothing justifies violence against the political personnel currently in place, who for the most part just happen to play by the existing constitutional rules. But just because a truth is painful and may be misused or misdirected does not make it less of a truth. The solutions put forward by populists of the left or the right are wrong-headed and dangerous. They are even self-contradicting to the extent that they typically call on us to, one more time, one "last" time, use elections to select the one good guy (always a guy) who will save us and "drain the swamp."

But their diagnosis—the excessive elitism of our current system, to which populism is, after all, largely a reaction—is not wrong. Politicians *are* part of the problem, if not the only problem. By politicians I do not mean any specific people, many of whom are, individually, decent. I mean politicians as a group, the group who run campaigns and need voters to elect them, and who stay in power so long that they become a class of their own. Whatever their personal, individual qualities, those do not add up to assemblies capable of either fully democratic representation or smart, optimally beneficial legislation.

I see "politics without politicians" in two distinct ways. The first—and most radical—is as an alternative to the status quo. It's an exercise in political imagination, a call to invent what doesn't yet exist while drawing inspiration from the past. It challenges the way we think of parliaments (my main focus in the book), but also the presidency, which is perhaps where our minds most naturally go when we think of elections. In a system where the legislature is randomly selected, would an elected president still make sense? Should that function be rethought? If so, how? Should we perhaps even rethink the whole articulation of the three branches of power, including the judiciary? This path is, therefore, revolutionary, maybe even utopian. It may serve best as a thought experiment—a way to step back, challenge the status quo, and expose its flaws.

The second approach focuses on creating opportunities within traditional political systems for ordinary citizens. Here, politics without politicians means carving out spaces, at all levels of the polity, where nonpoliticians can operate independently, even legislate, without the gatekeeping of professional politicians. While this approach remains radical—shifting power away from politicians to everyday people—it stops short of being revolutionary, at least in the near to medium term. Existing institutions are preserved, but adapted and hybridized to integrate these new citizen-driven spaces. Whether these changes help stabilize existing institutions—preserving the status quo while improving it—or eventually, in the long term, lead to their replacement and an entirely new institutional equilibrium is not something that is entirely predictable. Things could go either way.

I am compelled to step forward with these proposals, both the reformist and more revolutionary kinds, because what I have to say is starkly different from the views of many of my academic colleagues, both predecessors and contemporaries, who have put forward depressing and paralyzing treatises on the crisis, decay, or backsliding of democracy. Their solutions often consist in shoring up our existing model of democracy and trying to return us to some idealized good old times that perhaps never were, or were good for only some people. But if I'm right, and if this model of democracy is at least partly the reason why we are in so much trouble today, then we need to move forward, not backward. As you'll soon find out, I'm an optimist, but I'm no Pollyanna. I see the gulf between the ideal of democracy and the reality of plutocratic and exclusionary politics in the United States and elsewhere. But I also see that it's not too late for reform.

TWO

The Problem with Politicians

Did you hear my covert narcissism I disguise as altruism
Like some kind of congressman? (A tale as old as time)

TAYLOR SWIFT

We're electing idiots.

LIZ CHENEY

Politicians ▪ Ordinary Citizens ▪ The Shy ▪ All the Same ▪
Elections Produce Oligarchies ▪ Manin's Bombshell

In the fall of 2018, the French government passed a carbon tax, ostensibly to address environmental concerns but primarily, it seems, to close a two-million-euro deficit in the national budget. The move backfired spectacularly. By November, the Yellow Vests movement had emerged, named after the neon safety vests that all French motorists are required by law to keep in their vehicles and wear in case of emergencies, such as roadside accidents or break-downs. Protesters donned these vests both for visibility while blocking highways and occupying traffic circles across the country and as a symbol of their demand to be seen. The movement exploded, with demonstrators flooding Paris and marching on the Champs-Élysées every weekend for months. Their demands for social justice resonated, drawing support from over two thirds of the French population at its peak. But public sympathy faded as a violent faction emerged—torching public property, looting luxury shops, and threatening to storm government ministries. In a moment of chaos, panicked officials scrambled out of windows, a dramatic turning point that shattered the movement's image.

I observed the turmoil in disbelief from the United States, glued to the news. I remember thinking: Is it the French Revolution all over again? Are we headed for a civil war? It was clear that we were in a situation unprecedented since at least 1968, and I feared more violence to come. So did the government, which clamped down on the movement with brutal police tactics before turning to a more deliberative solution. In December 2018, President Emmanuel Macron announced the so-called Great National Debate, which consisted of a giant listening and talking session, pausing the country's politics for three months between January and March 2019. This new approach calmed things down for a while.

Meanwhile, in the United States, discontent was brewing as well, arguably culminating in the right-wing populist uprising that led to the January 6 insurrection. On that fateful day in 2021, a mob of Trump supporters—spurred on by the outgoing president, who refused to concede defeat—marched to the Capitol and stormed the building. The chaos ultimately left several people dead, multiple others injured, and countless members of Congress terrified. Whether we label this ultimately failed invasion an attempted coup or not, the violence was as real as what had unfolded in France. For many observers, this event marked the end of American exceptionalism. It exposed American democracy as being just as fragile and susceptible to demagoguery as any other. To me, it revealed strikingly similar fault lines in both France and the United States, even though their political movements stemmed from opposite ends of the ideological spectrum. The common thread seemed to be widespread discontent with a political system seen as detached, incompetent, corrupt, and fundamentally unjust.

All around the world, in fact, similar protests have been observed in the last few decades. In Taiwan, in 2014, students started what is now known as the Sunflower Movement by occupying Parliament for three weeks, to protest a free trade agreement with China but more generally in reaction to corruption in government and unrepresentative politics. In the United Kingdom, in 2016, the Brexit vote was the more procedural way in which the masses expressed their rejection of neoliberal politics, the lack of transparency and democratic accountability of the European Union, and the disconnection of the elites behind both. In Chile, in 2019, a small rise in the price of metro tickets spurred massive protests, a political revolution, and two failed attempts at rewriting the constitution. As I write, the government of Serbia (my husband's native country) just fell, after monthslong student protests—not unlike those that brought down the former dictator Slobodan Milošević—mobilized the country against corrupt politicians and democratic backsliding.[1]

Iceland, a tiny Nordic country, was the canary in the coal mine in many respects. While the bigger countries had to wait a few years for the consequences of the 2008 financial crisis to hit politically as well as economically, the tiny nation of Iceland collapsed immediately. In 2008, as the country suddenly incurred debts totaling seven times its GDP, the political elites were ousted from power, and thirty-six bankers were eventually imprisoned.[2] It being Iceland, the process was peaceful—using yogurt, bananas, and singing as weapons. But the shock waves were quite profound, leading the country to engage in a process of constitutional reform that, although it petered out after a few years, pioneered revolutionary ideas, such as the view that ordinary citizens should be involved in the writing of their own social contract.

What do these events have in common? Profound dissatisfaction with the economic and political system, and distrust of ruling elites. We can call this populism—of the left or of the right—and dismiss it as an irrational, obscure force to be squelched. We can minimize the problem as the normal way democracies function and adjust to changing circumstances, accepting a permanent state of crisis as an inevitable price to pay for the freedom to choose our rulers. Or we can ask ourselves: What isn't working in our systems that we get to this level of dissatisfaction, instability, and, in some cases, violence?

This chapter examines the systemic flaws in democracy by searching for a design defect at its core. Examining the history and theory behind our political institutions, I argue that the most glaring point of failure lies in how we select our ruling class. The issue isn't just governance—it's electoral representation and the professional class of politicians it perpetuates.

But first, to understand why a "politics without politicians" might offer a better, more democratic alternative, we need to define who "politicians" are and how they differ from ordinary citizens.

Politicians

Politicians are people for whom politics is a job. They are professionally involved in politics, typically as a holder of or a candidate for an elected office. I define politics here as the set of activities that revolves around making laws and policies for a given polity, at any level of the system. In representative democracies, politicians are typically elected. Some of them are also appointed—prime ministers in the UK or France, for example. But in representative democracies the legitimacy of politicians—what gives them the moral authority to hold power in the first place—is that they have been elected to the position by their constituents.

So, a politician is someone who is engaged in lawmaking or policymaking activities and is paid or otherwise derives an income for this job. The job arguably requires a number of skills, some of them acquired through practice. Politicians are expected to know how the political system works and how to get things done. A skilled politician knows not only how to win an election, but also how to get a law passed, how to build a coalition, and how to stay in power.

Note that someone who keeps running for elections but never wins or otherwise fails to access a political position of some kind would be no politician at all. Such people are at best aspiring politicians. You need to exercise, or have exercised, power, or held some kind of political role in order to qualify as a politician. People who lose power quickly after accessing it also qualify as politicians, albeit bad ones. Think of Liz Truss and her grand total of forty-five days as prime minister of the British government. At least she managed to get the job, if only to demonstrate her incompetence—or, if we're charitable, bad luck.

Now, what do politicians look like? Close your eyes and picture in your head "a politician." What comes to mind? Chances are it's someone in business dress (in the West, a power suit), speaking from a lectern, posing for pictures, cutting a ribbon, shaking hands, or kissing babies in a crowd. It's most likely a middle-aged white man, although, luckily at this point, a few women come to mind as well, and more and more people of color.

The figure of the politician sometimes also conjures up some unpleasant character traits, such as insincerity, hypocrisy, and lack of integrity. A politician is often seen as a smooth talker who will say anything to win your vote. Amid all the salient traits, however, there is one in particular that is perhaps the most widespread: boldness. Confidence, sometimes verging on entitlement. If there is indeed a unique trait shared by all politicians, it's not being male, or white, or even rich or educated. No, instead, what all politicians have in common is confidence.

Let's face it: Politics as we know it selects for the alpha types, the charismatic, the daring, the entitled, the arrogant, even those with no shame whatsoever, and sometimes even the downright psychopathic. Despite the fundamental differences in their views and personal styles, they are not wallflowers. This common trait— extreme confidence—is not necessarily a problem. It may even be an advantage in many situations, perhaps facilitating speedy and decisive action. But, as I'll argue later, it becomes insidious when it is a variable for which our system always selects, crowding out other types.

Ordinary Citizens

By contrast, what do I mean by regular or ordinary citizens? I mean, literally, a random selection from the general population. They could be anyone: nurses, engineers, construction workers, accountants, gardeners, restaurant managers, waitresses, Uber drivers, security guards, police officers, hairdressers, small business owners, students, doctors—you name it. They could be men, women, or nonbinary individuals. They could be any age and any skin color. They could be people who like to think with numbers or people who like to think in images. They could be social butterflies or introverts. They could be any one of us.

Only a tiny fraction of ordinary citizens in that sense are politicians, a number so insignificant that we can treat politicians and ordinary citizens as mutually exclusive groups. Ordinary citizens are those who are not professionally involved in politics. At most, they might participate temporarily as volunteers in political campaigns—usually unpaid—and with no intention of pursuing a government position. In contrast, politicians are a distinct class, separate from regular citizens. Regular citizens have political rights and responsibilities, like voting, but these are civic, not professional, obligations. Politicians, by definition, hold professional political responsibilities that set them apart from the rest of us.

The Shy

Among ordinary citizens, there is a subset I call "the shy." These are quieter people, who stand in sharp contrast to the category of "politicians." But shyness, as I define it, goes beyond innate reserve or natural diffidence—though it includes that. It's not simply a tendency to be "quiet," as the writer Susan Cain might describe introverts.[3] Instead, shyness reflects an attitude of humility and a sense of unease or lack of confidence about one's place and power in society.

Lack of confidence can be due to natural introversion, of course. But it is more often than not socially constructed and, indeed, ingrained in certain categories of people from a young age. As a result, the shy are not timid in all contexts, but primarily in contexts that structurally alienate them. Psychologists use the term "learned helplessness" to describe a mindset that develops in people who have repeatedly experienced a lack of control over their circumstances. Over time, they stop trying to change their situation, even when opportunities to do so are within reach. Learned helplessness is a form of shyness. It applies not only in regimes where people lack a sense of agency, like dictatorships, but in electoral democracies as well. Shyness, therefore, is not a vice or a character flaw, but neither is it a virtue. Rather, it is a symptom of political disempowerment and alienation.

Shy people in our societies are often young, female, poor or working class, people of color, LGBTQ+, or disabled, precisely because shyness is as much a result of one's social environment, with all its biases and prejudices, as an innate, genetic predisposition to being reserved or introverted. But "shyness," as I understand it, cuts across so many other dimensions than these classic markers of identity politics that I prefer to avoid this vocabulary altogether, especially because these labels can be problematically essentializing of those included in them as well as those excluded from them. White, heterosexual, older, able-bodied men can be shy, too, while young people, women of color, or LGBTQ+ people can be loud and proud. But on the whole, the vast majority of us may, at some point in our life, fall into the category of the shy. And when you know that at any point in time, between a third and a half of the population see themselves as "introverts," you start to realize that the shy are all around us.[4]

I will not parse out what is natural or socially constructed about the shy in this book. What interests me here is that the shy embody traits that stand in direct opposition to the characteristics required to be a politician. As a result, while an "ordinary" person might eventually make it in electoral politics, a shy person never will. The shy hate posing for pictures, shaking hands with strangers, asking for money, pretending to have levels of knowledge they do not possess, and vying for attention amid a shouting match. You will not catch a shy person shamelessly self-promoting on camera. Indeed, you will simply never catch a shy person seeking power if that power can be accessed only through public-facing elections.

All the Same

Viewed collectively—like Congress—politicians blur into sameness, and not just in appearance.[5] In the United States, they're overwhelmingly multimillionaires, highly educated (often lawyers), and products of private schools. In the UK, the ruling class is even more insular, with politicians cycling through elite institutions like Eton, Oxford, and Cambridge. In northern Europe, wealth is less of a defining trait, but elite education remains a constant. In newer democracies—whether in developing nations or post-Soviet states—the homogeneity is often even starker. Political leaders are almost always socioeconomic elites from the dominant ethnic group, and nearly all of them are men.

The homogeneity of the electoral class is so pervasive that we hardly notice it anymore. It becomes striking only in certain moments, often by contrast. One such moment for me came in January 2019, a few months after the Yellow Vests movement erupted in France, during the lead-up to the Great National Debate initiated by President Macron to quell the unrest. As a first step to rekindle national dialogue, Macron traveled across the country to meet with city mayors—France's last well-liked politicians. His goal was to regain popularity both among the mayors and, through them, the public. As I watched these events unfold from my computer in New Haven, one meeting particularly caught my attention: Macron's session with about six hundred mayors from my home region of Normandy, held in the small town of Grand Bourg-theroulde. For seven hours, I watched online as Macron conducted a marathon Q&A, deftly fielding questions from this critical and deeply engaged audience.

More important than the president's demonstration of retail politics, however, what stayed with me was the visual: a supremely confident white man, surrounded by a sea of middle-aged, bearded, graying white men in glasses and dark suits.[6] There were only a handful of women in the mix and not a person of color in sight—a perfect vignette of how patriarchal and homogenous the local hierarchies still are in France.[7] At the local level, it suddenly became very clear to me, the same old hegemonies still prevail.

I was struck in a completely different way by another image, which I ran across while researching the 2010 Icelandic constitutional process. It was a photo of the twenty-five-member Icelandic Constitutional Council—the group tasked with drafting a new constitution after the 2008 financial crisis. Something about it just felt . . . different. Of course, everybody in it is white—this is Iceland, after all, a small and not very multicultural country. But for one thing, almost half of the group is made up of women, who stand out in their colorful outfits. Second, in the foreground, lying almost flat on a reclining wheelchair, is Freyja Haraldsdóttir, a human rights lawyer afflicted by glass-bone disease. Meanwhile, even though most of the men obviously felt obliged to wear suits and ties for this official picture, not all of them did so. The overall effect is less like a gathering of politicians and more like a group of guests at a wedding.

These twenty-five Icelanders, beaming with pride in the picture, looked to me somehow, for lack of a better word, "normal." Ordinary. Just like us.[8] A look at the professions represented in that small sample also tells an interesting story: a mathematician, two pastors, a video game designer, a student, a union representative, a museum director, and a few academics, etc. In other words, none were professional politicians.

How did Icelanders manage to produce such a diverse group? Their method was simple, and quite brutal: They *banned politicians*. They literally legislated that politicians currently in office were to be excluded from the pool of people allowed to run for election to the council.

Why would politicians make such an anti-politician decision? Doesn't that prove they can, at times, act selflessly for the greater good? In theory, yes—but only under extreme duress. In fact, in Iceland, they hardly had a choice. After the disgust generated toward the political class during the 2008 crisis, which had revealed the levels of corruption and unethical collusion between politicians and the banking world, Parliament had to take drastic measures. If the constitutional process were to have any legitimacy, the new government ushered into power at that time reasoned, it simply could not be led by politicians. It had to be entrusted to regular citizens.

With this ban on politicians, Iceland took one step in the direction of what I call "politics without politicians." Their mistake, however, was to stay with the selection mechanism of elections. After all, you can kick politicians out of an election, but you cannot prevent an election from selecting for a certain kind of person. To go further, Icelanders should have tried doing politics without elections altogether. The fact that they did not shows just how hard it is to imagine an alternative. Before we explore such an alternative, however, we need to understand why elections are not all that democratic, despite the pull they have on us.

Elections Produce Oligarchies

Why are elections a problem from a democratic point of view? Despite being predicated on equality of votes, they systematically produce an unequal distribution of power, which ends up producing a distorted representation of the needs and preferences of the larger population. This distorted representation in turn produces laws and policies misaligned with and sometimes even contrary to the political interests of citizens.

Elections create this cascade of inequality through two mechanisms: one, the self-selection of the people seeking power; the other, human choice as a mechanism to identify who should be sent to power among that self-selected pool. Both mechanisms end up narrowing down the kind of people who can access power to a small portion of the population. The combination of those two factors creates a political class that is homogenous along too many dimensions to govern well and justly. Let me address each problem in turn.

That there is self-selection in electoral politics is undeniable. Electoral politics attracts certain types of people and repels others. The problem is not just that elections will attract people with such traits (even though there are no good reasons to think that such traits are optimal for successful governing) but that the overrepresentation of such people will dissuade other types of people—the unambitious, the selfless, and the accommodating—from running in the first place. In other words, the electoral selection mechanism, by itself, and quite apart from the additional difficulties of electoral competition, will dissuade many capable and talented citizens from seeking office in the first place. Among the first to self-select out of that dog-eat-dog competition are going to be women,[9] but so are, more generally, all those I call the shy.

As political scientist Brian Klaas acknowledges, this problem is more general: "There is always self-selection bias with power. Whether it's trigger-happy police officers or power-hungry tyrants in homeowner's associations, power tends to draw in people who want to control others for the sake of it."[10] Attracting the power-hungry may be problematic. But what is even more problematic for Klaas is that power may also attract the corruptible. Indeed, the more corruptible people are, the more they tend to be drawn to jobs where corruption is likely to exist. To be sure, not all electoral democracies suffer from high degrees of corruption, but the stakes of power are such that the possibility of corruption is much more likely in the job of politician than it is, say, in the job of kindergarten teacher or nurse.

More worryingly still, Klaas documents an overrepresentation of psychopaths among a number of professions—including salesmen, CEOs, lawyers, surgeons, and police—that share very similar traits with the job of politician. This would seem to indicate that psychopaths are also overrepresented in politics. Psychopaths are characterized, among other things, by an overconfidence in their own judgment, which, if anything, seems to be a job requirement in electoral politics. The reality is that we don't know for sure whether there is an overrepresentation of psychopaths among politicians because they form too small a sample within each country for which these studies have been conducted.

But it sounds quite plausible, doesn't it? And even if it turns out that electoral politics does not put psychopaths in power more often than other professions, it is bad enough that all evidence points to the fact that it selects for people who both want power and are easily corrupted by it.

Let us now turn to the second problem with elections. From among the pool of self-selected people, elections then rely on human choice: first, the choice of party hierarchies who select viable candidates; and second, the choice of voters.

Regarding the selection by parties, let me just quote here the point of view of Rory Stewart, a retired UK politician, in his aptly titled bestselling tell-all *How Not to be a Politician* (published in the UK as *Politics on the Edge*). The book damningly exposes the cynicism, careerism, and performative leadership that Stewart experienced at the heart of British government, in sharp contrast to the vision of politics rooted in integrity, public service, and moral responsibility that he initially believed in. Recounting his impression of party types he first came across, Stewart writes: "The particular compound of canniness and ignorance, fluency, misdirected loyalty and awkward dishonesties which made the modern MP, had evolved to survive the demands of the dominant party members, just as much as the unsanitary habits of wrinkle-lipped free-tailed bats were formed by their long years in deep Bornean caves."[11]

Okay, this is both delicious and probably *a bit* unfair. So let us charitably assume that the selection by party hierarchies does not necessarily worsen the oligarchic problem, though it may indeed lead to the selection of candidates with weird personalities. After

all, parties are supposed to function along "meritocratic" principles, whereby you have to prove yourself for a while within the
internal hierarchy before making it to the top. We could generously imagine that merit is randomly distributed and that tracking
it does not tend, in practice, to homogenize along gender, class,
race, or other dimensions (cough, cough).

But even in party-less elections (at the municipal level, say), or
assuming we could introduce quotas for underrepresented categories,[12] implement reach-out programs to diversify the pool, or
define the original pool of candidates on the basis of random
selection (with mandatory participation once candidates are identified), the real selection process at the end of the day is voters'
choice and judgment.

And relying on voters' choice has inegalitarian implications, as
it both systematically excludes the shy and tends to produce oligarchies.

We all instinctively know that electoral politics is oligarchic—
but what we fail to grasp is that this isn't a bug; it's a feature. The
politicians we elect are a tiny, unrepresentative elite, exceptional
in some ways—but not always in positive ways. And they know
they are exceptional. That's why every campaign is a sales pitch,
with candidates presenting themselves as being uniquely extraordinary, as if that's a virtue rather than a warning sign. "Vote for
me because I'm the best/I'm right/I alone can save the country/I
alone know X or Y/I alone can speak for you." This appeal to ex-
ceptionality is the rule of elections. François Hollande, the only
president of France who tried to sell himself as "normal" once in
power—though he was nothing like it—failed to be reelected. The
American equivalent was probably Jimmy Carter. Voters do not
usually like or choose "normal" or "ordinary."

Somehow, we persist in believing that this oligarchic dimension is merely an unfortunate by-product of preexisting inequalities—inequalities rooted in historical realities and socioeconomic forces. According to this view, the homogeneity of the political class is not a result of the mechanisms of human choice itself but rather the lingering legacy of past hierarchies. Surely, as we democratize our systems—expanding suffrage, removing wealth requirements for candidates, and encouraging broader participation from the working class, women, and minorities of all kinds—parliaments and local hierarchies will eventually come to reflect the diversity of the populations they serve. Isn't that exactly what we've seen over the past century in countries like the United States, France, and Germany? And look at Sweden, showing us what the future, or at least the potential, of electoral democracy looks like!

In the Swedish parliament, political scientists have found representation across social backgrounds to be "extraordinarily even," with nearly 30 percent of legislators lacking a college degree—a stark contrast to the United States, where 95 percent of legislators are college-educated despite only a third of Americans holding a degree. Consider Stefan Löfven, Sweden's prime minister from 2014 to 2021, a former welder without a college education. Remarkably, politicians in the Swedish parliament without degrees perform just as effectively as their more formally educated counterparts, demonstrating that true representation doesn't require a diploma.[13] So, no worries, it's just a matter of time and will! Sweden is the future. Voters are perfectly capable of choosing in a way that spreads offices and positions of power from the top to the bottom of the socioeconomic ladder and among all possible human types.

Except that's not really true. All that these examples from progressive Scandinavia prove is that in the best possible circumstances, where the right to run for election is universal, money plays less of a role, economic inequalities are moderate, the citizenry is educated, and so on, we can get professional politicians to look *a bit* more like a phenotypical portrait of the larger citizenry they serve. We can achieve a slightly less inegalitarian distribution of offices and positions of power across the citizenry. But consider that to get gender parity, even Scandinavian countries had to constrain individual choice, forcing parties to promote female candidates by implementing strict quotas.

The fact is that any selection mechanism for representatives based on human choice (and in fact any selection mechanism other than random selection) will have inegalitarian consequences. Why is that? Because human choice is inherently discriminatory and homogenizing. Whether the skew is rational or not (a separate question), choice is biased toward salient traits, or traits that are seen as superior in some ways, typically because they are rare and unevenly distributed. Those include wealth and social status, of course, but also charisma, confidence, eloquence, and height—all of which are positional qualities, i.e., qualities defined by their relation to other qualities.

As a result, elections are bound to generate an inegalitarian distribution of power that is not empirically contingent but structural. So even assuming ideal conditions, which are never found in real life, not even in Scandinavian countries, elections will send to power an unrepresentative group of people over-sampling certain traits, including those that are associated with being a confident elite, and under-sampling the shy.

This is a conclusion some politicians are sometimes willing to acknowledge publicly, at least once they have left power. Rory Stewart is one of those. So is Terrill Bouricius, a former Vermont state representative and now, like Stewart, an advocate for the alternative form of politics this book puts forward. Bouricius had an epiphany while working on a housing committee in the 1990s: "It became obvious to me that the 'people's house' was not very representative of the people who actually lived in Vermont. . . . The committee members were an outgoing and garrulous bunch. . . . Shy wallflowers almost never become legislators."[14] In other words, Bouricius came to the same realization this chapter has been leading to: Politicians are not like us. And shy people in particular—the "wallflowers"—can never make it in their world. Equally troubling, his fellow politicians were all homeowners, and tended, unsurprisingly, to legislate in favor of homeowners and against tenants. As Bouricius further remarks, "After that, I frequently commented that any 150 Vermonters pulled from the phone book would be more representative than the elected House membership."

Manin's Bombshell

The oligarchic nature of our current version of democracy becomes most clear when we look at the genealogy of this regime form. Here, I need to introduce and discuss the work of a French historian and political theorist named Bernard Manin, who, sadly, passed away as I was putting the finishing touches to this book. Some decades ago, Bernard Manin penned a groundbreaking book called *The Principles of Representative Government*, which came out in English in 1997. Though Manin was a mild-mannered and somewhat conservative scholar, his book—indeed his one and only book, but what a book—has been a bombshell for many of his readers. You start reading it confident in your understanding of democracy, only to finish wondering whether what we call democracy today is democracy at all. But so deeply ingrained is our commitment to the electoral model of democracy that it is only years later, in my case at least, that the full implications of this book became clear.

In the very opening paragraph, Manin remarks, "Contemporary democratic governments have evolved from a political system that was conceived by its founders as opposed to democracy." He goes on to say that while we commonly distinguish between "representative" and "direct" forms of democracy, as if they were varieties of the same type of government, the reality is that "what today we call representative democracy has its origins in a system of institutions (established in the wake of the English, American, and French revolutions) that was in no way initially perceived as a form of democracy or of government by the people."[15]

Manin's primary goal, however, is not to challenge the value or legitimacy of modern representative democracies, despite their nondemocratic origins. Rather, it is to identify and analyze the enduring features of representative governments since the eighteenth century—what he refers to as their "principles." Manin identifies four such features across time and geography, the first and most important of which is the principle of periodic elections. But in the process of doing this historical and descriptive work, Manin brings into relief the profound disconnect between the ideal of political equality, which we moderns claim to embrace, and the reality of our "representative democracies," whose core principle, periodic elections, has, in fact, an inegalitarian and indeed oligarchic character.

The gist of the problem is that elections rely on a principle of "distinction" between ordinary citizens and those fated to become a political elite. It is the problem with human choice that we discussed above, of which Manin was the first to remind us in the contemporary era: The distribution of power that results from elections will always be highly inegalitarian, concentrating power in the hands of a few people, those who "stand out" in some way. This produces oligarchy, or rule by the few, in the original sense, rather than rule by the many. Note that when the qualities possessed by the election winners correspond to true excellence, we should call this regime form "aristocracy"—from the Greek for "rule of the best people." But because Manin prefers to remain agnostic about the nature of the qualities that earn candidates people's votes, he favors the more neutral term "oligarchy."

The oligarchic feature of elections is what led the ancient Athenians to reject it as a way to distribute political offices and to prefer selection by lot, which both expressed and realized the ideal of political equality among the *demos*. The Athenians did use elections, but only for administrative and army positions, which were seen as requiring a particular kind of individual excellence worth the break from political equality. Manin quotes the famous phrase by Aristotle in the *Politics*: "It is accepted as democratic when public offices are allocated by lot; and as oligarchic when they are filled by election." The Athenians thus had various political institutions staffed by lot (through the use of a machine called a *kleroterion*): the Council of 500, which set the agenda for the People's Assembly; popular juries; and later the so-called *nomothetai*, randomly selected juries in charge of writing some laws. We will explore these peculiar institutions in chapter 4.

Describing these practices and inverting the modern puzzlement over the use of lot in ancient Greece, Manin asks the seemingly innocent but radical question: "Why do we not practice lot, and nonetheless call ourselves democrats?"[16] Conversely, one might ask: Why do we practice elections, and yet not call ourselves supporters of oligarchy?

What Manin shows is that representative government was meant to protect the interests of existing elites while securing an apparent form of popular consent, and none of the democratizing trends that came later changed that fundamental truth. As he further points out, even with the extension of the franchise or the abolition of parliamentary qualifications, two fundamental oligarchic features of electoral governments survived: "In governments based solely on election, not all citizens would have an equal chance of holding public office. And the position of representative would be reserved for persons regarded as superior or for members of higher social classes."[17]

Manin was probably the first scholar since the eighteenth century to emphasize the uncomfortable role that human choice plays in barring both the possibility of an egalitarian distribution of political offices and the possibility of a parliament that was a mirror image of the people. As he writes, "Since election involves a choice, it also includes an internal mechanism that hinders the selection of citizens who resemble others. At the heart of the elective procedure, there is a force pulling in the opposite direction from the desire for similarity between rulers and ruled."[18] In other words, even at the level of the ideal, elections systematically close off access to power to people who are too average and ordinary to stand out in the eyes of other citizens. The result of this selection mechanism is bound to be a demographically skewed representation of the people, under ideal conditions and even more so under nonideal ones.

Despite this radical conclusion about the core and irreducible

oligarchic features of electoral governments, however, Manin himself ends up defending a nuanced view. Unlike Aristotle, Rousseau,
and Montesquieu before him, who viewed elections as fundamentally oligarchic, Manin sees them as both oligarchic *and* democratic, a "Janus-like institution," he says, invoking the figure of
the two-faced Roman god.[19] The face turned toward democracy is
the principle of one person, one vote, which treats citizens as voters equally; the face turned toward oligarchy is manifested in the
fact that election treats citizens as candidates for office unequally,
giving only a handful of people a real chance to access power.

For Manin, this balancing act between equal voting rights and
the principle of distinction is what gives representative government its characteristic nature, that of a mixed regime, rather than
a pure democracy or a pure oligarchy. Manin was in fact quite
content with representative democracy as we know it. He even explained away its multiple crises as the growing pains of an adaptable system. I got a chance to interview Manin directly, in 2008,
for an online publication, on this question of whether or not representative democracy was in crisis then. He answered, "I don't
think that the conditions required to justify the diagnostic of a
crisis of the representative system are met." He thought that the
crisis threshold would be met only if too many people withdrew
from politics (by abstaining from voting altogether) and distrust in
government were much higher than it was back then. In essence,
he thought that a sense of permanent crisis is quite normal for representative government and the way the system keeps rebalancing
itself.[20]

Indeed, the mixed nature of representative government is what
explains for Manin its virtues of stability and durability, despite
the constant feeling of crisis it also generates, and its seemingly

universal appeal since the eighteenth century. The stability of representative government, in his view, is the result of the two classes of people—the masses meant to be ruled and the elites meant to rule—reaching a point of "argumentative equilibrium" around the institutional principle of periodic elections.

In this equilibrium, neither the group unlikely to be elected nor the elite destined to become rulers has an incentive to abandon periodic elections for another selection method. Despite their vastly different odds of being chosen as rulers, both groups benefit from sticking with periodic elections. For the elites, elections are preferable because they provide an impartial mechanism—giving the people the final say in the competition, rather than forcing elites to settle disputes among themselves through negotiation or conflict. As to the ordinary citizens, as Manin points out, they "are unlikely to insist that the power of selecting rulers be given to an authority other than the people." In this arrangement, citizens retain at least some power to choose their rulers, which is far better than having no choice at all.

Let us leave aside the question of the stability of this "equilibrium" for now and consider the political costs and consequences of doing "democracy" this way.

THREE

Democracy by Coincidence

It is accepted as democratic when public offices are allocated by lot; and as oligarchic when they are filled by election.

ARISTOTLE, *POLITICS*, BOOK IV

The rich have a slight edge.

MIKAEL PERSSON AND ANDERS SUNDELL

Democracy by Coincidence ▪ Plutocracy All Around? ▪ Money Corrupts ▪ Power Corrupts ▪ Lobbies ▪ Incompetence ▪ The Group Effect ▪ The Illusion of Choice ▪ Why We Hate Each Other ▪ The Road Not Taken

Most theorists of democracy assume that a democratic government is responsive to people's preferences in part *because* such preferences shape and guide politicians' behaviors. Bernard Manin, for example, assumes that representative government maintains a causal link between what the public wants and what representatives give them. His view of representative government as a mixed constitution is a lot less elitist in that sense than, say, Schumpeterian democracy, which assumes no such causal connection. On the contrary, it is essential for Manin's defense of elections, as it was for the Founding Fathers' defense of their republic, that representative government is at least minimally responsive to the wishes of the public, even if those wishes have been passed through the filter of more "enlightened" minds.

Manin even has a theory as to what allows for that linkage: "The central mechanism whereby voters influence governmental decisions results from the incentives that representative systems create for those in office: representatives who are subject to reelection have an incentive to *anticipate* the future judgment of the electorate on the policies they pursue."[1] This claim is purely theoretical, however, and Manin does not provide any evidence for it, in part because no empirical studies of this causal relation were available in his day.

In the last fifteen years, however, scientists and economists have started to put that conjecture to the empirical test. And what they have found out in many cases is far from reassuring. Not only do politicians not generate optimal laws and policies, they often do not even give us what we want, which—whether good or bad— one might expect in a democracy.

What's truly worrying isn't that politicians don't always give us what we want—they sometimes do. The real concern is *why* they give us what we want: It's not because we, the public, want it, but because the wealthy or other powerful groups do. Let me explain.

There is a difference between getting what we want because we want it and getting what we want only because someone else wants it, too, and is able to decisively shape the decision. In that second scenario, we get what we want only because we are the collateral beneficiaries of someone else's desires and influence. Our wants make no difference; they are not *causal*.

How do we know if what majorities want is causal in our democratic systems? It's actually very hard to measure. But attempts to do so have been made and yielded concerning results.

In 2014, two American political scientists, Martin Gilens and Benjamin Page, set off a debate about the plutocratic nature of American politics. Larry Bartels had already shown a few years prior that the votes of US senators better reflected the views of high-income citizens.[2] Gilens and Page now claimed to have found no correlation whatsoever between what majorities of Americans want and the public policies coming out of the American government during the period from 1981 to 2002, once they had controlled for the effect of the preferences of the wealthy and various economic and business groups.

They found, by contrast, significant correlation between the preferences of economic elites and organized groups representing business interests and government policy. In their own words, "economic elites and organized groups representing business interests have substantial independent impacts on US government policy, while mass-based interest groups and average citizens have little or no independent influence."[3]

What do these results mean? To the extent that people get what they want politically in the United States, it is only because their preferences happen to map onto those of economic elites and business interests, whose own preferences do causally shape outcomes. In other words, what we get in the United States is what Gilens and Page call "democracy by coincidence."

Democracy by Coincidence

Let's consider a classic example in US politics: gun regulation. Large majorities of Americans support tighter gun control. Yet, year after year, it doesn't happen. Even in the aftermath of shocking events like the Sandy Hook massacre, progress doesn't come when public support skyrockets to 90 percent for measures like universal background checks. Instead, it happens when billionaires like Mike Bloomberg throw their money and influence behind the cause, countering the dominant force in this debate: the National Rifle Association. In fact, even when the public does get what it wants—like deficit reduction or withdrawal from a foreign war—it's often not because the majority demanded it but because wealthier individuals or powerful groups wanted it too.

In cruder terms: The rich matter in politics, the rest do not. These results were so stunning that they landed Gilens and Page an interview on *The Daily Show with Jon Stewart*. On the show these cautious scientists carefully avoided using the word "oligarchy"—or, even more accurately, "plutocracy." But Jon Stewart's face and the audience's reaction reflected the proper level of shock at the implications of their claims: American politics is shaped by 10 percent of the population at most.

Of course, these results have been fiercely questioned. Several researchers have since offered different interpretations of the same data, arguing, for example, that the rich and the poor do not have terribly different preferences (although that seems a moot point if we care about causality) and that the gap in responsiveness is not as substantial as Gilens and Page make it appear.[4]

As of today, the literature seems to have settled on a more nuanced but still highly worrisome picture. The preferences of the rich may not be the sole drivers of policy and law, but they significantly affect the likelihood of implementation.[5] By contrast, the preferences of the poor and the middle class are much less impactful. According to the economist John Matsusaka, for example, policy congruence in the United States is 50 percent.[6] In other words, when majorities want something in the United States, they may or may not get it. It's essentially a coin toss. According to Matsusaka, one of the sources of this democratic deficit is the elitism of elected officials. The other two sources of the problem are, in his view, the emergence of an administrative state, whereby policymaking authority is delegated by Congress to executive agencies, and the excessive power of politicized judicial elites capturing authority over the interpretation of laws.

Even under the most favorable interpretations, majorities in the United States are causally influential half the time at best, while wealthy economic minorities—the top 10 percent—get their way the other half of the time. Is this a fair balance? Does it meet the standard of a true democracy? Perhaps, perhaps not. In the most optimistic interpretation, the United States is an inclusive meritocracy, where the more educated (who end up richer because of their education as well as talent and hard work) have greater influence. The reasoning for this interpretation goes like this: Raw majoritarian preferences might lack nuance, while the preferences of wealthy, educated minorities are more refined. In this view, the deliberative process in Congress might be justified in aligning with majorities half the time and elites the other half, following where better arguments and superior information lead.

But reading the US system as an inclusive meritocracy is taking the most optimistic and convoluted interpretation of the evidence. A simpler one is available, and that is the one some dissatisfied groups reach for: The United States is a plutocracy—that is, an oligarchy of the rich.

Plutocracy All Around?

The temptation is to assume that the United States is an "outlier," and that things are better elsewhere. Alas, it appears that most advanced democracies have a plutocratic problem too. Since Gilens and Page's landmark study, similar studies conducted in Europe found the same exact pattern everywhere they looked, including in the unlikely cases of Germany,[7] Denmark,[8] the Netherlands,[9] Norway,[10] Sweden,[11] and Spain,[12] as well as in EU-level institutions.[13] In all these countries, and at the EU level, policies and laws are more responsive to the preferences of rich voters and economic groups.

Finally, to cap it all, an ambitious study recently mapped the political terrain in thirty countries across a range of issues. In all thirty democracies, even arguably model ones, the authors find that "the rich have a slight edge,"[14] meaning that policies and laws are more congruent with—probably because they are more responsive to—the preferences of the rich. In the authors' words, "policies supported by the rich are more common than those supported by the poor whereas the middle class receives levels of responsiveness somewhere between the poor and the rich." If it's not as bad as the original Gilens and Page study made it appear for the United States, it's still far from great.

What is striking is that according to this latter study, it does not matter whether countries have strong unions or not, whether they finance their political campaigns privately or publicly, whether they are already characterized by high or low levels of economic inequality, or whether they are afflicted by low voter turnout or not—all factors long assumed to explain differences in policy responsiveness to different groups. These factors turn out not to matter at all. Either way, economic minorities seem to be calling the shots while everyone else gets a more limited share of influence.

There is something rotten even in the supposedly model democracies of northern Europe.

Adapting a famous line by the American political scientist E. E. Schattschneider, the electoral chorus "sings with a strong upper-class accent," leaving certain voices unheard. The United States, far from being an outlier, serves as a magnifying glass—its unique brand of capitalism possibly acting as the lens—revealing the true nature of electoral democracy. These empirical studies suggest that true power lies with the smaller, wealthier part of the population, and that electoral democracies are, indeed, plutocracies.

Such results map onto the subjective feelings of citizens in many democracies, as measured by a decreasing sense of individual political efficacy—the belief that one can have an influence on political decision-making—over time. The American National Election Studies document a decline in Americans' sense of political efficacy since 2002. Americans' political efficacy dropped from 60.6 on the index to 28.5, the lowest since the index was first created in 1952. Meanwhile, large majorities in the United States, France, and the UK feel that politicians are not responsive to their needs and are, by and large, corrupt.[15] Unfortunately, their perception of politicians' lack of responsiveness seems correct, even as the causal explanation—corruption—may not always be.

We now know that elected politicians form an elite group and that this is a problem because this elite group does not get us the policies we want or delivers them to us only because a minority wants them. What are the exact mechanisms that explain these bad outcomes? The studies mentioned above point to worrying correlations between economic elites and political outcomes. But inside the black box of political decision-making, what explains this disproportionate responsiveness of politicians to economic elites and their lesser responsiveness to majoritarian preferences? Is it corruption, incompetence, or both?

Money Corrupts

Plain and simple financial corruption is often the explanation many disillusioned citizens reach for. I'm not saying they are always wrong; in a number of young or recently transitioned democracies the corruption of politicians is a real, pervasive problem. In the United States and other rule-of-law-based democracies, financial corruption does not seem to be as pervasive, at least as measured by official studies. Then again, the revolving door issue—the fact that politicians and regulators frequently get cushy jobs with big business after they step down from politics and before they return to it—is an accepted feature of most electoral systems. Worse, it's not even illegal for members of the US Congress to make money on the stock market using the insider information they garner from occupying the halls of power. If that's not corruption, I don't know what is. Maybe we have set the bar so high for actual corruption that everything dodgy happening below that bar goes unmeasured and undetected.

The role of money is certainly a problem, especially in the United States, but one could imagine ways to curb it. Money *need not* be a problem for an electoral system, if only we could pass and implement the right kind of regulations on the revolving door phenomenon, insider trading, and campaign finance laws. In fact, as we saw with the case of the many Northern European countries mentioned above, where the wealthy wield disproportionate power despite the existence of healthy campaign finance laws, we can probably rule out money as the main causal factor, since, for example, German politicians are just as unresponsive to majorities as their American peers, even as they rely much less on private sources of funding.

Power Corrupts

Another reason elected politicians fail to act for the people who elect them is the morally corrupting effect of power (as distinct from the corrupting effect of money). One argument against professional politicians is that, as the hackneyed but eternally true phrase by Lord Acton goes, "power tends to corrupt and absolute power corrupts absolutely." And power *especially* corrupts the corruptible people who seek it in the first place, as Brian Klaas has reminded us. That is why the ancients knew not to leave people in power for too long. Their argument was both moral and cognitive—people who stay in power for too long lose their moral compass. And even if they were somehow able to retain their moral compass, their reasoning would become biased by groupthink and class interests. Susceptibility to corruption by power, however, would of course be a problem for anyone. The solution might not be to ban elections but instead to introduce term limits, recall methods, or oversight by ethics commissions.

Lobbies

Another, more specific explanation is the distorting influence of corporate lobbying. Politicians overrepresent the wealthy not because the wealthy buy politicians in a textbook quid pro quo, but because money buys the wealthy more access and influence, which is just short of legal corruption.

This particularly resonates in the context of the United States, though likely less in countries like Denmark and Norway. The 2010 Supreme Court decision *Citizens United v. Federal Election Commission* exacerbated this issue by protecting corporate spending on campaigns as free speech. Compounding the problem, US Congress members are required to spend hours each day fundraising, leaving little time for actual lawmaking. As a result, legislative responsibilities are often outsourced to lobbyists.

The influence of lobbies on US politics is actually *worse* than people imagine. In their recent *The Wolves of K Street: The Secret History of How Big Money Took Over Big Government*, two journalists, including the Pulitzer Prize–winning reporter Brody Mullins, show how political lobbying has evolved from a boutique activity in the 1970s to a full-blown industry, in a way that has led to the contemporary capture of government by big corporations, from Genentech to Google.

When you see who has a voice in Washington, the distorting effect of lobbies as an explanation makes sense. According to political scientists, a staggering 78 percent of the American adult population is represented by just 6 percent of the lobbying groups in Washington. Meanwhile, the remaining 22 percent—comprised of executives (8.5 percent) and professionals (13 percent)—command an overwhelming 94 percent of the lobbying influence.[16] To put it bluntly, more than three quarters of the US population is represented by a tiny fraction of lobbying groups, while a small elite— the white-collar professionals and their corporate bosses—enjoy near-total dominance, with 94 percent of the lobbying power aligned to their interests. It's only logical that those with greater access to representatives end up steering the decision-making process. The problem is stark: The average taxpayer simply doesn't have enough lobbyists advocating for their interests. Meanwhile, the people who *should* be representing them—politicians—spend most of their time interacting with, and inevitably being influenced by, advocates for corporations and the wealthy elite.

Incompetence

Another explanation for the political class's failure to deliver good governance on anything from climate change to social justice to economic policy could be sheer incompetence. Maybe the people we select through elections are just not good at governing. And indeed, if you pause to think about it, what ever made us think that people who are good at campaigning and making promises would be any good at governing and making laws? Who convinced us that there was any correlation between those two sets of qualities?

But why, you might ask, would incompetence translate into a systemic bias in favor of the rich? Incompetence should yield random results, perhaps complete inertia, unless maybe we accompany it with a story of capture by other actors. Still, we can't rule out individual incompetence as a part of the story. We all have examples in mind, whether incompetence is due to stupidity, absurdly old age, or some other reason.

But there is another version of the incompetence argument, which lays the blame not on individuals but on the group as a whole. Politicians, taken one by one, may be educated and know what they are doing. They may know the players, the rules, the system, their constituencies, and a lot of facts about the world. And yet, as a group, they can't get it right.

The Group Effect

In order to understand this possibility of a disconnect between the sum of individual competencies and the aggregate results, you need a new kind of political epistemology—which is a fancy word for "a theory of political knowledge." You have to accept the view that the competence of a group is not just a linear function of the competence of its average member. What matters is also certain group properties—for example, the diversity of perspectives and ways of thinking that are represented in the group. So when members of the political class are too similar (because of the homogenizing properties of human choice that we discussed in the preceding chapter), their group will tend to miss out on and misinterpret information. It's the theory of political knowledge of the antifederalists, who intuited that unless the government looked like us, it wouldn't rule in our interests. It's the theory of political knowledge of the ancient Greeks, who thought that political wisdom was produced by deliberation and voting among ordinary citizens, rather than independently accessed by experts. I will return to these arguments in chapter 5.

Ultimately, the real problem with elections might mirror the issue we identified with politicians earlier: It's not so much about *who* they are but *how* they are chosen. Elections inherently favor certain types of individuals while excluding others. Entire categories of people—most notably, the shy—are effectively repelled by the process. This systemic bias in access to political power lies at the heart of our challenges, driving the inequality and exclusion that lead to suboptimal policies and laws.

The Illusion of Choice

But isn't the ability to choose our rulers worth the cost of suboptimal policies? Wouldn't any alternative be worse? Before we explore such an alternative in the following chapters, let me ask you this question: Is the freedom to choose our representatives the ultimate value here? Or is it something else?

Americans tend to think that having more freedom and more choices is always better. But they are not better off for having entire aisles of various kinds of junk food and sodas to choose from at the supermarket. They'd be better off with a smaller selection of cheap, delicious, and healthy food. Similarly, the "freedom" to choose between elites is not necessarily real or healthy if this choice is ultimately largely disconnected from an impact on issues and policies. The freedom to vote directly on issues would be another matter, of course, and this is why I am in favor of the use of direct democracy mechanisms like referenda on many issues. But much of the business of politics needs to be conducted by representatives, which is why I focus on the question of their selection.

The point of elections, it is often argued, is to ensure a form of accountability; from that point of view, being able to choose one's rulers is indeed valuable, including from a democratic point of view. But are elections such an impressive mechanism for accountability? Given the various obstacles in the way of voter sovereignty, from how undemocratic the system of political parties is in choosing candidates to gerrymandering and the presence of filters like the electoral college, there are reasons to be doubtful. But even zooming out from the US case and looking at elections in a more theoretical, idealized way, elections are extremely blunt and inefficient tools, essentially because they punish politicians on the basis of bundles of policies rather than specific acts or behaviors. In practice, that means that politicians can get away with all forms of unethical, corrupt, and incompetent behavior for a very long time.

There exist other forms of democratic accountability than elections, which we will encounter in this book and which could be developed in the context of a non-electoral democracy. But, at any rate, it is important to recognize the trade-offs we are facing here. Do we want to preserve the individual freedom to "choose" our representatives, even at great costs to political equality, good governance, and, ultimately, collective freedom?.

Again, I don't mean to downplay the advantages of elected governments as we know them. Getting to choose one's rulers is certainly a vast improvement over systems where those rulers are imposed either by tradition or force. Being able to remove them from power at the voting booth also presents serious advantages over century-long dynasties. But that still just means we are enjoying the advantages of a liberal system that protects individual rights from too much encroachment by arbitrary powers. It does not mean we are getting closer to the ideal of self-rule in which we all share power equally. Self-rule may require not choosing our rulers but, instead, ruling and being ruled in turn. Or, as I prefer to say, representing and being represented in turn.

Why We Hate Each Other

There is, finally, a last point I want to make about elections, which is that even if they did not produce oligarchies, which they do, they also tend to have a terrible side effect: that of dividing us. Republicans and Democrats in the United States today hate each other. They don't talk to each other. They won't marry each other. How could we expect them to solve problems together in such a context? This problem of extreme polarization is starting to take root in other countries as well and is amplified by the media ecosystem and new technologies. The root cause, however, is not technology but electoral politics, which creates incentives to demonize the other camp, to argue in bad faith, to lie and distort the opposite camp's perspective.

Why? Because electoral politics is agonistic and adversarial by construct. The point is to win, not to be right, not to listen and learn or, God forbid, change your mind. There is an assumption behind the whole design that the clash of competing views will produce the truth and what's best for the country. That's a beautiful thought, and maybe that worked in the eighteenth century, when Parliament was seen as a place of highbrow deliberation where the natural aristocracy of the country would engage in lofty exchange of arguments and, in Madison's words, "refine and enlarge" popular judgment in the process. But alas, this idea has been completely falsified by recent history, if not since the invention of formal parties in the nineteenth century. Recent scholarship suggests that politicians not only don't enlighten us, they consciously cultivate our worst tendencies because they electorally benefit from them. According to the political scientist Steven W. Webster, party leaders have every incentive to keep feeding us political content that makes us and keeps us enraged, because anger makes us more loyal as voters.[17]

What we see today, as a direct result, is the triumph of lies over truth and "alternative facts" over actual ones. Again, we can blame technologies, the media, or foreign entities, but these external forces only accelerate and amplify a design feature of electoral politics. And while the situation is probably less dire in places like Norway, Denmark, Switzerland, or even France, my suspicion is that this is *in spite* of the electoral system, not because of it.

Does this mean that we should get rid of adversarial politics altogether? No, as conflicts of interests and values are here to stay. But surely we should strive, at the very least, to make room for another kind of politics, one that is more constructive, deliberative, and conducive to positive emotions that bring us closer to one another, rather than further apart.

The Road Not Taken

Let us briefly go back to a claim we accepted at face value in the previous chapter, namely that, as Manin posited, election is equally democratic and oligarchic. This conclusion is convincing only if you accept Manin's assumption of a perfect symmetry between universal suffrage and equality of access to power, as well as the story that there exists a perfect "equilibrium" between the arguments of the class of the ruled versus those of the class of rulers. Well, this assumption is problematic, and the story has holes in it.

First, the democratic principle of "equal votes" is not essential to the principle of periodic elections, which has long accommodated so-called plural voting—or unequal voting rights—both in practice (with many European countries distributing more voting rights to wealthier citizens until the middle of the nineteenth century) and in the theory of early liberal thinkers such as John Stuart Mill (whose influential *Considerations on Representative Gov-*

ernment made the case for giving more votes to more educated people). Periodic elections, in other words, do not in principle require "one person, one vote."

Second, and more important, the oligarchic aspect—the disproportionate amount of power distributed to a certain type of people—is bound to have a much larger impact on the nature of the system than the equality of citizens' votes. Politicians set the agenda and control the levers of power, with the ability to manufacture consent to a degree. By contrast, voters are a largely atomized bunch who can keep politicians on only a rather loose leash. Electoral accountability operates only at the level of bundles of policies over the period of an election cycle, never or rarely for singular ones.

Further, the assumption of argumentative equilibrium holds only if we assume that the selection of representatives must be performed by human beings. If human beings must make the selection, then it's probably indeed better for both the few (who buy social peace that way) and the many (who at least get to eliminate the worst options) that we all participate in the choice, rather than just let a small subset decide.

There is, however, another alternative, the one proposed by this book: letting chance take over and distributing opportunities for power equally across the entire population. This approach would disrupt the current equilibrium by significantly reducing elites' access to power while giving everyone else, however marginally, a better chance. Under such a system, any single member of the elite would have just one chance out of as many citizens as there are. Meanwhile, non-elites would move from having virtually no chance of being elected to the same chance of selection as anyone else—slim at the national level perhaps, but very real at the local level.

And while the odds for any individual non-elite remain small at the national level of a large country, the likelihood of someone like them reaching a position of power becomes remarkably high. For ordinary people, then, the shift from elections to sortition should be an appealing prospect. The current system's stability depends on keeping this lottery-based alternative either invisible or framed as entirely undesirable. Once recognized as viable, it challenges the legitimacy of the status quo.

If this is true, how come none of the French and American revolutionaries made the case for lot in the eighteenth century? Why did everyone converge on the idea of replacing selection to power based on tradition, divine authority, or bloodline with individual human choice? How come sortition, which for centuries was deemed the democratic option, is not an option for so many people today, as we have entirely embraced the view that democracy is inseparable from elections? This is a real puzzle, and one that Manin was among the first scholars to both spot and address.

Manin points out that talk of sortition entirely disappeared in the eighteenth century. And it is striking indeed that even the people whom lot would have served well ideologically did not even think of mentioning it. It just wasn't on their mental map of the possible. Consider the anti-federalists in the nascent United States. They were defending against what they saw as the elitism of the federalists, forwarding a vision of representation one would today call "descriptive." They wanted to make sure assemblies looked like the rest of the nation—or at least its white male part.

They wanted, in particular, the lower classes, including peasants and artisans, not just landed notables, to be able to shape national politics. Melancton Smith, a prominent American lawyer, politician, and anti-federalist leader during the founding era of the United States, wrote, "The idea that naturally suggests itself to our minds, when we speak of representatives, is that they resemble those they represent; they should be a true picture of the people: possess the knowledge of their circumstances and their wants; sympathize in all their distresses, and be disposed to seek their true interests." Similarly, John Adams, a federalist himself whose ideas later influenced anti-federalists, evoked representatives who would amount to a portrait of the nation and would "feel and think" like regular citizens. The representative assembly, he said, should be like "an exact portrait, in miniature, of the people at large, as it should feel, reason and act like them." Yet none of these great minds thought of lot as the best means to their end. Instead, they thought that only elections were an acceptable way to select representatives. Their solution for maximizing resemblance under an electoral system was to increase the number of representatives and to plead for small constituencies, so as to maximize the chances of lower-middle-class people being elected.

Manin's explanation for this eighteenth-century blind spot regarding lot places the blame on "social contract theory," a then-dominant theory of political legitimacy that traces the source of political authority to the consent of the governed—and to elections as its best proxy. This affinity between social contract theory and consent at the ballot booth explains both election's triumph over any rival selection mechanism for representatives, in spite of its oligarchic aspect, and the disappearance of lot, in spite of its egalitarian implications.[18]

It thus appears that the main reason why lot could not win in the eighteenth century is that it was understood mostly as an anticorruption mechanism meant to introduce some unpredictability but, crucially, no rationality in the political process. The unpredictability ensured protection against capture and gaming of the system. But it could also lead to the selection of incompetent leaders, which is why lot in the Italian republics was mostly used on a pool of carefully vetted participants.

The apparent irrationality of lot is presumably what explains its disappearance in the age of the Enlightenment, which celebrated individual reason above all else. But the science of statistics, which emerged in the following century, would demonstrate that there is, in fact, rationality in large numbers (the so-called law of large numbers) and that chance can, in fact, be "tamed" into a force for good.[19] In particular, statistics and probability theory would help justify the Athenian practice of using lot to staff assemblies, where the law of large numbers can do its magic, rather than individual positions, where you are at the mercy of a bad draw.

These historical and epistemological considerations explain why lot was abandoned yesterday, but they do not justify continuing to ignore it *today*. On the contrary, it is entirely possible that eighteenth-century thinkers made a terrible mistake in tying their fate to a theory of political legitimacy that ultimately entrenched an oligarchic form of representation through the ideology of the sanctity of individual choice. Or it could be that an electoral system was the best option at the time, given the lack of education of the general population, scientific ignorance of the properties of lot, and technological limitations in the implementation of a lot-based politics.

Either way, politics as we know it isn't delivering the laws and policies most of us want—and when it does, it's usually because a more powerful group happens to want the same thing. What we have is "democracy by coincidence," which, arguably, is no democracy at all. It's time to reconsider the choices made in the eighteenth century and to explore new ways of doing democracy—this time giving a central role to selection by lot—also known as sortition.

FOUR

Citizen Politics, Old and New

> *When the question is an affair of state, then everybody is free*
> *to have a say—carpenter, tinker, cobbler, sailor, passenger;*
> *rich and poor, high and low—any one who likes gets up, and*
> *no one reproaches him . . . with not having learned, and hav-*
> *ing no teacher, and yet giving advice.*
>
> PLATO, QUOTING SOCRATES IN *PROTAGORAS*,
> 319D (TRANSLATED BY BENJAMIN JOWETT)

The Athenian Revolution ▪ Ordinary Citizens as Legislators ▪
Experts as Slaves ▪ A Place for the Shy ▪ What About Accountability? ▪
Was Ancient Democracy Successful? ▪ Greek Lessons for Today ▪
Lot's Second Act ▪ Contemporary Revival

C lassical Athens (508–322 BCE) was by no means the first democracy. In *The Decline and Rise of Democracy*, the political scientist David Stasavage traces democratic forms of governance
all the way back to the third and second millennia BCE in the
Mesopotamian kingdom of Mari and to ancient republics in India
going back at least a few centuries before classical Athens. According to Stasavage, governance by assemblies of regular folks
was common in Mesopotamia until centralizing rulers destroyed
this pattern. Alexander the Great, as he progressed in his conquest
toward India circa 326 BCE, found institutions in some locales that

resembled, and most likely predated, the republican city-states that had existed in Greece—for example, the societies in the foothills of the Himalayas, in the eastern end of what is today Uttar Pradesh and Bihar. Today, the *gram sabhas* of India—open meetings that operate as legislative bodies at the village level—continue this ancient tradition of local popular assemblies, even as contemporary India has embraced the electoral model of democracy imported from the West at the national level.

Still, classical Athens remains the best-known and most sophisticated example of an ancient form of rule by ordinary citizens, and well worth looking back to. For my purposes in this book, Athens is also the first democracy we know of to have introduced a crucial innovation: the use of lot to assign political offices combined with a rotation of offices. These combined practices ensured that politics remained, for all intents and purposes, an amateur's sport. Politics was for everyone who counted as a citizen in Athens, not just social elites and gifted orators.

The Athenian Revolution

Democratic Athens was born first as a middle-class democracy when the Athenian lawgiver Solon, circa 594 BCE, made changes to the constitution that ended the exclusive control of government by the aristocracy (based on birth) and introduced a system where wealth played a role in political power. With this reform, political rights became accessible to the sufficiently wealthy.

Pericles, a Greek statesman and general during what is considered the golden age of Athens, introduced another set of reforms that further democratized the system by reducing the influence of wealth and property ownership on political participation and on eligibility to certain offices. In 458–457 BCE, Pericles reduced the property qualification needed to hold the office of Archon, one of the top political positions in Athens. This allowed more citizens, regardless of their wealth, to potentially hold important offices within the Athenian government.

After 454 BCE, Pericles implemented a system of payment for citizens who served as jurors in the Heliaia (the supreme court of Athens) and other public officials. This enabled even poorer citizens to participate in government without sacrificing their livelihood, as they could be compensated for their time spent on public duties.

Finally, Pericles extended citizenship rights to all free adult males, irrespective of their social or economic status. This reform, combined with paid public service, allowed lower-class Athenians to participate fully as citizens, including serving on juries and holding offices. Therefore, while property qualifications still existed for some roles, Pericles's reforms aimed to make political participation more accessible to all citizens, diminishing the significance of wealth and property ownership in determining an individual's ability to participate in and influence Athenian democracy.

Of course, the usual disclaimers apply: women, foreigners, and slaves continued to be excluded. But let us acknowledge that these exclusions were not peculiar to Athenian democracy. Every urban society in the world had slavery at the time, and Athenian democracy was simply not an exception. And in Athens, slaves had it better than they had it in, say, oligarchic Sparta: the Helots, the subjugated populations of Sparta, were harshly oppressed and, as a result, constantly rebelling, whereas there are no known cases of slave rebellion in Athens. As we'll see, some Athenian slaves even played key administrative roles in the city and were celebrated as such. What was truly unique in Athens is the way that the poor and the rich were actual political equals. This was unheard of at the city-state level in the ancient world.

Another unique feature of the Athenian system is that education and technical expertise were not prerequisites for participating in the assembly, nor, perhaps more surprisingly, were they required for exercising political functions. Citizen involvement was achieved through a combination of open public assemblies, where the masses directly made decisions, and a system of lotteries and rapid rotation for political offices. This approach ensured, as Aristotle famously defined ancient democracy, that everyone had the opportunity "to rule and be ruled in turn."

This Athenian approach to democracy is celebrated in the famous "Funeral Oration" in Thucydides's classic, *History of the Peloponnesian War*. In it, Pericles, a lauded Athenian general, credits the fact that in Athens everybody takes part proudly in public life for Athens' superiority—political military, and otherwise. "A man may benefit his country whatever the obscurity of his condition," Pericles remarks. And, as a result of a system in which everyone can see himself as an author of the law, "respect for the authorities and for the law" ensures public order. Meanwhile, life is made sweeter by a prosperous economy, as evidenced by the fact that Athens has "regular games and sacrifices throughout the year" as well as homes that are "beautiful and elegant." Additionally, "the greatness of our city" causes "the fruits of the whole earth to flow in upon us; so that we enjoy the goods of other countries as freely as our own." This good life is preserved by the valor of the Athenian army, whose military training is "in many respects superior to that of our adversaries" and which allows Athens, alone among all ancient city-states, to remain defiantly "thrown open to the world" and even welcoming of foreigners.[1]

While this description of the superiority of classical Athens may come across as typical patriotic bluster, there were objective reasons for Athenians' pride in their city and in their way of running things. Athens was both a flourishing commercial center and a feared military superpower at its peak in 400 BCE, standing its ground against other powerful cities like Sparta and, as a result, also more than willing to impose its imperialistic agenda on less-powerful city-states. Run and defended mostly by ordinary citizens rather than socioeconomic or military elites, democratic Athens proved to be a resilient regime as well as a cultural and scientific center and a magnet for foreign populations through its 250 years of existence.

Ordinary Citizens as Legislators

Ancient Athenians delegated agenda-setting power to a group of five hundred randomly selected citizens chaired each day by a different, also randomly selected, citizen. The Council of 500, as this assembly was called, was appointed by lot annually and deliberated over policy recommendations and law proposals. These recommendations and proposals were then passed on to a much larger body, the People's Assembly, which any citizen could join, up to the physical capacity of the venue.

The meetings of the assembly took place initially at the marketplace, the Agora, but were later moved to a bigger and specifically public-oriented space called the Pnyx, on a hill overlooking the city. The Pnyx could accommodate a maximum of around eight thousand people out of the sixty-thousand-strong citizenry. But somehow this subset was identified as "the demos" (the people), and their decisions were binding on those who didn't directly participate.

To reach a decision, the assembly members first listened to various orators arguing the pros and cons of policy recommendations and laws. Once they were done talking, the assembly voted through a mix of raised hands and the ancient equivalent of an applause meter.

Meanwhile, various citizens' juries ranging from five hundred to a thousand members were assembled daily to judge political trials, in which they listened to the accusations and rebuttals before casting a judgment (without deliberation).

In 411 and 404 BCE, however, Athenian democracy was lost to oligarchic coups by aristocrats who managed to convince the People's Assembly to vote for them. When rebuilding their democracy on the heels of these events, the Athenians decided to pass a series of reforms that transferred power from the People's Assembly to sortition-based bodies, called *nomothetai*.

While these reforms are sometimes understood to have weakened Athenian democracy, by moving legislative power from the open assembly to the lot-based juries, the changes may on the contrary be interpreted as a way of strengthening it, by preserving the principle of equality but protecting the decision-making from capture by gifted orators and demagogues. The Athenians seemed to have empirically arrived at the conclusion that randomly selected assemblies were not less democratic but less manipulable than large open ones. In fairness, there is some debate as to whether the *nomothetai* were appointed by lot or some other mechanism. But the key point is that they were supposed to be run by ordinary members of the demos.[2]

Experts as Slaves

Athenians knew of elections and used them in their system. But they reserved appointment by election for certain positions only, such as generals and top military administrators. These functions were vital and required a certain type of specialized competence. But they were not political—that is, pertaining to the articulation and promotion of the common good. The role of generals was not to decide whether to go to war, a decision left to the People's Assembly, but how to maximize the chances of winning the war once it had been declared.

Similarly, administrators' goals were to manage military manpower and resources according to political goals defined independently of them. Elections were thus seen as a good way to select for competence of a certain kind, but not the kind required for lawmaking. If anything, Athenians were suspicious of elections, which they saw as an oligarchic selection mechanism.

Not only did classical Athens make ordinary citizens the source of all laws, it also subordinated experts to their will. To the extent that magistrates and generals were experts, their decisions were in the service of citizens' ends. Even more fascinating, according to the historian Paulin Ismard, the only experts of any kind allowed to directly support the work of citizens as lawmakers were slaves. By turning to slaves rather than free men to occupy key positions in the technical administration of the city—such as archivists, accountants, and engineers—Athenians made sure that the inferior political and social status of their experts would prevent them from capturing power on the grounds of their superior technical knowledge.[3]

Why didn't they empower slaves as generals and military administrators, you might ask? Presumably because they knew that to put your life on the line you have to care more about your city than any slave could be reasonably expected to. That said, while they didn't elevate slaves to the position of generals, they did make them policemen—for example, the kind that prevented citizens from entering the People's Assembly meeting once the place was at capacity.

Slavery as a solution to the risk of expert capture is not morally commendable, obviously, but there is something interesting and even inspiring about how jealous early democrats were of the political prerogative of ordinary citizens over experts. As I'll argue later, a structurally similar, and more humane, solution for the modern age is to institutionalize the subordination of experts to citizens by placing them "on tap, and not on top."

A Place for the Shy

The Greeks understood political equality (for those considered free men) as the idea that no one was too humble to participate in politics. Poverty, for example—a common source of shame and political hesitation in most societies—was not seen as a barrier. According to Pericles, as we saw above, "obscurity of condition" was not an obstacle to a political career. It meant that in Athens even the dirt-poor citizen could find himself in the political spotlight—that is, visibly occupying a position of political influence—ruling, not just being ruled, as long as he had the desire for it.

Mere willingness to show up sufficed to access a key position of power in the polity, namely a spot in the People's Assembly, where the poor (again, as long as they were citizens) had the same opportunity as the rich to speak up and make proposals to the group, and at the very least could vote and shout and murmur to approve or reject a proposal. But citizens could also volunteer for a chance to serve on popular juries, in which they were part of a group that rendered important political judgments. Last but not least, if they put down their name for it, they might even be selected (by lot) for a spot on the Council of 500, on which they set the political agenda for the whole community. Over the course of a lifetime, these opportunities allowed any person counting as a citizen to feel that they were shaping political decision-making and to develop a real sense of political efficacy.

What's more, the desire to participate wasn't taken for granted—it was actively encouraged and incentivized, including through monetary compensation. Citizens were paid an obol per day (the equivalent of ten dollars today)[4] for attending the assembly or serving on juries. While this amount was insignificant to the wealthy, it was a critical incentive for the many poor citizens. For them, it was worth arriving at dawn to secure a spot, as latecomers were turned away once the assembly reached capacity—and without a spot, there was no pay.

What About Accountability?

How were the many randomly selected and self-selected bodies of classical Athens accountable in the absence of the electoral mechanism? First, randomly selected bodies in charge of lawmaking were protected from the risk of corruption by the very fact of their random selection. This made it impossible to predict who was going to be in charge and thus prevented the bribery of decision-makers ahead of time (for example, under the guise of campaign donations).

Random selection also made it impossible for any person to facilitate through donations the accession to power of his underlings. Additionally, facing a randomly selected group, any would-be corrupter would have had to bribe each individual one by one, in retail fashion, so to speak, rather than in bulk (as is made easier in elected assemblies, in which buying off the party hierarchy gets you all the votes at once). An additional accountability mechanism was periodic and frequent rotation of those same randomly selected assemblies, which made it difficult to build over time the relationships facilitating the desired quid pro quo arrangements. Additional preemptive accountability mechanisms included vetting of citizen volunteers up front for participation in the lottery.

To ensure additional accountability, classical Athens included a system of popular juries before which people accused of leading the city astray had to explain themselves and provide accounts of their proposals and actions, and by which these accused people would ultimately be judged. This was, infamously, what happened to Socrates, who was accused of impiety and corrupting the youth. Accountability was also facilitated by a practice called *euthynai* or "straightening," the examination of accounts that every public official underwent upon the expiration of their term.

In terms of a pure sanctioning mechanism—the threat of which also operated as a preventive mechanism—the Greeks resorted for a time to the practice of ostracism, in which each member of the assembly put down the name of the citizen deemed most dangerous to the city for that year. If enough people agreed on one name, that person could be banished for the next ten years. This is not a practice we would consider desirable today, but it illustrates the range of accountability mechanisms that can exist beyond elections.

Later, sometime after 417 BCE, the Greeks replaced ostracism, perhaps because they came to acknowledge its brutality, with the *graphe paranomon*, which consisted of the legal action taken against citizens who proposed motions violating existing legislation. The *graphe paranomon* was a sort of built-in judicial review procedure that was performed by democratic institutions themselves, as opposed to a task assigned to an external body such as a supreme court. It ensured that a person proposing a new law did their homework and verified that their proposal was in keeping with the existing laws of Athens. The *graphe paranomon* thus served as a deterrent to proposals that could have upset the Athenian democratic system, promoting its own self-regulation.

These practices and institutions functioned broadly as accountability mechanisms and, as far as we can tell, worked reasonably well. In fact, they may have been overly strict and punitive—ancient Athenians were held accountable not only for their actions but also for their proposals. Individuals could even be punished for bad outcomes stemming from sheer bad luck, regardless of whether incompetence or dishonesty was involved.[5] Nonetheless, their example suggests that accountability need not be a significant issue, even in a system where professional politicians, particularly elected ones, play little to no role.

Was Ancient Democracy Successful?

Classical Athens is the paradigmatic case of politics without politicians. Was Athens politically successful as a result of centering the political wisdom of ordinary citizens rather than that of professional politicians and even experts, as well as in making the knowledge experts statutorily subservient to the will of citizens?

Athenians and their contemporaries seemed to believe so, and modern historians concur. For example, Josiah Ober, a Stanford University scholar of ancient Greece, argues that it was the collective wisdom of Athenians and in particular the knowledge-aggregating properties of their democratic procedures that established the commercial, artistic, and even military superiority of Athens over rival city-states, including Sparta.[6]

Of course, superiority did not entail infallibility. Quite apart from and in addition to the moral bankruptcy of slavery, democratic Athens also made terrible political mistakes. Critics are fond of citing the 415 BCE invasion of Sicily, which resulted in a humiliating defeat for the city, though the army itself recovered relatively quickly, and the condemnation to death of Socrates by a popular jury in 399 BCE, which stained the reputation of democracy among philosophers pretty much forever (courtesy of Socrates's influential student Plato). Athens was not a flawless or entirely inspirational system, and it was ultimately taken over by the much larger Macedonian empire. But during the two hundred and fifty years or so of its existence, democratic Athens was still, on the whole, gloriously outperforming less-democratic regimes of similar sizes in terms of military might, economic prosperity, and flourishing of the arts and sciences.

Greek Lessons for Today

Assuming the Greek system worked well on the whole, what can ancient Athens possibly have to teach us today? We moderns live in huge, multicultural nation-states and in a postindustrial, globalized age in which problems are much more complex than those that ancient people had to face. What could still be of relevance in such ancient models of democracy, even if we ignore their repulsive reliance on and disenfranchisement of enslaved people? Would their form of politics without politicians be able to deal with climate change? Nuclear proliferation? An opioid crisis?

If your intuitive answer to the last question is that ordinary citizens would be incapable of coming up with solutions to these modern problems, you really need to read the rest of this book. For I will argue that what we can learn from the ancient Greeks and from all the people across history who have practiced a form of politics without politicians is that politics is not primarily a matter of expertise and professionalism. It is, instead, the business of every citizen. In ancient Greece, the definition of who counted as a citizen was certainly exclusionary. But once you counted as a citizen, your participation was not conditional on possession of knowledge and expertise any more than it was conditional on socioeconomic status or property ownership.

One implication is that the poorest of the poor had just as much of a chance as the wealthy to enter the People's Assembly, on a first-come, first-serve basis, since physical space was limited. In fact, a willingness to get up at dawn and wait at the entrance of the assembly site actually gave an advantage to the poor over the rich.

The poorest and the least educated also had the same chance as the wealthy of being selected, once their names were entered in the pool of viable candidates, in the lottery that assigned positions on the Council of 500 or on political juries. In fact, because attendance was paid (even if not much), the poor did, in practice, participate more than the rich. Thus, unsurprisingly, and unlike what happens in our modern societies, policies and laws were more responsive to their needs than to those of the rich. How else would you explain a system in which the rich were expected to pay, and were seemingly happy to pay, for their own expensive military equipment and all public religious celebrations?

The fact that political participation was not conditional on demonstrable expertise at the gate does not mean that ancient Greek democracy did not heavily rely on and make use of expertise. On the contrary, classical Athens was able to mobilize and use experts while keeping them subordinated to citizens' judgment. Many of these topical experts were slaves. Meanwhile, the practice of engaging in politics regularly educated citizens and created its own kind of expertise. As Ober describes it, "the Athenian system . . . provided citizens with an ongoing—indeed, potentially life-long—practical education in the workings of the democratic machine."[7] As a result, "individual Athenians became more politically capable—still amateurs in that they served occasionally and in rotation, yet possessing some of the decision-making characteristics associated with experts."[8]

In other words, what we can learn, or relearn, from the Greeks is that political expertise is also acquired on the job. The less we give people an opportunity to participate, the less capable they are. The more we ask of them, the more they learn.

A natural objection could easily arise: Aren't you then simply asking that every single one of us turn into an expert? Aren't you basically re-creating politics with politicians, just not the elected kind? Josiah Ober points out that in the Athenian context, learning from political practice did not mean turning into a politician: "The effective operation of democracy did not require each participant to be completely socialized into the routines of government or to understand all of the machine's complex workings."[9] Athenians, individually, did not have to turn into Pericles or Plato's philosopher-kings.

James Madison is famous for his criticism of ancient democracy on the grounds that "had every Athenian been a Socrates, every Athenian assembly would still have been a mob." It would be more accurate to say that "had Pericles never existed, the whole Athenian political system would still have been just as smart." This was arguably the view held by Pericles himself. In the previously mentioned funeral oration commemorating fallen soldiers of the Peloponnesian War, he is reported as celebrating the merits of public wisdom: "Ordinary citizens, though occupied with the pursuits of industry, are still fair judges of public matters."[10]

Lot's Second Act

Centuries after the Greek democratic period, selection by lot was used in several Italian republics, including Florence and Venice, between the twelfth and sixteenth centuries. Lot was used there not so much to distribute power widely as to fight corruption and monopolization of power among the groups of wealthy families who ran these cities. A complicated selection scheme mixing election and sortition ensured that no one family could capture power too easily, even as it was meant to be safely kept in the hands of the privileged.

The lottery system began to wane as the Medici family consolidated power in the early sixteenth century. By 1532, the Medici had transformed Florence into a hereditary duchy, ending its republican governance. In city-states such as Genoa, Siena, and Lucca, republican institutions were either weakened or were overtaken by neighboring monarchies in the late sixteenth and seventeenth centuries. Florence was the last to maintain its republican structures, including some uses of lot selection, well into the eighteenth century. However, when Napoleon invaded in 1797, the Venetian Republic fell, effectively ending its institutions, including its use of lot. After this, Venice was integrated into the Austrian Empire, and republican practices like lotteries were replaced with centralized governance.

The use of lot was also widespread in Switzerland from the Middle Ages until the early nineteenth century. In Swiss communities, particularly in rural cantons like Uri, Schwyz, and Unterwalden, lotteries were used to choose local representatives and officials in the early Swiss Confederation, beginning in the thirteenth and fourteenth centuries. Positions such as judgeships, memberships in councils, and other community roles were sometimes filled by drawing lots, ensuring that different families and regions all had a chance to participate in governance.

The Swiss cantons were relatively small and often had strong traditions of communal governance, with decisions made at the local level. Lotteries in this context served as a way to prevent certain families or factions from monopolizing power and provided a democratic means of representation.

As Switzerland evolved politically, especially with the establishment of the Swiss federal state in 1848, more formal and representative democratic processes, chiefly electoral ones, replaced the use of lotteries in governance. Voting systems based on majority and proportional representation became more common, and the use of the lot declined as a formal selection method for political offices. The legacy of rotation and equal opportunity to serve remained nonetheless a core principle in Swiss politics, influencing the Swiss tradition of direct democracy, where referenda and citizen votes became central to governance.

Outside the West, historians have also shown that lot was used in other countries, such as China. The historian Yves Sintomer documents that China occasionally used lot in military conscription, tax collection, public works, and local governance. However, it was never as widespread as in European societies. The dominant Confucian meritocratic tradition and the imperial examination system meant that lotteries played only a minor role in governance and were usually applied for specific administrative needs rather than as a routine part of political life.[11]

In the West, lot disappeared from politics sometime between the middle of the eighteenth century and the beginning of the nineteenth century, a puzzle that many authors are still trying to understand.

Lot nevertheless survived in the modern age in criminal and civil law, in the form of the jury, a Norman custom of law by peers (with no known connection to the Greek precedent) that traveled from France to England in the eleventh century and from there, eventually, to the United States and the world.[12] The idea of the jury is to have a group of equals decide a legal dispute, including criminal cases. The role of juror was initially reserved for elites but opened up to the larger population over time, so much so that it came to embody the democratic ideal for authors like Alexis de Tocqueville. Tocqueville considered the jury, as he encountered it in the nascent United States, a school of democratic education.

Despite their confinement to the legal realm, juries retain an important political dimension. Contrary to a common but mistaken view, juries are not solely in charge of "figuring out the facts" of the matter. As Jeffrey Abramson argues in his excellent study of the institution, *We, the Jury*, their judgment can take a political form, too, typically in the case of jury nullification, whereby a jury can choose to acquit a defendant, despite evidence presented, because they believe the law itself to be unjust or morally wrong, or because they disagree with the way it has been applied in the specific case.[13] This capacity of jurors to place their judgment above the letter of the law is a vestigial expression of political power.

Contemporary Revival

Recent decades have seen a revival of lot, inspired by both the Greek tradition of lot-based assemblies and the practice of small-scale randomly selected criminal juries, with the emergence of so-called deliberative minipublics. Deliberative minipublics—minipublics for short—can be defined broadly as a diverse, randomly selected body of citizens assembled for the purpose of deliberating about an issue of public concern. They are deliberative when their members are given time to educate themselves about an issue and exchange arguments, information, stories, and ideas with one another. Minipublics range in size, from a few dozen to a few hundred members, as well as in duration and purpose. From the 1990s onward, a variety of minipublics were experimented with, initially mostly in the Global North, including small-scale German citizen juries and Danish consensus conferences. Today there are two general types of minipublics: deliberative polls and citizens' assemblies.

Deliberative polls are the brainchild of the Stanford political scientist James Fishkin.[14] His idea was to bring a random sample of the public together over a weekend to learn from experts and confer with their peers about a particular issue or set of issues. Fishkin saw this method as a way to figure out what the public would think if its members had access to reliable information, experts, and enough time to discuss the issue with their peers.[15]

In deliberative polling, organizers select the sample of participants (usually several hundred people) using statistical methods that make the resulting group, in the words of the political scientist Jane Mansbridge, the "gold standard" of minipublics. The large group is given briefing materials and access to experts whom they hear from in plenary sessions, and is then broken down into smaller groups (at random). The aim is to give participants the opportunity to learn about the issues, discuss them with fellow citizens, and weigh different perspectives. You might say that deliberative polls are like standard polls if the participants met and talked to one another—in other words, nothing like polls at all (which is why the name is a little unfortunate).

One key characteristic of deliberative polls is that they include a control group, a sample of randomly selected citizens who are statistically identical to the people convened for the deliberative poll but do not get to meet with one another and deliberate. Both the deliberating participants and the control group are surveyed on the policy proposals in advance, and each group takes the same opinion survey again once the few days of deliberation are completed. The point of having the control group is that you can scientifically isolate and measure the impact of the deliberative process (which includes reading about the subject and listening to experts) on participants' beliefs and judgments by its contrast with the beliefs and judgments of the group that did not get to deliberate (but whose views may still have evolved under the influence of forces outside deliberation—for example, political news). To date, Fishkin and his team have successfully conducted more than 150 deliberative polls in over fifty countries, including in the Middle East, Africa, South America, and Asia.

Deliberative polls were initially designed—and are still conceptualized—as improved polls designed to help politicians' decision-making. Their purpose is mostly informational. But they are not meant to integrate citizens in the policy-making process. In fact, they are not always connected to an official government sponsor. For that, we need to turn to a different kind of minipublic: citizens' assemblies.

In 2004, the Canadian province of British Columbia embarked on a landmark democratic experiment known as the British Columbia Citizens' Assembly on Electoral Reform, which became the first-ever citizens' assembly. The assembly was created with the purpose of making recommendations for a possible reform of the province's electoral system.

The citizens' assembly consisted of 160 randomly selected individuals who represented a cross section of the population in terms of age, gender, and geography. These citizens were not politicians or experts; they were ordinary individuals from different walks of life.

Over several months, the assembly members engaged in intensive learning and discussion sessions. They received balanced information from experts and stakeholders about different electoral systems, including proportional representation, single transferable vote, and others. Through these sessions, the members gained a comprehensive understanding of the strengths and weaknesses of each system by weighing the pros and cons of each possible reform, learning from experts and one another's experiences and viewpoints. The citizens' assembly also sought public input to ensure broader participation in the process and make sure no obvious information, argument, or objection failed to be considered. It organized public consultations and received submissions from individuals and organizations across the province. This input informed the discussions and deliberations of the assembly members, providing them with a wider range of perspectives to consider.

At the end of their deliberations, the citizens' assembly members reached a consensus on recommending a specific electoral system for British Columbia. Their recommendation favored a form of proportional representation called the single transferable vote over the established system of first-past-the-post or plurality rule. This recommendation was presented in a final report to the provincial government. The recommendation was ultimately brought to a population-wide referendum, where it fell just short of garnering the required 60 percent approval to be passed into law (debate ensued as to whether that threshold was too high in the first place). Although the citizens' assembly's recommendation did not result in immediate electoral reform, it had a lasting impact on the discourse around electoral systems in British Columbia. It brought the issue to the forefront of public discussion, and its work laid the foundation for subsequent electoral reform initiatives in the province.

Since that somewhat ill-fated Canadian citizens' assembly, however, many more government-sponsored deliberative assemblies of this type, of various sizes, have mushroomed around the world—more than seven hundred, according to a recent OECD report that calls the phenomenon "a deliberative wave," with the wave gaining speed over the last ten years. Among the more famous cases are the Irish citizens' assemblies.

Irish citizens' assemblies are the jewel in the crown of deliberative assemblies because they have been conducted successfully on multiple issues and led to national referenda that resulted in important changes, including marriage equality and the loosening of restrictions on abortion. Ireland is thus the first country that truly put citizens' assemblies on the map.

It all started in 2012, when, in this country of five million mostly Catholic citizens, politicians were in a stalemate on a number of moral and social issues. A group of academics and activists, including the political scientists David Farrell and Jane Suiter, gave them a way out, convincing them to try out the new deliberative format of a citizens' assembly. Because politicians were not ready to let go of control just yet, the organizers proposed a hybrid assembly model, mixing two-thirds randomly selected citizens and one-third politicians. The two-thirds to one-third ratio was not scientific, just an intuitive way to trade off numbers and confidence, ensuring that ordinary citizens would not be overwhelmed by savvy politicians while at the same time ensuring that politicians' influence would not be completely diluted by large numbers of ordinary citizens.

This hybrid assembly was called the Convention on the Constitution and was meant to tackle topics ranging from the electoral system and the voting age to the place of women in the home and in politics, even the question of whether to allow same-sex marriage. In total, ninety-nine assembly members (plus a chair, an economist named Tom Arnold) deliberated about the topic of marriage equality over a series of ten weekends distributed over fifteen months between December 2021 and April 2023. Each weekend was devoted to a different topic. The citizens listened to expert witnesses and considered the pros and cons of a change to the law. Politicians and ordinary citizens also learned to trust one another. This first hybrid deliberative process ended, most famously, with a consensual recommendation to legalize same-sex marriage, which Parliament then put to a referendum, where that same recommendation was swiftly approved. Ireland thus became the first country to legalize same-sex marriage through a popular vote.

This first success set Ireland on a path to the normalization of citizens' assemblies as a way of doing politics that extends to this day. The next big success was the 2016 Irish citizens' assembly, which was exclusively made up of randomly selected citizens. This assembly tackled dozens of questions but is mostly remembered for addressing the topic of abortion, specifically whether or not to change the Eighth Amendment of the Irish constitution, which heavily restricted access to abortion.

The assembly ultimately put forward several recommendations, including the repeal of the Eighth Amendment and the provision of unrestricted access to abortion in certain circumstances. These recommendations led to the Irish government's decision to hold a referendum in 2018, which resulted in a historic majority vote (66 percent of the voting population) in favor of repealing the amendment, marking a significant turning point for Ireland's abortion laws.

Both of these Irish citizens' assemblies played critical roles in fostering public debate on issues where politicians had been stuck in a stalemate. They also demonstrated the competence and responsibility of ordinary citizens to tackle fraught moral issues and consider substantial social changes. Since then, Ireland has organized several more citizens' assemblies, respectively on gender equality, climate change, and the future of health care, most of the time with a successful referendum sanctioning the assembly's recommendations. Ireland today shows no sign of stopping.

Politics without politicians predates politics with politicians by thousands of years. Throughout history, lot-based assemblies of ordinary citizens played a central role—most famously in classical Athens—and have seen a surprising revival in the past forty years. But what makes this system so appealing? What could possibly be good reasons for empowering citizens on the basis of random selection rather than election?

FIVE

The Case for Lot

One principle of liberty is to rule and be ruled in turn.

ARISTOTLE

The jury is before everything a political institution; one ought to consider it as a mode of the sovereignty of the people, or place it in relation to the other laws that establish this sovereignty.

ALEXIS DE TOCQUEVILLE

Liberty ▪ Equality ▪ Fraternity ▪ Anti-Corruption ▪
Collective Intelligence ▪ Judging Juries ▪
Icelandic Wisdom ▪ More Empirical Evidence

My first real exposure to the world of deliberative minipublics was at a 2012 conference in Reykjavik, Iceland. The topic of the conference was the then ongoing constitutional process whereby Icelanders were aiming to rewrite their constitution in the wake of the cataclysmic economic and political crisis of 2008. I discovered in Iceland a lot of exotic things, including the glorious Blue Lagoon (before it was overrun by tourists), surprisingly good trout smoked with sheep's dung, and moonlike landscapes of dark stones covered in moss where there used to be, centuries ago, lush forests, apparently irreversibly destroyed by Viking shipbuilders.

Among the more surprising things, however, were the design choices made for their constitutional process, which included the public at various stages. One of the more innovative aspects was the empowerment of a large random sample of 950 Icelanders to set the agenda for the constitution makers. Among the recommendations that came out of that forum was the desire to nationalize all natural resources that were not already privately owned—a perfectly sensible move in light of the "tragedy of the commons" that a handful of giant fishing companies had caused by overexploiting fishing grounds at taxpayers' expense for decades. That recommendation would become the controversial Article 34 of the new constitutional proposal. When put to a referendum in October 2021, Article 34 would attract 85 percent of support among the voters. The Icelandic experience was one of the steps in my conversion to the idea that we should probably replace, or at the very least complement, elected politicians with randomly selected citizens.

But what are the actual reasons to prefer lot to elections? I believe they can be succinctly captured in the motto of the French revolution: "Liberty, equality, fraternity." In other words, the reasons that we should value lot are the same reasons through which we usually justify democracy: It is a condition of our political freedom, it expresses our standing as political equals, and it embodies our solidarity as members of a community. Additionally, lot has two more instrumental advantages: It is an anticorruption mechanism and it helps tap the collective wisdom of a given people.

Liberty

A democracy based on random selection arguably embodies a richer and more robust ideal of freedom than one rooted in elections—

something the Greeks clearly understood. Aristotle encapsulated this principle of Greek democratic thought with the idea that "one principle of liberty is to rule and be ruled in turn." For the Greeks, liberty inherently involved taking a turn in power. This stands in stark contrast to the modern notion of liberty, which centers on being ruled continuously within the protective framework of constitutionally guaranteed individual rights. While this modern liberty includes the occasional power to "kick out the rascals," it falls short of the Greek ideal—it does not equate to actively participating in ruling.

Modern freedom is often described as "negative" by comparison with the "positive" freedom of the ancients. Negative freedom is freedom from government, and best enjoyed in the silence of the law. This is the freedom that the tradition we call political liberalism emphasizes. By contrast, positive freedom is associated with ancient democracy and seen as too demanding for modern, industrial societies. It is a thicker kind of freedom that allegedly requires full-time devotion to the public good and political life. It is precisely because we moderns don't want this burden, busy as we are with personal and economic pursuits, that we have invented politicians. They do the ruling, under constraints and on the electoral leash that keeps them minimally accountable, while we are free to do our own thing.

But this division of labor is no longer working, if it ever did. Maybe we cannot really enjoy negative freedom unless we also actively shape its conditions and scope through the exercise of positive freedom. Maybe, in fact, we need to reclaim this positive freedom, because political autonomy can exist only when you have the possibility of doing the governing yourself. The beauty of a lot-based democracy is that it allows us to do just that, not all the time or all at once, but sometimes and in turn.

This is also exactly what Alexis de Tocqueville—the nineteenth-century Norman aristocrat philosopher and author—teaches us in the first volume of his *Democracy in America*, possibly the best book ever written about both democracy and the United States. In rather lyrical pages, he singles out the jury, both civil and criminal, as a key political (and not just legal) institution of the young American nation. Indeed, as the epigraph above emphasizes, the jury is for Tocqueville "before everything a political institution" and, specifically, a "mode of the sovereignty of the people" alongside the laws that emanate from Congress.

Of course, the jury, in its early forms, was not based on selection by lot. Juries in England and in the early United States were handpicked by a sheriff or some other authority. But over the decades, as the practice became more impartial and democratic and the selection method more random, the jury came to be equated with sortition. In fact, random selection was used as far back as colonial times in Georgia, where it is still used to appoint special county grand juries tasked with nominating or even appointing a variety of public officials.[1]

Tocqueville defined the jury as "a certain number of citizens taken at random and temporarily vested with the right to judge." Unfortunately, he did not tell us explicitly what it is about randomness that's important. But it is interesting that he did not insist primarily on the democratic nature of lot. After all, he recognized that the institution of the jury can be either aristocratic or democratic, "according to the class from which jurors are taken." In other words, for Tocqueville, what makes a jury democratic is how inclusive the pool from which the jurors are selected is, not how equally jury privileges are distributed within that group. In England, in the nineteenth century, the privilege of jury duty was reserved to an aristocracy. In the United States, this privilege extended to all white male citizens.

Strikingly, what Tocqueville sees as unique in the jury is its "republican character," by which he means that "it places the real direction of society in the hand of the governed or in a portion of them, and not in those who govern." This republican character is connected, for Tocqueville as for all republican theorists, not to equality per se but to the value of liberty as a capacity for self-rule. This is why Tocqueville approvingly quotes a judge of the Supreme Court of the United States when he writes about "the inestimable privilege of a trial by Jury in civil cases," itself only superseded by the even greater privilege of trial by jury in criminal cases, "which is conceded by all persons to be essential to political and civil liberty."

Why is the jury, both civil and criminal, essential to republican freedom? As Tocqueville sees it, it is because "the jury, and above all the civil jury, serves to give to the minds of all citizens a part of the habits of mind of the judge; and these habits are precisely those that best prepare the people to be free." These habits of mind include "respect for the thing judged and the idea of right." Respect for those two things, according to Tocqueville, preserves the characteristic love of independence found in democratic men and prevents it from turning into the destructive passion of "license," an excessive, lawless, unbounded form of freedom. In other words, the jury teaches men to accept seeing their negative, liberal freedoms tamed and constrained by a form of positive, republican freedom that is defined collectively and deliberatively.

That is not all that Tocqueville thinks is good about the jury. Serving on a jury also "teaches men practice of equity." It further teaches "each man not to recoil before responsibility for his own acts" and it "makes all feel that they have duties toward society to fulfill and that they enter into its government." Finally, "it combats individual selfishness, which is like the blight of societies." The jury is a school for various republican virtues, including basic fairness and a sense of responsibility and obligation toward the collective. But mostly it supports the capacity for freedom.

One hint of where random selection matters for Tocqueville is in the wide distribution—"across all classes"— of these republican teachings into the body politic. The jury diffuses the capacity for self-rule across all of society, not just a subset of it. That is arguably where the egalitarian aspect of lot-based selection kicks in, though Tocqueville hardly remarks on it. Interestingly, Tocqueville did not seem to notice either that the electoral system taking root in the United States at the time was likely not diffusing capacity for self-rule in the same way, "across classes"—instead concentrating power in the upper middle class.

We can blame this blind spot partly on Tocqueville's own aristocratic prejudices. The men he observed in local legislatures were already way too common for his taste, and he perhaps could not quite tell the difference between the various shades of plebeian on the lower rungs of the social ladder.

Consider what he writes, rather hilariously, of American parliamentarians. Upon entering the House of Representatives in Washington, he observes, "you feel yourself struck by the vulgar aspect of this great assembly." No famous and celebrated man in sight, he marvels. "Often the eyes seek in vain for a celebrated man within it. Almost all its members are obscure persons, whose name furnishes no image to one's thought." And forget about genius and manners, some of these people can't even read or write properly!

"They are, for the most part, village attorneys, those in trade, or even men belonging to the lowest classes. In a country where instruction is almost universally widespread, it is said that the people's representatives do not always know how to write correctly."

Tocqueville could not quite fathom that those who won elections in the United States in his time were not representative (in a statistical sense) of the entirety of the source population and already formed an elite of sorts. But the more plausible reason for Tocqueville's not remarking on the elitism of electoral democracy is his natural comparison point: the world from which his long ancestry came, that is, the ancien régime. Next to it the American representative government looked like a massive democratization of legislative power.

From where we stand, however, two centuries later and with the benefit of hindsight, we may want to ask why we did not extend the institution of the jury to the sphere of lawmaking as well, and why, if anything, the use of legal juries is now under threat.[2] It appears instead that the capacity for self-rule, which includes the capacity to shape the laws constraining and enabling our individual, negative freedoms, is an ambition we renounced in the eighteenth century, in exchange for the lower-hanging fruit of being able to elect our rulers and kick them out at regular intervals—a form of freedom, no doubt, but not the highest or most extensive one.

Equality

A second argument for politics by lot is that it is also a better embodiment of the ideal of political equality. For a given group, lot distributes power among all of the members of that group, on the basis of "one person, one lottery ticket," by contrast with election, which spreads power to the social elite, with the occasional working-class person attaining power to maintain the illusion of accessibility to all.

As we saw in chapter 2, elections are particularly inegalitarian because they combine a self-selection of candidates, which favors the rich or ambitious and the power-hungry, with the bias of voters' choice, which is more likely to award power to the social elite, the rich, the charismatic, and the tall, even as our rational selves know better: There is zero empirical evidence to date of a correlation between those features and the ability to govern well. So, if we're honest with ourselves, we should recognize that "one person, one lottery ticket" is a no less plausible and a more democratic way of distributing power.

Indeed, random selection has the merit of giving everyone the exact same mathematical chance of occupying a position of power. It is arguably as important an expression of political equality as the principle of one person, one vote. That is why ancient Greeks favored lot over elections, deemed too oligarchic, as a way to distribute power among citizens. They combined it with financial incentives, to make sure even the poor participated, and the principle of rotation, to prevent the corruption of the selected and maximize the breadth of power distribution over time.

Sortition was also put in the service of more oligarchic regimes, in which only a few had the full rights of citizenship. For example, the Venetian Republic empowered only a few families among all the citizens. But among these elites, sortition equalized the chance of each individual member accessing power. In that sense, even when used within oligarchic regimes, the formal properties of chance have egalitarian implications for the group in which it is used.

In the context of societies where rights of citizenship are equal and more universally distributed than in ancient Greece, lot has even more democratic potential. Because it is an embodiment of formal equality, if not democracy per se, random selection, combined with rotation, ensures over time an equal distribution of political office across the entire citizenry, rather than its top 10 percent.

Of course, this egalitarian potential of lot-based democracy can be realized only if people are willing to participate. One problem currently with lot-based minipublics is that only a fraction of the people invited to join them is willing to participate, typically under 20 percent. Different groups also participate at different rates. Specialists like Tiago Peixoto and Paolo Spada suggest that so-called conversion rates of up to 80 percent are theoretically achievable, as they are in surveys, but even then, the amount of negative responses or nonresponses creates problems for representativeness.[3] Mandatory participation, as in jury duty, would, of course, offer a straightforward solution to these problems, although it does not seem desirable until the place of minipublics in existing political orders has been meaningfully institutionalized, legitimized, and stabilized.

Another problem with the egalitarian promise of lot-based democracy is that, in order to produce panels that are sufficiently descriptive of the larger population despite the limitations of size and self-selection, organizers usually resort to statistical sampling methods making use of quotas for certain demographic categories (gender, race, geographic origins, socioeconomic level, political ideology, etc.). However, the problem with quotas is that they tend to bias the probability that members of certain demographic groups have to be chosen, in violation of the principle of democratic equality, which should stay at or as close as possible to "one person, one lottery ticket." Quotas, in other words, "almost always necessitate selecting people with somewhat unequal probabilities, as individuals from groups that are under-represented in the pool must be chosen with disproportionately high probabilities to satisfy the quotas."[4] As democrats, however, we should not have to accept this compromise. There should be "no stratification without representation."[5]

Luckily, algorithms have the capacity to solve this complex optimization problem. A group of mathematicians and computer scientists working with the Sortition Foundation has recently developed an algorithm called LEXIMIN that relies on close-to-equal representation probability for all agents while satisfying meaningful quotas.[6] To date their algorithm has been used to select more than forty citizens' assemblies around the world.

That said, given the opacity of algorithms to most people, and the accusation of manipulation this might trigger, it may be preferable to resort to simpler methods, like drawing balls from an urn or papers from a hat. Another solution is to educate the public, guaranteeing the reputation and impartiality of the scientists designing and running the algorithms, and being transparent about the exact probability of being chosen for each demographic group considered for a given minipublic. The team behind LEXIMIN use a live lottery for an assembly in Michigan, allowing participants to observe the probabilities according to which each pool member was selected.

Fraternity

Lot is also a way to manifest solidarity and civic friendship—what the French revolutionaries saw as an indispensable complement to liberty and equality, and which they called *fraternité*: brotherhood or fraternity. The masculinist assumptions of those terms may not work as well today, but what they really refer to is a universal form of civic friendship, a bond of solidarity and mutual care among members of a community. They express the idea that citizens should treat one another not as competitors or strangers but as fellow citizens or, metaphorically, as siblings—with a sense of shared belonging and responsibility.

Selecting representatives by lottery is a way of showing that we are all in this together, like a family. It doesn't ask who's the smartest, loudest, or most connected. It simply says: "You're part of this community, so you have the right—and the ability—to take part in decisions that affect us all." Lot also implies and requires a deep trust in others: that they will take their turn and lead, responsibly, when called upon.

But lot is not just symbolic of fraternity. When ordinary people are selected to participate in citizens' assemblies, they often discover that, despite their differences, they can work together. They learn to listen and compromise. They stop seeing politics as something distant or toxic—and start seeing it as something shared. In this way, sortition helps create fraternity as well.

Indeed, politics by lot may be the only way left to heal the deep divisions that electoral politics have created. In my experience, the beauty of random selection lies in its ability to bring together people who would otherwise never meet. Freed from partisan labels, they begin by listening without prejudice, working toward a shared purpose. And by the time their differences surface, they've already learned to respect—sometimes even love—those who see the world differently. I've witnessed this kind of civic friendship firsthand:

fierce, unexpected, and real. Chapter 7 explores how this bond emerges within citizens' assemblies.

Anti-Corruption

The beauty of lot, however, is not just the way it expresses and fosters the flourishing of these lofty ideals of liberty, equality, and fraternity. More pragmatically, lot has important instrumental properties. The first one is that it is, by itself, an anti-corruption mechanism.

First, you can't bribe a lottery. If no one knows in advance who will be chosen, no one can buy influence. There are no campaigns, no donors, no promises made behind closed doors. The process is simple, clean, and impossible to rig in the usual ways. Of course, at the point where they access power, lot-selected officials may be vulnerable to bribes and corruption, but as lot-based officials rotate more often than elected ones, the corruption becomes very costly for the would-be corrupter, who cannot count on long-term relationships with people in power.

Second, lot combined with rotation reduces careerism by ensuring a constant renewal of the pool of decision-makers. People who are randomly selected aren't climbing a political ladder. They're not trying to please donors or win reelection. They're here to serve and then go home. That also makes them more likely to make decisions based on what's right, rather than what's popular or profitable.

Third, a lottery makes it much harder for power to concentrate in the hands of a few. When the same kinds of people—wealthy, connected, outspoken—are always in charge, they often form tight circles of influence. These circles are easy to corrupt and hard to break. But if political roles are filled with ordinary citizens, the system stays open and remains less prone to backroom deals among the usual suspects.

The prophylactic properties of lot were the primary reason that the Venetian and Florentine elites used elements of lot, in combination with elections, to distribute political positions among themselves. It is also the argument of a number of lot supporters today, including those who still see value in the electoral system and those who do not.[7] Their common point is that lot would be a welcome corrective to some of the undeniable defects of our electoral democracies.

Collective Intelligence

A second, much less intuitive instrumental argument for lot is that it plays a key role, via deliberation, in the capacity of a democracy to produce good results and generate what is sometimes called "collective intelligence." Collective intelligence, defined as a capacity to achieve one's ends and solve problems successfully, is the intelligence of the group, as distinct from, and indeed superior to, the average intelligence of its individual members. My own research (for example, in my book *Democratic Reason*) has made the case for the collective intelligence of democracy and for studying the mechanisms that are conducive to it.

Several mechanisms in politics produce collective intelligence. One is simple judgment aggregation through majority rule, as in voting. Since the eighteenth century, we have come to understand the law of large numbers, a mathematical phenomenon whereby, given a sample of independent and identically distributed values, the sample mean converges to the true mean.[8] This mathematical law, it turns out, applies to human judgment as well. In 1785, nine years before dying in a revolutionary jail, the Marquis de Condorcet, a French aristocrat and brilliant mathematician, formalized this property of group judgment in a theorem known to us today as Condorcet's jury theorem. This theorem states that as long as voters are smarter than a coin flip (i.e., have a probability of getting a prediction right more than 50 percent of the time), vote sincerely (their true belief), and vote independently of one another (not copying one another, for example), the majority's probability of being right increases as the group size increases and, at the limit, reaches 1. (Note that this makes sense only where we are willing to assume the existence of something like a "right" answer, which will apply only to certain political questions.) Despite its limitations, many scholars, including myself, consider Condorcet's jury theorem and its many variants a strong justification for the use of majority rule.

Another mechanism of collective intelligence in politics is deliberation among all. Before (and sometimes instead of) aggregating their judgments through voting, citizens talk to one another. Ideally, this process would result in group consensus. If not, deliberation at least formulates the options between which voters must decide. Voting is an incomplete decision-procedure because it can aggregate judgments only about predefined options. Deliberation, by contrast, creates the options over which we make judgments. Deliberation is how an agenda is set and is where much of political power, and I will argue the promise of collective intelligence, reside.

Of course, deliberation has always been an important element of democratic life. But some political philosophers, such as Joshua Cohen from the United States, Jürgen Habermas from Germany, or Carlos Nino from Argentina, among others, have made it the cornerstone of political legitimacy. And for good reason. If we are going to impose coercive laws on one another, directly or via our representatives, shouldn't those coercive laws be backed up by the best possible reasons, produced through a process in which all can participate? That is the intuition behind the ideal of democracy that I subscribe to—namely "deliberative democracy," which has emerged since the 1990s as an alternative to Schumpeterian and aggregative democracy. In Habermas's famous phrase, what makes deliberation particularly attractive is that it roots even coercive policies in the "forceless force of the better argument."

But as a number of democratic theorists, including myself, have argued, deliberation is attractive not only because it ensures that we justify to one another why we should be bound by certain laws; it also helps the group produce better laws and better solutions to political problems, at least on average and in the long term.

When it comes to the outcomes produced by deliberation among citizens, my research has convinced me that their quality is not merely a linear function of the intelligence of its individual participants. It depends even more on the group's properties—particularly the diversity of perspectives and ways of thinking within the group relative to the problem that it faces. I owe this intuition to the pioneering work of Scott E. Page on the benefits of what he calls "cognitive diversity" in group problem-solving.[9] In his book *The Difference*, he shows how, under certain conditions, it is more useful for a group trying to solve a difficult problem to include people who think very differently from one another relative to the problem at hand, rather than to include only the smartest people, who are likely to think similarly (because, say, they went to the same elite school). To crack a code, for example, it could be more useful to have a mathematician, a poet, and a linguist working together, rather than three top mathematicians. The friction between the three different ways of thinking may be productive in a way that having similar forms of individual intelligences seamlessly interact is not.

Scott E. Page formalized this argument as the so-called Diversity Trumps Ability theorem, a now-famous and much debated result meant to apply to the context of engineering and business. For me, it unlocked the following thought: Maybe one of the reasons we should want to include even the most ignorant citizens in a political deliberation—not just the smartest ones—is precisely because we are, paradoxically, more likely to smartly solve our problems that way.

The importance of the cognitive diversity found in larger numbers of deliberators is arguably why Aristotle claimed in the *Politics* that democracy had the superiority of a potluck dinner, which can never disappoint, compared to feasts organized by one person only, which can go awry if the host's tastes are too specific, however refined.[10] (What would you think of a feast of snails, veal sweetbreads, strong-smelling aged cheeses, and a fennel tart to top it off?) In other words, "the more, the smarter," because everyone contributes a different perspective, piece of information, or argument to the political question of the common good, whereas even the smartest few are likely to miss elements of the big picture. This is also why ancient democracies all had some sort of open "assembly"—a place for all people to talk—at the heart of their design.

As the group grows in size, it becomes impossible and too time-consuming to include everyone. So the question becomes: What is the next best thing to all-inclusive deliberation? How should we select a sufficiently small subset of the community so that they can engage in productive deliberation while preserving, or at least not losing too much of, the rich knowledge and diversity of thinking contained in the larger population? How should we move from assemblies open to all in small-scale societies to assemblies of representatives in large, modern ones? Historically, as we saw, we have done this through elections. But there is a good case for why we should do it by lot instead.

Lot's instrumental value for collective intelligence comes from its ability to reproduce at small scale the cognitive diversity present in the larger group. Indeed, given the variety of political issues, any other method is likely to homogenize the set of representatives along some dimension (in practice, often by gender, wealth, and education) that will likely correlate with certain blind spots, sometimes huge ones. Assemblies that oversample homeowners, for example, as Terry Bouricus noted of the American House of Representatives, are less able to understand and address the problems of renters, the poor, and especially the homeless. Assemblies that include mostly urban people might not anticipate the impact of, say, a carbon tax on rural dwellers who need their car to get to work every day (which is partly how we got the Yellow Vest revolt in France). This is not to say that only renters can understand and properly represent renters or rural dwellers other rural dwellers—that is a variety of identity politics that has its limits. But it is just as likely that, when a category of people is missing, their views won't be represented well. The solution, therefore, is to sample widely and equally from the whole population as opposed to the most educated or the most charismatic or the best informed on this or that particular subject matter. In other words, we are better off choosing our representatives at random.

I like to illustrate the merits of deliberation among a random sample through a slightly idealized but still relevant example: the fictional jury in *12 Angry Men*. A classic of American cinema, *12 Angry Men* depicts the deliberations of a twelve-man jury following the closing arguments of a murder trial. The film is usually interpreted as a celebration of civic dissent, with the focus on the smartest, bravest juror in the room, Juror Number 8, played by Henry Fonda. Fonda, in the typical fashion of American heroes, stands up to the early majoritarian inclination to vote guilty at the beginning of the movie.

But in my view, the movie can also be read as a celebration of the collective intelligence of a group of ordinary citizens talking to one another, even as they are limited and biased in all kinds of idiosyncratic ways. It's not one man against all. It's *all* of these men, flawed and complex as they are, helping one another figure out the truth of the matter. And while Juror Number 8 might stand as the figure of the group "leader," the deliberative group dynamic is truly the hero of the movie.

A pivotal moment in *12 Angry Men* occurs when Juror Number 8 produces a copy of the murder weapon—a cheap switchblade he bought for a few dollars at a store near the court—disproving its supposedly unique and incriminating nature. However, the jury's shift toward reasonable doubt owes just as much to subtler contributions from less-prominent figures. Juror Number 5, who grew up in a violent slum, explains how a switchblade is properly used (upward, not downward), casting doubt on the eyewitness's account, which described the knife descending on the victim. Later, an older juror, dismissed by some as feeble, observes that the main witness wears glasses—evident from red marks on her nose—and likely couldn't have seen the murder clearly without them. These interventions, combined with mounting doubts, lead the jury to a unanimous verdict: The young man is not guilty.

In the film, all twelve jurors matter, in all their differences, because it is only through the interplay between their conflicting interpretation of the evidence and arguments—colored as those are by their personal histories, socioeconomic backgrounds, and types of intelligence—that something like the truth is revealed. The capacity of deliberation to produce good outcomes manifests even though the protagonists are far from ideal human beings (and all are white men). One juror just wants to be done with the deliberation and go to a baseball game, one is a bigoted racist, another is biased by irrelevant fatherly emotions. . . . Deliberation, in other words, can overcome many moral and cognitive limitations.

The power of deliberation is at its greatest when the group is cognitively diverse, even if this diversity comes at some cost to average individual competence. If the group had been made up only of clones of Juror Number 8, it is unlikely that they would have gotten to the right conclusion. And even if some jurors are not all that useful (say, Juror Number 12, the advertising executive who says only dumb things and brings down the average, so to speak), the fact remains that there is no way of knowing in advance who is going to be useful or not out of a particular group. And even the arguably least-useful juror is ultimately capable of recognizing the force of the better argument, adding a crucial vote to the final tally.

Deliberation, in this setup, finally has the merit of empowering the shy, both the natural introverts and the ones made shy by their position in society, in ways that benefit both them and the group's collective intelligence.[11] Juror Number 2, a quiet and self-effacing bank teller, slowly gains the courage to stand up to both the overly confident salesman and the xenophobic garage owner. Similarly, Juror Number 6, a blue-collar worker of few words, stands up to another, more articulate juror when the latter starts verbally abusing the older gentleman of the group. The shy become more vocal and more assertive over time, including in support of one another, when they realize they have a voice, and that it matters as much as anyone else's. The whole plot, in fact, strikingly turns on the voice of the juror with the lowest socioeconomic status, who, after staying silent for the longest time, comes to recognize the value in his experience of poverty and violence—a past he once regarded as shameful. He *alone* knows how to properly use a switchblade, and that knowledge is ultimately key to saving an innocent's life. Far from being just a celebration of the bold dissenter, the movie could also be subtitled "The Triumph of the Shy."

Judging Juries

So, the key component of politics without politicians is assemblies of randomly selected citizens. Lot, or random selection, is desirable for the values it promotes (liberty, equality, fraternity) and the outcomes it serves (anti-corruption, collective intelligence). Now, that all sounds good and well in theory, and in fiction. But what does the empirical evidence say, especially about the instrumental properties, which are arguably easier to measure?

The empirical evidence about juries supports theoretical predictions about the reliability of jury deliberations. In their seminal 1966 study *The American Jury*, Harry Kalven and Hans Zeisel show a high level of agreement between jury verdicts and the judges' pre-verdict opinions, suggesting that juries are generally competent and reliable in deciding cases, at least as much as individual judges. The book also finds that juries understand the legal instructions and evidence presented in a trial, answering any criticism that jurors often lack the necessary understanding to decide complex cases. More generally, juries appear to offer several systemic advantages, including a more trusted, timely, and generally efficient criminal justice system compared to countries that rely solely on judges for decisions,[12] as well as reduced levels of corruption.[13]

But minipublics—the type of juries I envision for a system of politics without politicians—address a different set of questions than determining the guilt or innocence of individuals on trial. This distinction requires us to define new standards for what constitutes a successful political outcome. While spillover effects, such as a more effective political system or reduced corruption, would be welcome, the primary focus lies elsewhere.

Specifically, we aim for citizens' views to become more informed through the deliberative process. Additionally, the recommendations, decisions, or legislative proposals emerging from these minipublics should be "good" in a meaningful way—ideally better than, or at least on par with, those produced by politicians in comparable circumstances. Equally important, they should avoid being "bad" in ways that undermine the political process.

There are various ways to go about measuring the quality of outputs generated by deliberation among ordinary citizens, from the more indirect to the more direct. A first proxy for the substantive quality of deliberative outcomes is, for example, the objective level of (accurate) information people have post-deliberation as compared to pre-deliberation. The presumption here is that as people's views are more (accurately) informed, they are also more likely to be right—although there is, of course, no guarantee.

Another route is to measure the procedural properties of deliberation, as in the so-called discourse quality index (DQI), which is an index recently developed by political scientists to capture various features of a debate, for example, how equal, respectful, and argumentatively sophisticated people's speech is.[14] Finally, one can measure the quality of deliberative outcomes in terms of the corresponding decision's impact on the world. Are the solutions put forward validated by the outside world, by actual empirical success? This strategy has already been successfully pursued by the economists Simon Johnson and Daron Acemoglu, who earned the 2024 Nobel Prize in economics for their work showing the positive effects of democratic political institutions (specifically the features they call rule of law and individual rights) on long-term growth and prosperity. Do democracies that practice more deliberation do better (say, on welfare, health, or happiness indicators, corruption levels, or environmental sustainability) than non-democracies or less deliberative democracies? These general effects cannot be measured today, as there are not enough democracies, perhaps indeed none, that qualify as "deliberative" in the sense proposed in this book. But evidence is accumulating about the local effects of deliberative assemblies—in terms of individuals' information levels or the quality of the policies these assemblies put forward.

Icelandic Wisdom

In published research, I myself have tried to gather some evidence of the superiority of deliberations among laypeople over deliberations among experts on political matters in the context of the 2010–2013 Icelandic constitutional process described earlier.[15] Recall that in this process, twenty-five relatively ordinary citizens wrote a new constitution on the basis of the recommendations of a random sample of 950 Icelandic people as well as the online contributions of the public on their crowdsourced drafts.

Since the proposal was never enacted into law, the only outcome we can analyze and compare is the text itself, rather than its real-world effects. The Icelandic setup offers a unique opportunity as a quasi-natural experiment, allowing us to compare three proposals: two drafted by experts and one drafted and crowdsourced by laypeople. All were created around the same time, under similar conditions, and using the same original input from 950 randomly selected Icelanders. A key distinction lies in the process: The citizen proposal achieved consensus among its twenty-five writers, whereas the seven experts were so divided that they produced two separate texts. This contrast highlights a fascinating difference in collaborative dynamics between experts and laypeople.

I painstakingly compared, line by line and article by article, the production of the twenty-five citizens to these two expert drafts.[16] The conclusion I have drawn from this comparison is that the proposal written by the twenty-five is superior to the expert-written drafts, even as the twenty-five citizens had only four months to write their proposal when the experts took a full year. All proposals were arguably quite good, and true, the citizen draft is not strikingly better. But it is better in ways that are crucial.

First, the citizen draft is the only one that addressed the problem of a handful of corporations exploiting the national fishing grounds for free, at the expense of the public, through the bold proposal to nationalize all natural resources not already privately owned and demanding a rent to the nation for any private exploitation. One can disagree with this particular solution, but none of the other drafts offered one.

Second, even when the citizen draft and the expert proposals offered similar answers to an existing problem, the citizen solutions were arguably more sophisticated—for example, in addressing the long-standing problem in Icelandic constitutional theory of the place of the Evangelical Lutheran Church in a secular state. Instead of removing any mention of the national church, as one of the expert proposals did, the citizen draft maintained a recognition of its existence in the text. But instead of entrenching its privileged status in the fundamental law, as the more-conservative expert proposal did, the citizen proposal specified that the status of the national church ought to be decided by Parliament.[17]

Third, the citizen draft develops a longer and richer list of citizens' rights than the experts' proposals, causing the Venice Commission, a body of legal experts at the European Union level who were asked to evaluate the proposal, to praise it for the way its new provisions, among other things, "aim to better reflect international human rights obligations."[18] The proposal also includes rights that are not listed in either the original constitution or the expert proposals, such as the right to access the internet (article 15), which was suggested on a Facebook post at a time when the Egyptian president, Hosni Mubarak, turned off the internet to stifle dissent during the Arab Spring. The proposal is also more attuned to certain gender issues, mentioning explicitly "sexual violence" as a type of violence the state should protect individuals from, and the needs of children, devoting a separate and extensive article to their rights. The proposal mentions still more sources of discrimination than the expert drafts, including genetic character, ancestry, and political affiliation. Finally, the proposal offers a more "open and comprehensive approach to the right of freedom of religion" in that it extends the scope of this freedom to "view of life" and "personal conviction." According to the Venice Commission, this extension of the scope of religious freedom as well as the inclusion of the right to change religion or faith form "a substantial improvement compared to the current Constitution."[19] Given that both expert-written drafts merely reproduced the content of the original constitution on this point, the citizen proposal is markedly better in this respect.

Last but not least, the citizen proposal is more democratic, in that, as noted by constitutional theory specialists,[20] it creates institutional avenues for popular participation. Important elements of direct democracy are introduced in the crowdsourced constitution, allowing the public a role in the determination of the status of the Evangelical Lutheran Church as the national church (any change to the status quo introduced by Parliament must be approved by referendum) and the approval of certain treaties (such as a treaty to enter the European Union). The text also includes a "right of referral," by which 10 percent of voters may demand a referendum on any bill within three months of its passage, subject to some exceptions, such as the budget.

Additionally, and most innovatively, the draft introduces what is elsewhere sometimes called a citizens' initiative. This participatory mechanism allows 2 percent of the population to present an issue to the Althing, the national parliament of Iceland, which the Althing is free to ignore. If 10 percent of the population present a bill to the Althing, the Althing must either accept it or make a counterproposal. In the latter case, if the bill of the voters has not been withdrawn as a response, the Althing must present both the popular bill and the Althing's counterproposal to a referendum. These elements of participation in the crowdsourced constitution have been internationally celebrated, including by the Venice Commission.[21]

What explains the superiority of the more inclusively written proposal over the expert-written one? In my research I trace the superiority of the text in part to the crowdsourcing phase that the twenty-five members of the council included as part of their writing process. The twenty-five, far from isolating themselves from popular input, regularly posted the version of the draft they were working on online. All in all, they posted twelve drafts, at various stages of completion. Anyone interested in the process could send feedback by posting comments on social media platforms like Facebook and Twitter, or by posting on the council's own web page or by using regular email and mail. Foreigners were free to participate if they could find a way to overcome the language barrier (e.g., Google Translate). For example, an American citizen with property in Iceland wrote on the Facebook page that she hoped the new constitution would consider the interests of people in her situation. Among the key ideas that emanated from the roughly thirty-six hundred online comments were the previously mentioned addenda to the list of rights, including children's rights and a right to the internet.

I believe the superiority of the crowdsourced draft is also due to the greater diversity of the constitution drafters. The group included a Polish, culturally Catholic mathematician, whose ideas turned out to be crucial to the way the proposal handled the delicate question of the place of the Evangelical Lutheran Church as a state church in secular Iceland. Similarly, the presence of a union leader with experience handling difficult negotiations, the only working-class representative on the council of twenty-five, helped the group settle on a consensus. (Incidentally, this union leader is also the father of the international rock star Björk. But as I can confirm after he gave my graduate student and me a ride in his normal car to his modest house near Reykjavik, where we interviewed him over tea, he is entirely down-to-earth and unassuming.)

The Icelandic experiment shows that ordinary citizens can do as good a job as professional politicians. But the Icelandic drafters were still elected (from a pool of nonpoliticians), not randomly selected. They were, as a result, more educated than average. Additionally, the task of writing a constitution is perhaps easier than that of ordinary lawmaking, as some critics have argued.[22] What do we know about the competence of truly randomly selected bodies in the context of ordinary politics?

More Empirical Evidence

The empirical evidence in favor of lot-based bodies deliberating on ordinary political issues has started to accumulate over recent years. Research on deliberative experiments based on surveys and case studies provides evidence that participants experience growth in knowledge and sophistication.[23] Experiments—carefully designed scientific processes based on randomization and involving a control group to isolate the proper causal effects—also show that deliberation increases participants' knowledge of evidence and shifts their attitudes regarding the role of evidence in policymaking.[24] These experiments also show that deliberation is conducive to persuasion (a change of opinion that results from the rational effect of arguments) rather than polarization (an irrational amplification of the group's pre-deliberative beliefs) through the mechanism of rational justifications.[25]

Deliberation has also been shown to have a beneficial impact on the relationship that participants have with their community. Studies summarized in a recent *Handbook of Citizens' Assemblies* show that participants display greater tolerance toward other people's political views, come to trust others more, develop a greater sense of their own political efficacy, develop practical civic skills and a desire to act politically, and generally become more politically engaged.[26] In addition, deliberation seems to prod people to want to talk more in general, whether in the context of political debates or giving advice to family members, or even giving talks in the workplace.[27] Finally, deliberation seems to have a long-term positive impact on participants' interest in politics, political engagement, and opinions about policy.[28]

The most convincing evidence we have for the properties of deliberation among ordinary citizens comes from the study of deliberative polls. Like some of the experiments underlying the results I have discussed, deliberative polls always include a control group of people who are not made to deliberate but demographically match the deliberating group. By comparing pre- and post-deliberative answers for both groups (where the second group does not actually deliberate but is just asked to repeat the questionnaire at the same time as the deliberating group), we can measure the presumed impact of deliberation on the deliberative poll members.

Those differences are often significant. The political scientist James Fishkin has conducted such deliberative polls in over 150 countries, and the data seems irrefutable.[29] Deliberation educates, depolarizes, and additionally aligns fundamental preferences by, for example, transforming narrowly self-interested preferences into more socially oriented ones.

Rather than bore you with more figures and statistics, let me take you straight into the deliberative minipublic I know best: the 2019–2020 French Citizens' Convention for Climate.

SIX

Another French Revolution?

What will come out of this convention, I promise, will be submitted without filter to either a vote in Parliament, a referendum, or direct regulatory application.

EMMANUEL MACRON, APRIL 25, 2019[1]

The 2019–2020 Citizens' Convention for Climate ▪ Why the French Example Matters ▪ Citizen Legislators ▪ Did It Work? ▪ Were the Law and Policy Proposals Any Good? ▪ Aftermath ▪ Experts on Tap, Citizens on Top ▪ Governing Citizens' Assemblies ▪ Great Disillusion or Inspiring Precedent?

As recounted earlier, the fuel tax that the French government tried to implement in the fall of 2018 triggered the massive social response known as the Yellow Vests movement. By November, France appeared to many—including myself—to be on the brink of revolution.

Faced with the crisis, President Macron had to choose between repression and negotiation. Initially, he opted for repression, employing a harsh use of force during the Yellow Vests demonstrations. This approach left many protesters injured and provoked fierce criticism from both the left and the right. In December 2018, Macron shifted his strategy. In an open letter to the nation, he condemned acts of violence against elected officials, the media, and public administrators while also acknowledging the widespread sense of injustice felt by many French citizens. To address the unrest, he announced a new initiative: the Great National Debate, a nationwide dialogue set to take place in the early months of 2019.

The Great National Debate was an ambitious, rushed, grandiose mess, combining all sorts of consulting methods without a clear sense of hierarchy, as if the government had thrown everything at the wall to see what would stick. All in all, around five hundred thousand people were involved in about ten thousand local meetings. Between five hundred thousand and 1.5 million people contributed online, though the exact number is unclear because the website did not track unique contributors. Additionally, approximately fourteen hundred individuals took part in twenty-one randomly selected regional assemblies. What's more, the Great National Debate triggered further conversations among roughly forty-five thousand participants in the so-called True Debate, organized in parallel by the Yellow Vests and other critics of the Great National Debate. In some fashion, one can conservatively estimate that around 1.5 percent of the total population directly participated in the debates, though many more were affected indirectly.

Later, in spring 2020, the televised reveal of the Great National Debate results felt momentous, if a bit too staged. Frustratingly, the interpretation of the results by the government—"We heard you, you want fewer taxes" seemed to be the main takeaway—was one-sided and simplistic, considering the massive and complex amount of content generated by the population. The process helped President Macron regain popularity in the polls, and as a result, critics dismissed the process as a diverting strategy. But it also objectively brought some temporary reprieve to the country and was met with relief and gratitude by a large percentage of the population. Importantly, the Great National Debate provided the occasion for President Macron to evoke the possibility of what he called "a republic of permanent deliberation," a promising if somewhat mysterious phrase. But more important still, the Great National Debate paved the way for the next big step at the national level: the Citizens' Convention for Climate. In my view, this Citizens' Convention was truly revolutionary. It introduced a new political actor into the game—transforming a random sample of 150 citizens into a de facto legislature that rivaled Parliament.

The 2019–2020 Citizens' Convention for Climate

On April 25, 2019, inspired by the Irish precedents, President Macron announced the Citizens' Convention for Climate. This convention was, in many ways, the real, albeit delayed, response of President Macron to the Yellow Vests movement, and more generally to the nation that had widely supported it. Essentially he said: "So you think my fuel tax is a bad idea? You go and figure out a better answer to climate change, then." You may recall the Irish politicians who could not see a traditional path to the decriminalization of abortion and gave the hot potato to a citizens' assembly. The French government admitted to a similar impotence: "We don't know how to pass climate reforms that will be acceptable to the larger population. So, you do it."

On the first weekend of October 2019, 150 randomly selected individuals from all over France, including its overseas territories, met for the first time in the Iéna Palace in Paris, the seat of the Economic, Social, and Environmental Council (CESE), which had been put in charge of the hosting and logistical organization of the convention.[2] (If you're curious about the selection process for that sample, I'll get to it in chapter 8.)

I, too, was there on that rainy morning, when umbrellas were lining up at the entrance of the building, with the Eiffel Tower and the French flag soaring in the gray sky. As one of the twenty-five researchers allowed to follow the convention, I wouldn't have missed that occasion for the world.

These citizens were embarking on a nine-month process that spanned seven weekends—each an intensive two-day session. Together, they formed one of the most representative cross sections of France ever assembled.

Throughout these weekends, they moved between small-group workshops, full plenary sessions, and dynamic discussion formats. Other discussions unfolded more informally, over coffee breaks, meals, and late-night hotel conversations. The formal deliberations were guided by facilitators from three well-established firms: Eurogroup Consulting, Missions Publiques, and Res Publica.

In June 2020, after several months of hard work (not just during but also between physical meetings, from home and during online webinars), the convention voted on and approved 149 proposals. Among them were, for example, an ambitious proposal to render global housing renovation mandatory by 2030 under threat of sanctions, a ban on publicity for heavily polluting goods, the promotion of vegetarian meals in public schools, constraints on soil artificialization, and a proposal to add a paragraph to the first article of the French constitution specifying that the French Republic "guarantees the preservation of biodiversity and the environment, and fights against climate change" (my translation). Strikingly, none of these 149 proposals included a carbon tax.

Why the French Example Matters

While France wasn't the first country to experiment with citizens' assemblies—and unlike Ireland, it has yet to link them successfully to a process of mass and direct participation, such as a referendum—it has been the most ambitious in terms of scale, cost, duration, and citizen empowerment.

This is important because, due to its size and cultural diversity, France is arguably a better proof of concept than Ireland, let alone tiny Iceland, for the viability of politics without politicians. It is both large (with sixty-seven million inhabitants) and multicultural, with a large minority of Muslim citizens (about 8 percent) and close to 30 percent of the population being first-, second-, or third-generation immigrants.[3] As recent news illustrates, from the 2023 riots taking place on the heels of monthslong demonstrations against President Macron's pension reform to the political turmoil caused by the dissolution of the National Assembly after the triumph of the far right in the European elections, the political, economic, and social situation is quite explosive. The degree of political polarization is constantly rising (though perhaps not quite to US levels), and there is a sense that the country is at a boiling point. If citizens' assemblies can offer some relief in such a tense context, they might in many others as well.

For other countries, the worry might be that France is too rich and too stable for the experiments that succeed there to be replicable in less-privileged circumstances. It is true that the French model is the Rolls-Royce of deliberative assemblies. The climate convention cost upward of six million euros and required a strong state and functioning bureaucracies. Still, there seems to be something universal about both the power of ordinary citizens coming together to solve problems for their countries and, beyond this more instrumental concern, the therapeutic effect of deliberation among ordinary citizens who are currently divided by increasingly bitter partisan and polarized politics. And similar experiments have been successfully conducted, with local adjustments, in much more difficult contexts and on shoestring budgets in countries like Bosnia, Colombia, and Lebanon.[4]

More important, the French Citizens' Convention for Climate was, to my mind, the first citizens' assembly to give so much power to ordinary citizens. Indeed, the task that the convention members were given went way beyond the advisory policy role that most citizens' assemblies are confined to, even as it was not strictly equivalent to the work of elected parliamentarians. Fulfilling a legislative function comparable to that of both parliamentarians and ministers, the citizens in the French convention were given the prerogative to initiate and formulate the law, and ultimately to authorize it in a formal vote (even if this vote, as we'll see, was not legally binding within the constraints of the French constitution). In a recent paper, my coauthor Théophile Pénigaud and myself propose to call ordinary citizens placed in this position "citizen legislators."

Citizen Legislators

The label "citizen legislators" refines a category already well-established in the literature: "citizen representative." Coined by Mark Warren, the term refers to laypeople who act or speak on behalf of other laypeople. Representation, in its basic sense, means standing in for others—something politicians often claim only they can do, though it is not inherently exclusive to elections.[5]

Warren developed the idea of citizen representatives through his study of citizens' assemblies and participatory budgeting processes— settings where ordinary people make decisions about public resources. He argued that even without being elected, such citizens represent others in a meaningful political sense. In *Open Democracy*, I reached similar conclusions, defining representation as "standing for" others in a way that is recognized by a relevant audience.[6] Under this view, representation is not mysterious or reserved for elites—anyone can do it, provided they are seen as legitimate.

Citizen legislators, then, are a specific subset of citizen representatives: their function is to formulate legislative proposals and to draft laws. The term "citizen" signals that these actors are laypeople—not professional politicians or members of a demographically distinct elite.

What evidence is there that members of the French Citizens' Convention for Climate acted as citizen legislators, in the sense I've just defined? The first clue lies in President Macron's now-famous "no filter" promise. When he announced the convention in April 2019, Macron pledged that its proposals would, "without filters," be submitted either to a vote in Parliament or a referendum, or applied via executive actions. This implied that the proposals needed to be near-legislative in form—effectively draft bills. Participants were expected not only to deliberate on climate policy but to formulate it in legal terms. They were asked, in short, to act like lawmakers.

This promise was quickly walked back. When the prime minister met the participants in October 2019, he clarified that constitutional "filters" would still apply. Much subsequent commentary has focused on the gap between Macron's promise and what was delivered, which was interpreted as a betrayal. But that focus misses the real point: the promise, even if impossible to fulfill legally, had a profound empowering effect. It conferred public legitimacy on the convention and raised its status in the national imagination. In practice, it treated citizens not merely as advisers but as lawmakers of a new kind.

Second, the convention's official mandate supported this legislative framing. The Prime Minister's mission letter charged the convention with identifying "structuring measures" to reduce greenhouse gas emissions by 40 percent (relative to 1990 levels) by 2030, and with producing a set of "legislative and regulatory measures" to that end. Unlike most citizens' assemblies, this one was not asked to offer general recommendations—it was asked to produce concrete, legally actionable proposals.

To support this, the government established a legal committee whose role was to assist in translating citizen proposals into draft legal text. According to the convention's governance charter, the legal committee was tasked with helping citizens craft proposals "as close as possible to a bill or regulation."

Third, the convention was deliberately politicized. Unlike the Irish model, which emphasizes protected deliberative space, the French process encouraged public engagement. Citizens could speak to the press, share their experiences on social media, and meet with stakeholders, including elected officials and lobbyists. This visibility amplified their role—not just as deliberators, but as political actors shaping public discourse. Many observers noted how unusually political the convention felt compared to other climate assemblies. This politicization further reinforced their status as legislators.

Fourth, the internal workings of the convention resembled

legislative practice.[7] The participants were divided into thematic subgroups—on housing, labor, food, transportation, and consumption—mirroring parliamentary committees. Toward the end, the convention adopted a formal amendment process inspired by legislative procedure. Thierry Pech, cochair of the governance committee, would later call the assembly "a Parliament of citizens"— even as he cautiously framed it as "prelegislative" in nature.

Fifth, the question of authorship brought the convention's legislative identity into sharp relief. After the legal committee translated the proposals into legislative form, debate erupted over whether citizens should formally vote to "appropriate" the legal drafts as their own. CESE members on the governance committee argued against it, insisting legal authorship belonged to the experts. The rest of the committee argued that unless citizens could approve the final wording, the process would lack democratic ownership. In the end, the citizens voted, block by block, to formally adopt the legal versions. This authorship claim would later be acknowledged in the preamble to the 2021 Climate and Resilience Law, which explicitly linked the legislation to the work and "spirit" of the convention.

A sixth and final piece of evidence comes from what followed. During the governance committee meetings of the second French Citizens' Convention (on the End of Life), the question of authorship arose again. A senior CESE official, recalling the difficulties of the earlier convention, made the new mandate crystal clear: "We are not going to write a law. We already tried that, with all the frustrations it caused. We are going to give a political answer."

This was a telling moment. It revealed just how seriously the first Convention had been taken—not merely as a deliberative body but as a lawmaking one. And it shows that the label "citizen legislator" captures something real and disruptive about that experience.

To be sure, the convention's legislative authority was more de facto than de jure. It had no constitutional (and ambiguous legal) standing to initiate, let alone author, law. But that made the experiment all the more important. It created a precedent—a proof of concept—that could, with the right reforms, be institutionalized into something more permanent and binding.

The term "citizen legislator" helps us name what happened in France, but it also points beyond. It describes the radical innovation of the French case while also resonating with other examples—from British Columbia's Citizens' Assembly on electoral reform to Iceland's citizen-led constitutional process. And just as important, it draws a clear line between purely consultative assemblies and truly empowered ones.

Did It Work?

The climate convention was founded on the hope that deliberation among a randomly selected group of French citizens, supported by expert input, could generate smart and efficient solutions to reducing greenhouse gas emissions—solutions unlikely to provoke a social revolt, such as the Yellow Vests movement. Was this faith in collective intelligence validated?

The convention succeeded in producing 149 proposals, most of which were internally approved with overwhelming support (over 80 percent in favor) and externally approved by the larger public with a lesser but still very high degree of support (as evidenced in polls). This achievement is even more striking given the disruptions caused by the COVID-19 pandemic, which forced some meetings online—a steep learning curve for both organizers and participants—and the social protests that necessitated rescheduling, with echoes of the Yellow Vests movement still reverberating in the background.

It succeeded despite deep disagreements—over the scale of change needed, whether to persuade or compel their fellow citizens, and the inevitable clashes of interest. Property owners and renters were at odds over a nationwide housing renovation plan. Urban and rural residents debated the role of cars in modern life. Even the divisive issue of a carbon tax didn't derail them. Though President Macron likely hoped they'd endorse it—and experts kept pushing it—they rejected it as a national solution, considering it only at the EU level. Instead, they forged consensus around 149 other measures.

Were the Law and Policy Proposals Any Good?

Now, maybe the process worked in the rudimentary sense that it was brought to completion and produced a unified outcome. But were the proposals generated by the 150 people under such conditions any good? Surely, before we consider replicating the French attempt at turning ordinary citizens into full-blown legislators, we need to know how good their "laws" were, and how they compared to those produced by professional politicians.

Evaluating the quality of legislative proposals is inherently complex and often controversial—much like assessing the work of professional politicians. A relatively uncontroversial benchmark, however, is to ask whether the proposals created by the 150 citizen legislators were at least comparable in quality to those drafted by professional politicians. On this front, the answer is yes. The proposals were honed over several months of hard work, reviewed, annotated, commented on, and assessed by various experts—in the same way that experts are brought in to help parliamentarians working in parliamentary commissions.[8] Ultimately the proposals were translated into legal language by the legal team supporting citizens' work.

The substantive and formal quality of the proposals enabled 10 percent of them to be implemented as regulations or otherwise directly applied (bypassing Parliament) by late summer 2020. Official government sources claim that, as of 2023, 100 of them (67 percent) had been implemented partially or in full.[9] Not a single measure was publicly dismissed by a qualified expert on the grounds of technical deficiencies or impracticality. Even the three proposals vetoed by President Macron were, by all accounts, rejected for political rather than technical reasons.

Another way to assess the quality of the proposals is to ask whether they were likely to meet the ambitious target of greenhouse gas reduction. Here the answer is less conclusive. The support team of experts did provide a rough assessment of the fitness of the proposals for the greenhouse gas reduction target (on a rough scale of 1 to 3, 3 being the highest contribution). But there was no external, independent, and public evaluation of the measures. The reality, however, is that no one knows how to make precise assessments in a domain where uncertainty is so great. And ultimately, the fact is that these proposals would have brought the country closer to the goal than any existing legislation ever passed by the French Parliament. In February 2020, a group of one thousand scientists urged the government to implement the proposals as they were at the time.[10]

A third way to evaluate the quality of the proposals is to ask about their political viability. If viability is defined as the likelihood of being supported by the French population, then yes, the vast majority of them were viable. In June 2020, a first poll revealed that 70 percent of the French had heard of the Citizens' Convention for Climate and that 60 percent considered that body legitimate to produce recommendations on behalf of the French public.[11] A second poll revealed that all fourteen of the Citizens' Convention's main proposals, except one, had majoritarian support in the population, including the rather coercive proposal of a mandatory global housing renovation, which had 74 percent support in the general population (against 85 percent among the convention members).[12] From this perspective, the limited implementation of the proposals by the current government—estimated by nongovernmental sources to range between 10 percent and 40 percent— reflects poorly on the government's responsiveness to majoritarian preferences, rather than on the quality of the proposals themselves.

A fourth criterion for evaluating quality is more substantive: Were the solutions proposed by the 150 citizens sophisticated enough to address the problem effectively while also demonstrating creativity? Simply recycling existing proposals wouldn't necessarily qualify as innovative or "smart" in this context. An independent indicator of success lies in the response from an established think tank, which praised the proposals for their originality, coherent trade-offs, and systemic approach to ecological transition.[13] Furthermore, in the aftermath, many environmental associations and political parties adopted the proposals as a morally authoritative foundation for their claims, underscoring their perceived value and impact.

In summary, when compared to current legislation, the proposals exhibit a decent level of technicality, strong democratic credentials, and more ambitious ecological content. The 149 proposals were, undeniably, of a quality comparable to what could have come out of a parliament.

Aftermath

In June 2020, after the Citizens' Convention for Climate concluded, President Macron welcomed the 150 participants to the Élysée gardens. Researchers like myself were not invited, so I followed the event through media coverage. Macron immediately broke his "no filter" promise, announcing he would adopt only 146 of the 149 proposals. He rejected three: reducing highway speed limits to 110 kilometers per hour (the least popular proposal, with 57 percent support inside the convention), a 4 percent capital gains tax to finance the green transition, and a constitutional amendment that would have subordinated public freedoms to environmental principles.

The remaining 146 proposals underwent a protracted and chaotic amendment process, culminating in the "Climate and Resilience" bill presented to the Ministers' Council on February 10, 2021. Some convention members were invited to meet with ministers, but they reported feeling sidelined and powerless as government officials and lobbyists diluted or overturned many of their measures.

In February 2021, an eighth and final session allowed the citizens to respond to the government's handling of their proposals. They rated the government's efforts a dismal 3.3 out of 10, reflecting widespread frustration. Many activists and observers accused the government of using the convention, like the earlier Great National Debate, as "participation-washing"—a performative attempt to appear responsive while pursuing its own agenda. Despite delays, the bill was passed by Parliament on July 20, 2021. It acknowledged the 150 citizens as being "associated with" the legislative process and its "spirit," though the French constitution prevents formally recognizing them as coauthors. Nevertheless, their influence was undeniable. Another bill proposing a national referendum on the convention's constitutional amendments passed Parliament in January 2021 but was vetoed by the Senate.

A lingering question remains: Should credit for the law's foundation go to the 150 citizens or to the experts who supported them? This debate highlights the tension between the contributions of ordinary citizens and the expert guidance shaping their work.

Experts on Tap, Citizens on Top

The relations between experts and citizens in the CCC were deeper than in any comparable precedents in that the experts were embedded in the protocols at almost every stage of the process. A natural worry is the perception that given their role in the climate convention, the process was in fact entirely expert-led, so whatever outcome came out of the process, it should be credited to the experts, not the citizens. I studied this convention with a focus on this question of experts and their relation to lay citizens, and my observation, as well as that of the twenty-five researchers who observed the convention alongside me, was that experts were not in charge. Remember how the ancient Greeks chose their administrators, experts, and top-level bureaucrats from among educated slaves to ensure they would not be able to take over the polity? Well, the French assembly similarly tried to keep its experts "on tap, not on top."[14] Meaning, the experts were kept in a position where they were offering support, information, clarification, and ideas, but they did not decide for the citizens, whether directly or indirectly (through manipulation or undue influence).

This inversion of the traditional relationship between experts and amateurs was purposely put in place by the organizers to subordinate expert advice and knowledge to the ends defined by the citizens. This required a transformation of both groups and a relationship of trust and respect, anchored in a clear acknowledgment that the citizens provided the direction while the experts were there to help actualize their visions. To the extent that the experts stayed "on tap, not on top," the result can arguably be credited to the citizens and them alone, because it is ultimately the filter of their collective judgment that shaped the proposals.

What ensured that the citizens were not dominated by the experts?[15] First, the citizens never manifested the sort of blind deference that one could expect. If anything, they were defiant. They certainly did not take it well whenever experts waltzed in unprepared or arrogant. The Paris airport CEO learned this the hard way. Dressed in a three-piece suit, he began pontificating about the progression of climate change since the dinosaurs. He was promptly interrupted by a polite but firm remark: "We already know all this. Can you please get to the point? What would it take to reduce the number of flights for short distances?" When he went on to argue that the Paris airports were a model of environmental responsibility and cleanliness, he was met with undisguised skepticism.

Second, when the citizens adopted expert recommendations, it was typically for sound, objective reasons. For instance, during the discussions of the working group on housing, they quickly embraced an idea introduced by experts in the first two weekends: a comprehensive renovation plan mandating energy-efficient up-grades to homes by a specific deadline. What drove their agreement was not merely the charisma of the experts but the strength of the argument itself. This is evident in the widespread recognition of comprehensive renovation as one of the most effective and equitable public policy tools for reducing greenhouse gas emissions.[16]

The idea wasn't adopted uncritically. The citizens considered the imperative of social justice and, after hearing feedback from a representative of an agency supporting low-income families, developed a plan to subsidize the comprehensive renovation initiative, ensuring it would be free for those unable to afford it. Similarly, the citizens embraced the concept of recognizing *ecocide*—a term describing environmental destruction as akin to murder—and not because of the influence of a charismatic expert, though the former environment minister Nicolas Hulot did speak to them about it at their request. Instead, they supported the idea out of a deep conviction that it was the right thing to do. One citizen in particular became known within the assembly as the idea's most passionate advocate.

On many occasions the citizens rebelled against expert advice, which suggests that when they followed the experts, it wasn't out of sheer inertia, apathy, or deference. The emblematic case in this respect was the position of the convention on the principle of a carbon tax. This option, though defended by experts at every turn, was spectacularly rejected in a plenary session during the second weekend, after the expert who presented it was berated by a few infuriated citizens ("Don't treat us like children!").

Finally, the citizens expressed their independence in the way they increasingly challenged the governance of the assembly over the course of the whole year. Almost from the beginning of the process they asked about the possibility of inviting experts of their own choosing as opposed to the governance committee's choosing. They also extended, without prior approval by the governance committee, direct invitations to various people, including President Macron, who obliged with a much-publicized visit to the convention in January 2020, and Greta Thunberg, who never replied. Additionally, the visit of President Macron was conducted on their terms, not the governance committee's or even the president's. In response to their invitation, the president had sought to bring them over for dinner at the Élysée Palace. The citizens did not like the idea and thought that he should come to them for a work session on equal terms, seated at a table with them rather than lecturing from a podium. The governance committee was appalled, arguing, "You don't say no to the president!" But in the end, after some very delicate negotiations, the citizens won. President Macron came to the Iéna Palace and sat down at a table with them to talk.

During a special session on COVID-19's impact on their work, the citizens pushed back against what they saw as the governance committee's attempt to pressure them into publishing proposals before a vote. Resistance grew against the so-called Squad—a select group tasked with issues like financing and constitutional matters—forcing the governance committee to dissolve what was perceived as an elite faction and issue an apology. Tensions also flared over the organizers' preference for apparent consensus, especially when they closely monitored the collective drafting of a letter urging the French public to consider climate change in post-pandemic economic plans. Surveys later revealed that most citizens favored more formal voting procedures to resolve disagreements, signaling a broader push to reclaim control over the convention's decision-making process.

Overall, it seemed that they would not tolerate any attempt to guide or nudge them in a direction not of their choosing. All of this bears testimony to the capacity of the citizens to keep the upper hand and to maintain the experts in the position of advisers and support staff.

Governing Citizens' Assemblies

A greater challenge to the 150 citizens' claim of authorship came from the governance committee—a fifteen-member body that controlled key aspects of the process. It shaped the boundaries of deliberation, for example, deciding whether nuclear energy was within the mandate, or if citizens could propose financing mechanisms. The committee also set meeting agendas, structured discussions, determined session procedures, and selected experts and interlocutors. Acting as the main link to the government and institutions, it held significant sway over the process.

The committee included two co-presidents, five CESE members, and three climate experts—two of whom were already affiliated with CESE—alongside three participatory democracy experts. Representatives from the private organizations Missions Publiques and Res Publica, responsible for organizing and facilitating the sessions, attended meetings and took part in discussions but lacked voting rights.

The convention was therefore governed by experts and not internally autonomous. The fifteen people on the governance committee were able to impose a number of procedural decisions as well as the selection of a number of key experts. Additionally, all these choices were made without much justification or much accountability to the citizens, although the added presence of two randomly selected citizens after the first session possibly helped on that front. These two citizens, rotated after each session, were meant to serve as a direct liaison between the governance committee and the 150.

There was little transparency about the functioning of this governance committee, as researchers were not allowed to observe them or their deliberations. We don't know, as a result, how the balance of power between the various factions on the committee worked and to what extent the introduction of the two citizen representatives was able to influence the dynamics.

But there were possible conflicts of interest built into the leadership structure. For example, the CESE members on the governance committee had an interest in the convention's being a success, as their institutional survival depended on it. In the past, President Macron had floated the possibility of dissolving this chamber—seen as costly and of questionable utility—and the CESE's main way to save its institutional skin was to show it could serve as an organizer of citizens' conventions going forward. At the same time, it was not in this institution's interest for the citizens to emancipate themselves from the tutelage of the organizers, lest Macron consider, as he had also suggested, replacing half of the CESE with randomly selected citizens.[17] Interestingly, some surprisingly specific recommendations about making the CESE a future chamber of participation could be found in the final citizens' report, even as the future of the CESE as an institution had no direct link to the mandate of curbing greenhouse gas emissions.

Similarly, the partisan beliefs of some members of the governance committee, as well as of one of the so-called guarantors of the process (honorary observers appointed by the CESE), sometimes led them to act in intrusive and manipulative ways, as if they were more concerned about prodding certain results out of the convention than impartially facilitating a democratic process and staying committed to it, regardless of its outcomes. One of the governance committee members publicly cried in disappointment after learning that the citizens had decided against putting most of their proposals to a referendum.[18] Similarly, one of the co-presidents actively encouraged the citizens to be more ambitious, whether through public statements or informal conversations. In the working group on food, for instance, she lamented that the topic of meat had not (yet) been included in the agenda.[19] While that might have been a valid point, the fact that this remark came from the top of the hierarchy could be construed as a form of undue influence.

So, there were undoubtedly opportunities for capture in the design. That said, my observations as well as my direct experience of being on the governance committee of the second French citizens' convention have convinced me that these opportunities for capture can be and likely were in this case counterbalanced by other forces, including the pluralism of the members of the governance committee, the presence of the two randomly selected citizens on it, and a vision of the role of experts in general as facilitating the work of citizens rather than guiding it. More important than anything, however, was the strong will of citizens as a collective. They felt entitled and empowered by the initial presidential promise of "no filter" to be in charge, and contested the limits put on their agency at every turn.

Nevertheless, the current model placing the citizens' assemblies under the guardianship of the governance committee raises fundamental questions about the kind of power such assemblies can and should be granted going forward. Consider that parliaments do not have a governance committee. They are not told what to legislate about from an outside authority. They have full sovereignty over their agenda, their deliberations, and their ultimate decisions. Their self-rule is facilitated by party hierarchies and impersonal rules of order, which it shouldn't be impossible to either replicate or find a functional equivalent for in randomly selected assemblies. After all, we know that the Council of 500 in ancient Athens managed to self-organize efficiently from within even without external governance, facilitation teams, or the modern communication technologies we can rely on today. It's a matter of will, not of feasibility.

Why would we want to move toward a greater self-regulation of citizens' assemblies, you might ask. It is the right thing to do, for one thing, if we take seriously the idea of citizen legislators. But, as a member of the climate convention put it to an interviewer, it's also the condition for results more aligned with the values of the assembly members, and generally for greater speed and efficiency of the process. Asked what he thought of the role of the governance committee, this citizen remarked, "I think we lost a lot of time with this type of functioning. . . . A governance committee is necessary, certainly, for general stewardship purposes, but here it was also piloting our intentions. . . . In a real citizens' convention, I think that governance must be done by the convention itself. . . . I'm convinced we'd move forward, perhaps differently, but faster too."

Great Disillusion or Inspiring Precedent?

To this day the French media and chattering classes (including some corners of academia) have considered this first, historic, and uniquely ambitious citizens' convention a half-success at best, a failure at worst. The French parliament, meanwhile, saw the convention all along as illegitimate competition. As a result, few elected representatives bothered to attend its meetings, and many of them actively tried to undermine the convention's work. The government, for its part, was disappointed that the convention's members bit the hand that fed them by giving them a low grade on implementation. As to the 150, many of them seemed to regret having made the mistake of placing more faith in politicians than in their fellow citizens by forgoing the possibility of a referendum on their main proposals. They realized that if they had gone to a referendum, their work might have ultimately gained in both legitimacy and impact. A subset of them ended up publishing a collective book of testimonies about the process, which they titled *The Great Disillusion*.[20]

Despite this negative overall assessment, however, this first French convention shines as a beacon of hope. Consider that the work of the 150 forced the French parliament to produce its most ambitious climate bill to date. It changed the public conversation around climate change, now fully established in the French national consciousness. And in just the nine months that the Citizens' Convention for Climate existed, it radically improved the attitude of the public toward the very concept of a citizens' assembly. This attitude went from ignorance, suspicion, or downright hostility to support.[21]

Most important, the Citizens' Convention for Climate performed a novel legislative function without a clear equivalent in existing systems. It mirrored the traditional activity of parliamentary commissions, where experts are interviewed, as well as the role of the office of the prime minister, which in French law can also initiate so-called law projects. Most strikingly, no doubt, it evoked the role of Parliament, where laws are debated and amended.

Ultimately, the climate convention is perhaps best described as the first example in the modern age of an assembly of "citizen legislators" in a large, multicultural nation. It is not exactly a parliament, but it is definitely not just a focus group or a merely consultative body. Now, imagine if this assembly of citizen legislators had included 500 citizens, rather than just 150. Imagine that participation had been mandatory, ensuring even greater representation in the sample. Imagine that the citizen legislators had full control of their agenda instead of being constrained to address one particular problem within the parameters set by the executive. Imagine that their proposals had been sent to a referendum and endorsed by a majority of French citizens. Imagine all that—and realize that France came very close to fundamentally changing our vision of democracy.

SEVEN

The Power of Love

Omar, I love you.

FRANÇOIS, RETIRED FRENCH BUSINESS OWNER IN THE FRENCH
CITIZENS' CONVENTION FOR CLIMATE

Can I give you a hug?

OLDER WOMAN TO YOUNGER WOMAN IN THE FRENCH CITIZENS'
CONVENTION ON THE END OF LIFE

I'm going to throw him out the window.

FINBARR, FIFTY-SOMETHING MALE PARTICIPANT IN THE IRISH
CITIZENS' ASSEMBLY ON MARRIAGE EQUALITY

Civic Love ▪ "Where Are You, Nicolas?" ▪ Omar ▪ "You Can't
Lift a Stone with One Finger" ▪ "A Communion of Souls" ▪
Curing Prejudices ▪ Deliberation in Fragile Contexts

Despite its critics, the first French citizens' convention was
successful enough—logistically, politically, and otherwise—
to warrant a second try. In October 2022, I received a call from the
cabinet of the CESE president inviting me to join the governance
committee for a new convention, this time on end-of-life issues.
The mandate was to assess whether French law should be revised
to allow assisted suicide and euthanasia.

I had observed the first convention as an outsider, but when asked to help guide a second—even on a topic I found daunting—I said yes. There would be fourteen of us: six CESE members, three researchers (myself included), two medical ethics experts, one specialist in palliative care, and two citizens who had participated in the climate convention, there to represent the citizen perspective. For six months, I was immersed in Zoom calls—often at ungodly hours—and frequent weekend trips to Paris.[1]

The second convention brought together 185 citizens, selected by the same method as the first. We had wanted a larger group, to boost representation and visibility. Like the climate convention, this one wouldn't lead to a referendum—French law prohibits such votes on life-and-death issues. Still, the process was widely seen as smoother and more successful than the first.

Logistically, I agree. There were setbacks, but the meetings ran relatively well, press coverage was mostly positive, and public opinion strongly backed the issue: over 80 percent supported some form of assisted dying. Compared to the climate convention, our task was far easier.

Democratically, however, the second convention marked a retreat. President Macron did not offer a "no filter" pledge this time. And under a 2021 law, all future conventions were now formally subordinated to the CESE—a consultative body. Their recommendations would be filtered, folded into official CESE opinions. Whatever legislative ambition the citizens' assemblies once had was effectively gone. Sure enough, when Parliament passed assisted dying legislation in May 2025, no one mentioned the convention. Politicians claimed the credit. The convention had been "one voice among many"—and, in the end, a voice that hardly counted.

Nevertheless, this second convention still mattered—both to

the citizens and to me. For the participants, it felt like a real opportunity to shape policy. And it proved just as transformative as the first. For me, it revealed how difficult governing by committee can be—but also how meaningful it is. And it confirmed a deeper intuition that I had begun forming during the first assembly: citizens' assemblies are valuable not only for the arguments and proposals they produce but for the emotions they foster.

Most surprising, they make room for one emotion that is vanishingly rare in politics as we know it: love—specifically civic love. That love was healing for the participants and instrumental to their deliberations, allowing everyone, including the shy, to contribute their views.

Civic Love

The emergence of love between participants in citizens' assemblies is not something I was expecting to witness going into these conventions, let alone have to conceptualize. In fact, this is something that wasn't even part of my theoretical framework as a scholar, which was mostly focused on questions of knowledge, information, and expertise, and the capacity for deliberation among a diverse sample of citizens to generate a form of collective intelligence.

The belief that love is a central emotion of citizens' assemblies, however, started dawning on me shortly after the end of the Citizens' Convention for Climate. At the time, in the United States, a daring Democratic candidate in the presidential elections, Marianne Williamson, was talking about a "politics of love" as the only viable alternative to the politics of hatred arguably put forward by Donald Trump, and more broadly the politics of rage some political scientists claim is intentionally cultivated by all politicians.

Even though I had initially dismissed her as unrealistic and naïve, after the convention I started thinking she might be onto something.

The steps leading to this realization crystallized as I boarded a plane back to the deeply polarized and partisan world of Trump-era impeachment proceedings in the United States.

On November 14, 2019, just days before the third session of the climate convention began, I attended a conference in Aubervilliers, near Paris, titled Locating the Democratic Experience. The event focused on the Yellow Vests movement, specifically their experiences at traffic circles from November 2018, when the protests began, to the summer of 2019, as the movement waned following the conclusion of the Great National Debate. The speakers—primarily ethnographers and anthropologists—offered vivid accounts of the human connections formed in the occupied spaces of the Yellow Vests. They analyzed observed interactions, rituals, and unspoken forms of communication, enriching their presentations with photographs and detailed descriptions.

The portrait of the Yellow Vests that came through was that of people desperate and grateful for a human connection, who wore yellow jackets to express their membership in the tribe of the oppressed, the angry, the people to whom injustice had been done. But it was clear that they also came to find acceptance and companionship. Despite the anger that brought them there, the lack of naïveté ("None of us here are angels," "We are not teddy bears"), what the Yellow Vests seemed to experience and come back for was, generally, a form of civic bond and, more deeply still, a form of love.

Sometimes this happened literally: Some younger protesters met their future spouses at the traffic circle groups they had joined. But for most, the feeling described was something softer, akin to what Aristotle calls civic friendship. The speakers at the Aubervilliers conference thus quoted the Yellow Vests as moved by the desire for a different, deeper, more spiritual human relationship, at an existential level: "Through a word, a gesture, a look, you feel it, you are here, you exist." "Yellow Vests are reinventing a human society." "The vest, it's our soul." "We are touched in our heart." "Every traffic circle has a soul." "I felt something vibrating in my gut." "When I had to get rid of my vest [to escape encirclement by the police], it's as if I got rid of a part of myself."

What was also striking was how transformed by the discovery the researchers themselves seemed to be, in the way they described their findings. These were serious, professional researchers used to keeping their own subjectivity at a distance. Still, the awe with which these seasoned researchers spoke of what they saw was striking. They were not just reporting on the love they observed—they seemed profoundly touched by it.

At the beginning of the movement, in the early months of the peaceful occupation of traffic circles, the Yellow Vests had generated massive support for the movement in the larger population, a support that started decreasing only when some violent as well as anti-Semitic and racist incidents tainted the movement's demonstrations in Paris and other cities in the later months. Listening to the testimonies about those early months of the movement, when something special was blooming, it was easy to understand its massive popularity. The Yellow Vests sounded like they could have been our neighbors, our friends, our relatives, or our family, just fallen on hard times. With a bit of bad luck, any one of us could have been them.

A few days after that conference, I showed up at the Iéna Palace to attend the third session of the Citizens' Convention for Climate.

I had been able to watch the second one only online due to my teaching obligations. As soon as I arrived at the convention, I was immediately struck by the difference in tone between the first session, where people had seemed shy, cautious, and vaguely skeptical, and the first morning of that third session. It felt like a successful third date.

Everyone was giddy, expressing how happy they were to be back in the same building, the same room, together again. Somewhere between the first and third sessions, the participants had clearly bonded, forming a genuine connection. I felt it too. Returning to the Iéna Palace stirred a mix of emotions in me—a blend of happiness and pride, akin to patriotism. It was a love for my country, my people—a healing sense of belonging for someone who had left France with lingering resentment. In short, it was *civic love*.

"Where Are You, Nicolas?"

During the first plenary session of the third weekend, the two citizen representatives of the 150 who had been selected (by lot) to join the governance committee at the last session, and had attended every meeting of the governance committee since then, reported on that experience to the rest of the group, perched at the podium at the center of the main auditorium. One of them, Aurélie, started by expressing her happiness to be back at the convention and choked up as she searched the room for the youngest member, a seventeen-year-old teenager who had been nicknamed Little Nicolas (after the character drawn by a famous and beloved French cartoonist named Sempé). She said, "I hope you will have a long life and your blond hair will turn a lovely gray."

The addressed Nicolas wasn't there yet. Ironically, he had been stuck on the metro by Yellow Vest demonstration–related delays. As Aurélie scanned the rows filled with people—"Where are you, Nicolas? I don't see you"—the organizers, who misunderstood the situation, pointed her to Nicolas Hulot, the former minister of the environment who was the guest of honor that day. Upon seeing him, Aurélie disappointedly said, "No, not you, the little Nicolas." At which point the whole room erupted in laughter, Hulot included.

Shortly after, it was Hulot's turn to address the room. His speech was marked by a lot of bitterness, sadness, disappointment, and regret about his abortive bout in politics as President Macron's minister of the environment and a lifetime of caring about nature yet seeing it savaged and destroyed a bit more every year. But amid all the hand-wringing and angry denunciations, Hulot said something striking: "What I hated the most about the French National Assembly is the atmosphere. *People hate one another over there.* Here, you are positive. It gives me hope."

Primed by those striking few exchanges, I started paying attention to the markers of love and affection between the citizens. In the working group on housing, I noted the time when an older, retired woman from the Savoy (who charmingly insisted on being called by an Americanized version of her first name because she had spent a few happy months in the United States in her youth) stood up and said to the rest of the group: "I love you, you are amazing." Others in the group exclaimed in turn, "Mary is a beautiful soul," "She has a good heart," and other terms of endearment.

Later, I interviewed a young woman about the role of the experts in the convention. But again, the conversation took a surprising turn toward emotions. I asked her how she found the atmosphere at the convention. She said: "Between us, we are all in solidarity—we have created an intensely close, passionate connection."

At that point, everything that was happening still felt very new to me. Before the Citizens' Convention for Climate, I had read and heard about similar experiments, but even my relatively firsthand knowledge of the Icelandic constitutional process was not through direct observation, because I met people and conducted interviews only after the fact. What interviews revealed about the dynamic of the Icelandic constitutional council (a nonrandom but diverse group of twenty-five people who were not professional politicians) was that it was also a place of love, if also of great conflict. They had fought, argued, and screamed at one another a lot. But they always found a way to patch things up at the end. Several people told me they had rituals, like singing at the beginning and end, and that after a fight they always ended up at the pub. Music and alcohol were thus the cure to their core political disagreements. This is Iceland, I thought; how quaint, how charming, how hopelessly unique.

That's probably why, now, as a direct observer, the warmth and earnestness over the course of the convention surprised me. What happened to the familiar French reserve and distance? The Parisian snark? The blasé, cynical attitude I grew up immersed in? Instead, this felt like a family reunion. The whole day was like that: lots of hugs and touches, greetings by name, laughter, gentle remarks, and jokes. In the few interviews I managed to conduct despite the mad pace of the convention, the solidarity of the group, the respect, and the love were palpable.

Omar

What clinched this conclusion, finally, was a conversation over lunch during that same third session, with one particularly vocal member of the convention. Let us call him Omar. I was struck by this angry character, whose regular outbursts were somehow tolerated by the rest of the group even as, from where I stood, he seemed like a rather aggressive and unpleasant character. He had been immediately noticeable for posing a pointed question during the Q&A session with Prime Minister Édouard Philippe on the first day of the convention; he stood out also during a plenary session at the second meeting when he heckled an expert talking about the carbon tax: "Stop treating us like children!" In one small group, he had also shot down an expert with "Mrs. Expert, you're spouting nonsense."

I was puzzled by the reaction of the other citizens, because even as they protested and even once booed him into silence in one of the working groups, most of the time they gently tried to deflect his anger with humor or calm him down with injunctions such as "Be positive, Omar" or "Come on, Omar." It turned out that Omar was very much respected and liked within the group. When I sat down with him for lunch that day, I learned that he was a pediatric surgeon from a small town in the northwest of France. He was also a second-generation immigrant from North Africa who had experienced discrimination throughout his life and had seen his parents suffer from it. He had also recently gone through a divorce and remarried. He cared passionately about his patients. There was a lot of pent-up anger in Omar, about his life, the state of French hospitals, and the way old people in France, in his view, were left to die alone.

But while people were initially annoyed by his temper, they also came to appreciate Omar's passion, his courage, and his role as protector of the most vulnerable among them. As he told me over lunch, he thought the organizers were pressuring the participants too much with the workload, the long days, and the expectations. He said that he saw a participant leave and a couple of others break down in tears. He said that as a surgeon he could, of course, take this pressure ("And even a lot more!"), but that some people were fragile. He sounded incredibly protective of his fellow citizens, and angry on their behalf too.

Later, after I felt I had gained enough of his trust, I dared to ask him the question on my mind: "Omar, you've been banging your fist on the table frequently in this assembly, and it doesn't always go well. Can you explain why you are doing that and how you think other people perceive your attitude?" His answer was: "It's because I'm passionate. I care."

At that point, another member of the same working group sat down to join us, a big, friendly sixty-year-old business owner on the verge of retirement named François. I jokingly turned to François and asked, "So, François, what do you think of Omar and his contribution to the group?" I was expecting him to tease Omar about his bad temper. Instead, without pausing, François said, "Me, I admire Omar." And then he looked Omar right in the eye and said, "Omar, I love you."

Not fully realizing what was happening, I mused out loud about how much love seemed to be a theme in this convention. But when I turned to Omar again, he was all choked up and his eyes were full of tears. He very soon could no longer speak. I may or may not have started tearing up at this point too.

I took his hand and asked, "How many children do you have, Omar?" He squeezed my hand back and then hid his eyes in his hand. He showed me with his other hand: five fingers. Five children. Still choked up, he explained: two from a previous marriage, two from his new wife's previous marriage, and a child with her, now five years old. He eventually softly said, tears streaming down his face, "That's why I'm here, it's for the human exchange, the connection." Meanwhile, François said, "You can't imagine the hope I have." But he immediately followed with, "But it's always disappointed."

This was an incredible moment of humanity, indeed the most profound moment I experienced at this convention. To me, it showed how closely love is running under all the apparent anger, just looking for an outlet to express itself. Love also creates conditions from which hope can emerge, even though this hope, as François's last remark illustrates, also opens a fear of being betrayed and disappointed.

A few days later, of course, I could not help but wonder whether this love was maybe the result of the naïveté of new beginnings. As soon as they have to make collective decisions, I thought, disagreement and partisan camps will emerge, and resentment and suspicion will come to replace love and solidarity, as they always do. And to some degree, that is what happened. Partisan logic reemerged, and intense battles were fought. But somehow, the group did not give in to bitterness and suspicion. Instead, it stayed whole until the end, and voted with 80 percent approval margins on all but one of 150 proposals that came out of their deliberation. So, love grew and matured—it didn't die. In fact, it helped the group navigate the passionate disagreements that continued to take place until the end.

My conviction now is that the bond between the citizens flourished and lasted until the end because it was left to grow in this unique space of the randomly selected assembly. In the context of the convention, people overcame the barriers artificially created by status inequalities and partisan affiliations, among other constraints. Even as people figured out over time who was rich or poor, who was progressive or conservative, these labels were not part of the way people identified and came to know one another initially. They identified only, at least initially, through their first name and region of origin. This allowed friendships to bloom between people from very different backgrounds who otherwise might not have talked so easily.

Many of the citizens used the term "family" to refer to the convention. This was beautifully illustrated when one of the citizens, a beloved architect from Nantes, welcomed his second child halfway through the convention. Everyone chipped in for a gift, and the little boy, named Oscar, was informally adopted as the 151st member of the group. The CESE even planted a tree in the courtyard of the Iéna Palace in his honor.

"You Can't Lift a Stone with One Finger"

Equipped with that first experience at the climate convention, I came to the second convention expecting love to emerge in that context as well, albeit perhaps in a more subdued form, given the depressing nature of the topic of end of life. But love came gushing out there, too, and quite early on. For example, during the second weekend, when people still barely knew one another, an older woman spotted a younger woman looking quiet during the break after a difficult story had been shared in their small working group. The older woman, who identified herself as a mother when she told me this story, came to the younger woman and asked, "Can I give you a hug?" The young woman opened her arms and said, "I was waiting for someone to offer."[2]

Later in the convention, when people had started developing deeper friendships, a widow from the north of France, who used the opportunity of her weekends in Paris to visit the tomb of her late husband, confided to a peer that she didn't have the courage to go alone that day. Shortly after, ten other citizens showed up and accompanied her to the cemetery.

But in this second assembly, I saw love surging most spectacularly during the last session, when we gave participants a chance to share their thoughts about the process they had just gone through. This moment of self-reflection and opportunity for self-expression had been missing from the first convention, which was always pressed for time and too focused on output. In our case, the governance committee wanted to give our participants a chance to decompress and an occasion to reflect upon the process.

In a private (i.e., not filmed or streamed) plenary session, the citizens were thus invited by the facilitating team to answer questions like "What was the most important thing for you in what you experienced at the Convention?" "What was the most exciting thing? The hardest?" "What are three things you are going to take with you going forward?" The participants mostly ignored the questions and turned this occasion for self-expression into an unadulterated lovefest.

An older gentleman, who said he was too emotional to improvise, read a text that included the following passages: "I lived through this convention one of the most beautiful experiences of my life" and "We have become the members of an improbable family born out of the works of chance and necessity."

A young man cited the French historian Ernest Renan's idea of the "common heritage" and the "everyday plebiscite" that the convention had reaffirmed. Mathéo, a thirty-something-year-old Black man and one of the few citizens who came from the French overseas territories, in his case, Guadeloupe, said, "I have to be eight hours on a plane one way every other weekend" but that he was coming out of the experience "a bigger man" with more self-esteem because "with this convention, at least once in your life, you feel useful." He also hinted that the self-esteem of people from overseas territories was boosted through his presence at the convention. "We represent France, and that's extraordinary."

A woman celebrated the "consideration for citizens" she had felt throughout the convention. Several people recalled how their doubts and skepticism at the beginning—"I thought it was a scam"—had given way to pride and a sense of civic engagement. One celebrated the collective intelligence of the group. Several sent their love, wishes for good health, and kisses. After thanking France for making her a citizen, a woman shared a proverb from her native Mali: "You can't pick up a stone with one finger." An older man said that he'd been initially unsettled by the methodology of the convention yet had later felt rejuvenated by it. He also said that the topic of the convention stayed with him every day for the 120 days since it started and that he had worked throughout, not just during the weekends.

A woman in an African head wrap mentioned that sometimes hurtful things had been said during the convention. She wanted to ask for forgiveness if she had offended anyone, and in turn, she was forgiving everyone else. Laughter and applause ensued. A Muslim participant known for vocally opposing assisted suicide thanked the facilitation team for their work, "especially with me, who must have been exhausting," and ended with an "I love you" to the collective.

Iris, a Black woman who had never spoken in the plenary meetings before, said, "I experienced unforgettable moments with some citizens." She also emphasized the kindness she had felt from other people, including people from the majority she disagreed with. "What struck me is that once I was the only one against [assisted dying] in a group for it. I received benevolence. . . . I spoke about my faith with atheists. They understood my love for my God. Thank you for hearing that."

As you can see in this mix of testimonies, people expressed their love for one another in different ways, layering it with other feelings, ranging from pride to gratitude. Gratitude, interestingly, at least in this sample, seemed to be voiced most explicitly by women of North African descent. The undergraduate student of mine, Thalsa-Thiziri Mekaouche, who pointed this out to me, is herself a French woman of Algerian descent. She ventured the thought, based on her own experience, that maybe the extent to which immigrants feel unloved and unwanted in their day-to-day life, as she had sometimes felt herself growing up, partly explains these bursts of emotion. She conjectured that love is likely to be even more powerful for ordinary citizens who are traditionally excluded, simply because they are likely to feel gratitude. I do not know if this conjecture is warranted, or whether it would be truer of immigrants than other categories of "the shy," but I find it plausible and worth exploring (as I hope she will!).

In any case, upon hearing all those testimonies that day, we on the governance committee could not have been prouder. What became clear for me in that moment is that far from being an epiphenomenon, love and bonding are essential to the work that is accomplished in citizens' assemblies. It also proved that the shy will willingly come out of their shell when the tone of exchanges is appropriately respectful, benevolent, and indeed loving. It showed that a different kind of politics is possible than the bitter, alienating kind we're all too familiar with.

"A Communion of Souls"

One of the most remarkable effects of the assemblies I observed was how they brought people into the deliberative fold, reconnecting them with politics. Participants embraced the deliberative process within the convention. They even found renewed interest in electoral politics as usual.

What stands out is the commitment shown by participants. They returned every weekend, often traveling great distances— like Mathéo from Guadeloupe—and worked long hours when they could have been spending time with family and friends. Despite the intense demands on their time and cognitive energy, only about 10 percent dropped out of the first convention—a relatively low number given the challenges. The second convention, however, probably because it was better paced, enjoyed a truly extraordinary retention rate: 184 of 185 participants stayed through to the end. The sole dropout left reluctantly, as a new job conflicted with her participation. This dedication endured despite numerous setbacks and crises, both internal and external, that could have easily derailed the process. It's a testament to the power of meaningful engagement in fostering commitment and resilience.[3]

Why did people care so much? Here, I'd like to share an exchange I had toward the end of the Citizens' Convention for Climate. On the last day of the fifth weekend, as I was leaving the building, I ran into Jules, the most visible and vocal climate skeptic in the convention and initially an angry man disaffected with politics. He had been on TV to explain his climate skepticism to puzzled journalists. He had also spent the first weekend with a frown of disgust and skepticism on his face, taking his carry-on everywhere instead of checking it at the door because, as he explained, he was going to leave any minute now. He ended up staying and was actively involved until the end, even though he remained a committed climate skeptic throughout. He also went on to run for office in his home region shortly afterward.

I interviewed him on the fly as we were both leaving the building that Sunday afternoon, pushed out by the CESE's ushers. He explained how he hated "partisanship," "club spirit," and "indoctrination," and that is why he had been so very suspicious of the convention to begin with. I remarked that despite all of this he was still here and seemed well integrated in the group. He replied, "Not only am I well integrated, but I'm passionate. So, the convention, once I feel free to express what I want, and I feel loved . . ." I couldn't help but interrupt him: "You feel *loved*?" I asked. He explained, "I feel loved by . . . there are a lot of members who love me very much and whom I love very much. . . . There is a communion of souls. You feel it."

I wish I hadn't interrupted him, though, because I'll never know what he meant to say happened once he felt free and loved. A plausible interpretation, based on the rest of the conversation and his subsequent behavior, is that once he felt free and loved, he felt motivated to participate and contribute to the common good in ways he would never have contemplated, or perhaps even felt capable of, before.

Curing Prejudices

The most striking example of the transformative power of civic love comes from an assembly I did not observe myself, the 2012–2014 Irish Convention on the Constitution (the first Irish citizens' assembly), which tackled, among other topics, the question of marriage equality. The story is worth recounting because I now firmly believe that it is representative of the transformative power of citizens' assemblies more broadly. In this particular case, the assembly allowed two radically opposed people, and beyond them arguably an entire country, to come closer to a form of political reconciliation.

On the one hand, there was Finbarr O'Brien, a disgruntled Irish voter, a loner, someone disaffected with politics (not unlike Jules above). Finbarr is also someone with a tragic history: He was sexually abused as a kid by one of his parents' friends. On the other hand, there was Chris Lyons, a young gay man with a history of being bullied by homophobes.

According to the journalist who reported on the story,[4] Finbarr saw Chris Lyons arrive at his table on the first morning of the first day of this Irish convention and tensed up immediately. All he saw were the lip piercings, the Mohawk hairstyle, the eye makeup and rainbow-colored painted nails. Realizing that this man was gay triggered Finbarr: "My first thought was, I'm going to throw him out the window. My thoughts were out of control." And while Chris triggered Finbarr's childhood trauma, Finbarr similarly triggered Chris's fears: "I looked at him, and he stared off into space. So, I thought, okay, gentlemen's agreement, you don't look at me, I don't look at you. . . . I could see it all clearly, anyway: older Irishman, I'd spent my whole life fighting against these people and their values, repeatedly having to say, you know, I'm not a pervert, I'm a person whose life has value."

What kind of deliberation, understanding, and consensus can we expect between a man who thinks men who are attracted to other men and paint their nails are like the pedophile who abused him as a child, and a man whose experience has taught him that so many older white men hate him and wish him dead?

Yet, as David Farrell and Jane Suiter recount in their book, *Reimagining Democracy*, something remarkable happened at the end of the weekend devoted to marriage equality. Finbarr, who had not spoken until then, stood up to make a statement. "He spoke clearly," they write, "but with some emotion: it was obvious to all in the room that he wanted to make a strong point." The group listened intently as Finbarr opened up about his childhood trauma, sharing how it had shaped his views and attitudes toward gay people. In this space, he felt compelled to make a declaration: He fully supported the proposal for gay marriage. As Farrell and Suiter, who witnessed this moment firsthand, soberly describe it, "The hair rose on the backs of our necks. Applause broke out. Members rose to their feet, clapping." Finbarr had gone from wanting to throw Chris out of a window for speaking up for his right to love, to standing as one of Chris's most ardent supporters. Chris, in turn, had gone from fearing older white men like Finbarr to finding a friend in him. What happened?

What happened was the transformative power of civic love. Over approximately six days of deliberation (spread from December 1, 2012, to April 14, 2013), these two individuals bridged the gap between them by learning together and bonding over a shared goal. Without that bond, there would have been no understanding, no growth, no opportunity for either of them to challenge their assumptions. Together, they moved closer to the truth—about each other, about the reality of homosexuality, and, arguably (though perhaps more controversially), about what it means for a democratic, liberal society to treat all its members with dignity and respect, regardless of sexual orientation.

Deliberation in Fragile Contexts

Are such moments of reconciliation possible only in the privileged context of established and stable democracies, where peace and law and order are a given and individuals can additionally count on a social safety net of sorts? Could civic love emerge in more challenging contexts, such as poor and war-torn societies? Empirical evidence suggests that human nature is the same everywhere. The sociologist Nicole Curato has conducted extensive observations of deliberative assemblies in what she calls "fragile contexts," that is, contexts characterized by sources of instability such as civil war, drug violence, and poverty. She describes how even there, divided communities can come together and start healing deep and sustained wounds.

Curato has for years conducted fieldwork in her native Philippines among low-income communities recovering from armed conflict and police brutality in the wake of President Rodrigo Duterte's brutal crackdown on the drug trade. Among many examples, she documents the case of a deliberative assembly in Quezon City, in the northern Philippines, that brought together the parents and spouses of drug dealers and their victims. She reports how, after two days of intense listening and painful and initially acrimonious exchanges, the two sides came to a better understanding of the larger circumstances that constrained their children's and husbands choices.

The supporters of the drug war started accusing mothers and wives of suspected drug dealers of being irresponsible for not doing more to stop their sons and husbands from selling drugs to young people in the village. But in the course of the deliberation, as stories started pouring out unveiling the complexities of individual situations and as other ways to improve the security of their community emerged, the two sides "developed empathy for each other." They realized their children had all been at risk of being recruited into the drug trade. The victims could have been the perpetrators and vice versa. Meanwhile, the parents and spouses of the drug dealers broke down, acknowledging that their sons' and husbands' involvement in the drug trade put their neighbors' children at risk and asking for their forgiveness. In turn, their neighbors fell into their arms, not only forgiving but extending compassion for lives lost to drug gangs. They even reassured the mothers and widows that they could still be proud of their sons and husbands, "for they did everything they could to provide for their families." As acrimony gave way to understanding, "the forum ended in tears."[5]

This striking example is just one among many. The late political scientist Jürg Steiner and his collaborators have similarly shown that deliberative dialogues can start a process of reconciliation and healing in post-conflict Colombia, the post–civil war Balkans, and Brazilian favelas devastated by gang violence.[6]

Contrary to what politicians have led us to believe over the years, politics does not have to be only about conflict, polarization, rage, and resentment. In the context of citizens' assemblies and other spaces designed for deliberation across differences, ordinary citizens are perfectly able to engage with one another, listen to one another, and solve problems together. And one of the reasons why they succeed in solving problems, often precisely where politicians fail, is because they bond and learn to care for one another, and even to love one another.

EIGHT

Bringing the Shy People Out

You're speaking, Denise, you're growing!

LUC, FIFTY-SOMETHING MAN IN THE FRENCH CITIZENS'
CONVENTION FOR CLIMATE

*It's the first time I'm speaking in the auditorium, to say
thank you.*

IRIS, THIRTY-SOMETHING BLACK WOMAN

I have nothing to say.

GÉRARD, RETIRED MILITARY RESERVIST IN THE FRENCH
CITIZEN'S CONVENTION ON THE END OF LIFE

The Guest List ▪ Curation and
Facilitation ▪ Giving the Shy a Shot ▪
Ideological Minorities ▪ Center Versus Periphery ▪
Feeling Excluded ▪ The Forgotten Butterfly

I once attended a workshop at an Ivy League law school, after
which we were taken to dinner to continue discussing the work
of the scholar who had spoken. The topic was populism, something
I thought I had things to say about. But while I was able to ask my
question in the facilitated context of the workshop, I could barely

make myself heard during the dinner itself. Participants, all legal scholars except for me and the speaker, were constantly interrupting and talking over one another. At first, I did try to insert myself into the conversation. But my voice is soft and I dislike shouting over others so, after a while, I gave up. My left-hand dinner companion noticed and told me, in a gently scolding tone, "You have to get in and impose yourself."

Slightly annoyed that the burden was placed on me to assert myself rather than on the dominant voices to pay attention to others, I nevertheless tried to step in more aggressively—to no avail. Seeing that I wasn't succeeding, the same dinner companion eventually took it upon himself to say, "Come on, guys, let her speak." I was able to make my point, aware that people received it with some impatience. But once that courtesy was out of the way, the belligerent style took over again for the rest of the evening. I can't remember if we made any progress on the concept of populism in the end. All I remember is being put off by this battle of egotists, all trying to speak at the same time, more concerned with making their points and sounding smart than with learning from or just listening to others.

My own experience in this setting and many others has made me sensitive to the fact that it's not enough to invite people to the table. You have to go out of your way to make them welcome and to include them in an intentional, thoughtful manner. Otherwise, they will do what I did and clam up. And it will be as much your loss as it is theirs.

Bringing the shy people out takes thought, intention, work, and structural and institutional design. The shy will not willingly come out. You have to bring them out of their shells, lower the entry barriers into the conversation, and make sure the methods you use to lower those barriers are actually working. All of this is part of an effort to create new behavioral norms that make the shy, and everyone else, comfortable. It is what is required for them to feel at ease in a workshop, at a dinner party, or as part of a citizens' assembly—to feel that they belong and the shared space is theirs too. I now turn to the various ways in which citizens' assemblies achieve this.

The Guest List

A lot of the inclusiveness fostered by citizens' assemblies has to do with how the guest list is constituted and how representative it is of the larger country. Ideally, the invited group would be large, the take-up rate high, and as a result the sample would be as statistically representative as possible.

In practice, citizens' assemblies are never perfectly representative. Since participation is not mandatory—though, ultimately, it probably should be, as it is for jury duty—the sample is inevitably characterized by a large amount of self-selection. But these assemblies are not highly unrepresentative by any means, especially not in comparison with elected chambers. Quota sampling and incentivization via honoraria, paid day care, and other measures allow the samples to capture many dimensions of the target population, including a range of incomes, education levels, and sometimes ideological leanings. Additionally, within such assemblies, procedures are in place to avoid domination by some subset of the group. The most empirically sophisticated studies available, of deliberative polls, show no greater influence of the wealthy and educated.[1] Finally, the setup of citizens' assemblies in general empowers those I call the shy, including traditionally oppressed minorities, more than any comparable environment.

There are many methods out there to achieve a diverse and maximally representative sample. The simplest, theoretically purest one is "one person, one lottery ticket." In practice, however, this ideal gives way to what is called stratified random sampling, because the sample is usually too small for the law of large numbers to work its magic; even when the sample is sufficiently large, there is still a probability that the law of large numbers would produce an outlier sample that overrepresents or underrepresents certain categories of people in ways that could be seen as problematic. So, to be sure that the singular sample is sufficiently representative, one usually defines at the start a number of demographic categories that need to be filled with a certain number of people: for example, gender, age, geographic origin, and level of education. Sometimes it is possible to track things like race or religion.

The methodology that James Fishkin uses for his deliberative polls has been described as the "gold standard" of population sampling.[2] Its method of recruitment consists of sampling participants from existing panels of the public willing to share all kinds of information about themselves to create a sample that almost perfectly approximates a portrait of the larger population according to a series of demographic characteristics. The problem with this method is that restricting the pool to people already willing to volunteer their information creates a bias in who ends up participating in the deliberative polls. In some countries, there are no preexisting panels, and other, more costly and time-consuming methods, such as mailing letters and door-to-door recruitment, must be resorted to.

In France, the use of panels was rejected in favor of the costlier but more accurate method of random dialing. The polling institute Harris Interactive and its partner Le Terrain worked with phone companies to identify all 260 million existing cell phone numbers, and excluding from them unused numbers. Two random samples of one hundred thousand each were created, one being the one from which 170 people would be recruited at random. The other served as a backup pool.

As a member of the governance committee for the second convention, I had the opportunity, along with a few colleagues, to visit the Paris office of Le Terrain, the company responsible for recruiting participants for the Citizens' Convention on the End of Life. In a dimly lit basement room, we observed a team of twenty young people, all seemingly under twenty-five, working in cubicles with headsets, making muffled phone calls to people across France. Calls were made between 5:00 p.m. and 9:00 p.m. to increase the chances of reaching people at home. The operators didn't dial numbers themselves; a computer system handled the dialing, connecting the recipient to the next available operator to minimize errors.

The calls all started the same way "Hi, my name is X, I'm calling on behalf of the society Le Terrain to let you know that you have been randomly selected to take part in a citizens' convention organized by the CESE. Would you be interested in hearing more?" At this point people who picked up (about 10 percent of the people called) often hung up because they thought it was a scam or commercial spam. Even when they stayed on the line, they often rescheduled the call to a better time, perhaps hoping never to pick up again or just postponing the conversation.

During the half hour we observed the young operators at work, most calls ended in brief refusals or rescheduling for a better time. Later, we were invited to listen to full exchanges, including the participants' responses.

In one call, a woman with a heavy North African accent, working as a caregiver, showed initial interest in both the process and the topic of end-of-life issues. However, when the operator explained that participation required more than four meetings, including weekends away, her enthusiasm waned. In a subdued tone, she said, "It's too much, I can't." When asked if her employer was the obstacle, she confirmed, "Yes." The operator assured her that explanatory documents would be sent for further consideration, though it seemed unlikely she would accept the invitation.

Another call offered more promise. A young man from Calvados—my home region—who happened to be born in 1982 (he could have been my brother, so I paid close attention!) took the call seriously. He listened carefully to the operator's explanations. Surprisingly, he already knew about citizens' conventions, likely because of the climate convention three years earlier. However, his interest dipped when he learned the topic: "The subject doesn't interest me much, and I don't have much to say about it." Just as the operator seemed ready to give up, he added, "Well, if I've been selected by lot, I'll do it. I'll give my opinion."

It wasn't clear if he felt obligated, as for jury duty, or if he appreciated the rarity of being selected, though he did remark on how "lucky" he was to be "given this opportunity." His reaction, at any rate, confirmed a suspicion I and other colleagues have long held: Operators shouldn't reveal the topic until participants commit. Knowing the subject in advance likely skews participation. For instance, during the climate convention, more climate advocates participated than skeptics, as those dismissing climate change were far less likely to volunteer for such a discussion.

During the call, the operator also gathered demographic details—gender, age, education, income, and rural versus urban residence—

that would later help fill quotas. Political ideology, you might wonder? It wasn't included, though the question feels worth asking.

Political ideology is a category that could have been sorted for. In France, however, neither convention used that criterion. This was probably more of a mistake for the first convention, which, as a result, likely under-sampled climate change skeptics. In the case of the second convention, positions on assisted suicide and euthanasia seemed to track the distribution of views in the larger population, which would seem to indicate that the lack of stratification on political ideology was less of a problem.

What about race and religion? In France, race is not recognized as a legitimate category. In fact, under President Macron, the term "race" itself was erased from the French constitution.[3] Religion, meanwhile, is not a category that the state has the right to keep statistics on. It is therefore impossible to directly sample for those categories. This was problematic in the context of the Convention on the End of Life, a topic that obviously raises spiritual and religious issues and where one would want to make sure that the various religious affiliations of French citizens are represented in a fair way. (For example, while there are no official statistics tracking people's religion, we still know through unofficial calculations that there are roughly five million declared Muslims in France.)

The governance committee of the Convention on the End of Life considered sampling participants based on religious and spiritual affiliations, with the operators asking about individuals' beliefs. However, without official statistics to verify proportional representation, this would have been tricky. Another concern was the potential backlash: "See, I said I was Catholic/Muslim/Jewish, and they excluded me." While I thought this fear was overstated—

particularly given my perspective from the United States, where the opposite criticism of neglecting religious balance might arise—the committee ultimately chose not to include religion as a selection criterion. To this day, I'm unsure if it was the right decision.

In any case, because of the limitations of size and methods, the samples produced by the two French conventions were undeniably far from perfect. But they still offered a vastly more representative picture of the population than the French parliament itself and the group of professional politicians running the nation.

What helped bring out the shy, in particular, is the fact that participation was financially incentivized. The rate was around eighty-four euros per day for the first convention, close to ninety-five euros for the second convention. For the nine weekends of two and a half days each that the citizens had to devote to the Citizens' Convention on the End of Life, for example, the total compensation, if you attended all sessions, was around twenty-five hundred euros, a solid month's salary for most people. Transportation, hotel nights, meals, and childcare were also covered.

But even with good statistical methods and well-structured incentives, you might not reach all the categories of the population you would want represented on the assembly. The shyest of the shy may not have a cell phone to begin with, or if they do, they might not pick up. Both citizens' conventions strove to include marginal populations. The CESE worked each time with charitable organizations to find homeless candidates. These people were accompanied throughout by representatives of NGOs and civil associations because they required heightened care and support in order to stay until the end of the process.

You might wonder what the contribution of homeless people to such assemblies can possibly be. The fact is, most dropped out early in the process. But their sheer presence reminded those who encountered them of what the implications of housing policies—a central question in the climate justice debate—can be. It is one thing to deliberate in the abstract about the policy implications of higher rents among people who are all safely housed. It is another when you have to look someone in the eye who's been living on the street for months or years and explain to them why their being homeless is an unfortunate side effect of the policies you defend. The knowledge that homeless people are in the room can change the nature of the conversation. At the very least it changes its tone, to a more respectful one. No one in a citizens' assembly where homeless people are present would dream of calling poor people the "toothless," as former French President François Hollande (a socialist at that!) infamously did.[4]

Curation and Facilitation

Bringing the shy to the table is one thing. But you also need to encourage them to participate. There are many ways the French conventions tried to do so. A key factor was facilitation. In both conventions facilitators were essential in both reining in the outspoken people and spotting and encouraging the wallflowers. Facilitators are professionals trained to distribute speaking rights in a fair way: to identify and counter predictable gender dynamics whereby, for example, men speak and women nod; to handle the hecklers in plenary sessions and the troublemakers in small groups; and generally to create conditions in which norms of mutual respect and listening are established and maintained throughout.

This curation of the deliberative space ensures that the shy flourish and gain in confidence over time, carried by the trust placed in them by the very design of the assembly as well as the love and emotional support of other participants.

One striking example took place halfway through the process, in one of the meetings of the working group on housing. The organizers were asking everyone in the room to speak in turn to express an opinion about the morning debate in the plenary session. When it came time for Denise, an elegant white-haired lady, to take her turn, everyone stood still, as if paying extra attention and making room for her. She gave her opinion in a soft voice. When she was done, you could have heard a pin drop. Luc, an older, tough-looking guy, then said loudly, with affection: "You are speaking, Denise, you are growing." A murmur of approval followed, and joyful laughter erupted. I learned only later from others that Denise was a former stutterer and almost never spoke in public.

Facilitators are key in nudging people out of their comfort zone. For example, a woman was selected by lot to join one of the so-called debrief meetings that we on the governance committee held after each session to assess what had gone well, what had gone not so well, and what could be done better next time. This woman found the courage to show up, perhaps because it was a small group of around twenty people. But when the facilitation team said to the participants that day that they would have to give a public account of the meeting to the rest of the group during the first day of the following session, she exclaimed, "That will be without me." Obviously, the perspective of speaking from the elevated lectern at the center of the imposing amphitheater where plenary meetings took place paralyzed her. The facilitator next to me whispered: "She's afraid of going onstage. I'll talk to her." I don't remember if she ever walked onstage in the end. But facilitators can provide the nudge and encouragement that the shy, whose first impulse is to retreat (as I did myself at the dinner after the law seminar), often need.

Facilitation, especially good facilitation, is labor intensive and costly. In the first convention, the choice was made to not have facilitators at all tables, partly for economic reasons and partly because of a faith in the self-discipline of citizens, once norms of mutual respect and good listening were established. That design choice was not entirely successful. In the second convention, tellingly, the choice was made to have facilitators at each table (though, according to some citizen reports, they were of uneven quality).

Ideally, other advocates for the shy would be present besides facilitators, who may be too busy taking notes or coordinating activities to prevent some voices from being ignored. In the Convention on the End of Life, a committee of four guarantors, playing the role of impartial umpires of the whole process, also took on the role of advocates for viewpoints expressed by shy people when facilitators failed to amplify them.

Here is one particularly good example of how these advocates for the shy worked. At the beginning of the Citizens' Convention for Climate, President Macron had evoked the possibility of submitting the citizens' proposals directly ("with no filter") to a referendum. One question debated during the process was the possibility of a multiple-question referendum on the model of what had been done in Ireland, rather than the classic yes-or-no model used in France until then. For some reason, the governance committee members had no interest in exploring the possibility of a multiple-question referendum.

During a presentation on referendum options, a citizen posed a question in the Zoom chat: Had a multiple-choice referendum ever been organized in France, and would it have a better chance of being accepted today? The facilitator deflected, explaining that the legal committee had decided not to include this option because it was considered "uncertain," given its lack of precedent in France. Another citizen followed up in the chat: "What is it that's 'uncertain'?" The question went unanswered for several minutes until Cyril Dion, one of the process guarantors, stepped in. He asked, "When you say the legal committee sidelined the possibility of a multiple-choice referendum, does that mean it's not technically possible? It seems to me this decision should be up to the citizens, not the legal committee." The organizer responded defensively: "I didn't say the legal committee sidelined it, but that they chose not to explore this possibility." Dion persisted: "It's important to keep this an open hypothesis—it's up to the citizens to decide." Several citizens in the chat expressed agreement.

This episode highlights two key points. First, citizens are capable of challenging experts' conservative frameworks—in this case, the preference for sticking to established French procedures. Second, it underscores the importance of individuals who can amplify quiet voices or questions that might otherwise be overlooked. Thoughtful institutional design, such as the inclusion of impartial guarantors, can play a crucial role in ensuring these voices are heard.

In both conventions, an effort was also made to meet people at different levels of formal education and in different cognitive modes. The work of graphic designers, for example, considerably helped participants less comfortable with reading understand the logical progression of arguments and ideas. For the Convention on the End of Life, the graphic designers came up with a "deliberation tree" that visually captured the various argumentative paths that had been taken until then and helped structure the rest of the conversations.[5] The graphic designers also captured the humor of situations in witty cartoons regularly shared on the big screen during plenary sessions. This created lighthearted and laughter-filled moments throughout the proceedings that indirectly helped the process. During the last session, their work got the first standing ovation of the weekend.

Giving the Shy a Shot

Finally, other design choices matter, like making sure the shy themselves are also represented in the governance structure of the assembly. In the French conventions, the governance committees mostly included appointed experts. But the organizers of the first convention decided to include two randomly selected citizens in the governance committee meetings, rotating them after each session, to make sure the citizens' perspective was taken into account as well. Unfortunately, those citizens were picked at random from only a limited pool of volunteers, the natural leaders of the group. This led to a sense among the rest of the group that people who attended the governance meetings were somehow more special than others, which created some resentment. In the second convention, even though we only included them in debrief meetings, we insisted on choosing the citizen representatives by lot from among the whole group instead. This was not only to preserve the principle of equality, it was also to make sure the shy people got their shot. That's how we ended up with someone like Gérard, a retired army reservist, who was present at the debrief meeting during the seventh weekend. Note that in France the army is nicknamed "The Great Mute" because its members were denied voting rights until 1945 (one year longer than French women!). Soldiers in France are historically used to being, literally, second-class citizens and, consequently, silent.

When given the floor at the debrief meeting, Gérard first claimed, "I have nothing to say." But then, as we politely waited for him to expand on that first thought, he haltingly launched into a *long* tirade about various complaints he had, including the fact that some dominant voices were slowing down the process and taking up too much space in the proceedings. "I'm used to being quiet because of my job. But some people talk too much." The only reason why he was in the room that day was that we randomly selected from the whole group of 184 people, and then gave them the option to opt out. The nudge of being selected tipped Gérard over into participation, despite his professional reserve. His presence and testimony helped us on the governance committee to better appreciate the complicated dynamics of a large, deliberative group of people and how some people in it might feel silenced.

To make sure the shy show up, though, including them in the pool by default and counting on random selection to pick out some of them won't be enough. The shy might still decline your invitation, so you need to work on providing them incentives to participate. Shyness is not something that one overcomes in a day or on the first invitation to participate.

Ideological Minorities

One way to empower the shy is by helping them connect with one another. In the Convention on the End of Life, one category of the shy was the minority who opposed assisted dying. They self-censored during the first couple of sessions. Then, during session 3, a piloting committee member improvised a vote—neither discussed nor approved by the governance committee—on the blunt question, "Are you for or against assisted dying?" The vote, intended to gauge the room's general sentiment, showed 76 percent in favor. However, it left many deeply uncomfortable. Some citizens called it "a catastrophe," and at least one considered not returning. The outcome itself wasn't surprising; national polls at the time showed 80 to 90 percent support for assisted dying, which the assembly largely reflected. The issue was the perception that the vote prematurely shut down the debate, undermining the deliberative process and causing frustration among a significant portion of the group.

Some citizens defended the vote as a necessary part of the democratic process, and it's unclear how the majority felt about its value. However, the strong opposition from a vocal minority was enough to highlight its divisiveness. In hindsight, I believe the vote should have been delayed by one or two sessions.

Halfway through the debrief meeting after weekend four, several citizens voiced concerns that those opposing assisted suicide still didn't feel heard or confident enough to raise objections. This issue had also been raised previously during office hours—ninety-minute sessions that gave anyone who wanted to speak with us (typically three governance committee members) direct access to share their concerns. About fifteen to twenty citizens usually attended, and we reported key feedback during the debriefs. One citizen suggested meeting with like-minded individuals. The governance committee was divided on this idea, fearing that opinion groups might reintroduce the partisan divides that citizens' assemblies aim to avoid. However, given the citizens' request and the need to rebuild trust after the contentious vote during session 3, we decided to experiment with opinion groups in session 5.

These opinion groups went remarkably well, and session 5 was probably the turning point that allowed minorities to feel fully at home at the convention. These groups allowed all opinion minorities (those against both assisted suicide and euthanasia; those against euthanasia but in favor of assisted dying under conditions; and those in favor of both assisted suicide and euthanasia as universal and almost unconditional rights) to find one another and work on their counterarguments. The opinion groups allowed dissenters to come and listen, sometimes interjecting in helpful ways to make the arguments presented stronger. They also ensured that the minority opposed to assisted dying ultimately rallied behind the group project, despite their opposition to some of its recommendations. Indeed, over time, a form of consensus emerged. The citizens' final report,[6] along with their sixty-five proposals, was approved by an overwhelming 92 percent of the convention. Seventy-six percent of participants voted for a change in the law to introduce a French model for assisted suicide and euthanasia. But a large chunk of the report also focused on what the minority had been arguing for all along: better access to quality palliative care at the end of life, as a way to save people from having to consider tragic choices. On the last day of the convention, the (informal) leader of the minority stood up to say, "I want to thank the 75 percent for giving us 50 percent of the speaking time and 50 percent of the final document."[7] To us on the governance committee, this reconciliation of majority and minority was one of the convention's biggest achievements.

I should acknowledge, however, that reintroducing partisan logic did come at some cost to the harmony of the group, as we found out later in interviews.[8] Further, when directly asked about the opinion groups (at a conference that I organized at Yale University in February 2024), the previously mentioned minority leader said that despite the gratitude she had wanted to express publicly with her speech, she recognized that the opinion groups had substituted a logic of "winning" against the initial logic of collaboration and had entrenched minority and majority opinion groups as "warring sides."[9] These were strong words. Harmony and collective spirit, she implied, started fading the minute we reintroduced the possibility of a partisan orientation toward winning.

So, were opinion groups a mistake? I don't think so. They empowered minorities and forced majorities to seriously engage with dissent. The real issue may have been letting these groups persist too long—perhaps their purpose was fulfilled after a few sessions. An alternative might have been to create opinion groups through random selection, encouraging participants to "role-play" opposing views. This approach could have made minority perspectives more visible and understandable without entrenching divisions or solidifying "camps."

Center Versus Periphery

As we saw, the first French convention was an imperfect process in many ways. In my view, one of the less remarked upon problems was the limited inclusion of the views of inhabitants of the French overseas territories. On a topic like climate change, which extends to questions of biodiversity loss, you would think that the views of people from territories where 70 to 86 percent of France's biodiversity resides would be central and centered. Yet citizens from the French overseas territories were not given a space, voice, and role in that first convention commensurate to their firsthand knowledge of this reality. In fact, the organizers of the convention, despite a budget of six million euros, had not even flown out anyone living there at the time, considering it too costly. They had included only people from overseas territories who had already moved to the metropole in order to reach the quota of overseas representatives.

While this may seem like a problem specific to a former colo-nizer like France, the point I want to make here is more general: It is about the place of the shy, namely people at the margins of a system, whatever this system is. So let us explore the consequences of the marginalization of certain groups within the two French conventions.

A researcher from Réunion, Christiane Rafidinarivo, who also observed the Citizens' Convention for Climate, noted that it counted seven representatives of overseas territories versus 143 from metro-politan France. Of those seven overseas representatives whom she followed during the convention over its nine-month duration, Ra-fidinarivo notes with appreciation that they were spared "tokeni-zation" and "did not serve as alibis of diversity."[10] She also found that the Convention for Climate successfully reduced the injustice typically suffered by overseas citizens in France, when their expe-rience is found unintelligible by the metropolitans and their testi-monies are discounted.

Still, the final document of the Convention for Climate in-cludes very few of the concerns about seas (except for a few provi-sions on fishing) that are paramount for the overseas territories (most of them islands).

When I was brought onto the governance committee of the sec-ond French citizens' assembly, the Citizens' Convention on the End of Life, one of my hopes was that we would not make similar mis-takes. And, indeed, in this area the second convention improved somewhat on the previous one. Unlike the climate convention, ours flew in people who lived on the islands, ensuring a better represen-tation of this part of the population. I have already recounted how proud I am of our including ideological minorities. These ideolog-ical minorities cut across race, ethnicity, and geographic provenance, and it appears to me, on a superficial level at least, that the nonwhite members of the convention were not treated any differently than the white ones and were not markedly less vocal or engaged in the process.

Of course, it would be hard to demonstrate such a claim, even if some researchers had paid attention to and tried to measure that dimension of the second convention (which, to my knowledge, none did). It would be hard because, as previously reported, France, unlike the United States, cannot identify people through their "race." So "race" was not a category the polling company that built our sample of 185 participants could use. It is also not a category that French researchers are generally comfortable with, unless they have studied in the United States.

There was nevertheless a substantial number of people of color in the convention just by virtue of the law of large numbers and the geographic criterion that ensured representation of French citizens from our overseas territories, who are predominantly Black and brown (I would say the only truly underrepresented category was people of Asian descent).

However, my trust that minorities, including racial, ethnic, and geographic minorities, had been treated relatively fairly in the process was shaken by two particular plenary interventions at the end of the process.

Feeling Excluded

During the final weekend, as we gave participants free rein to express how they had felt through the process and what they had learned from it, one citizen, the first Black woman to speak in this session, said, with visible emotion: "My feeling in this convention is that the minority against assisted suicide and euthanasia was crushed by the majority in favor. I felt completely excluded in this convention." Polite applause ensued, and she was thanked by the facilitator for sharing her feelings with honesty. Later, she interrupted other citizens from the minority camp when they recounted different, much more positive experiences than hers.

Witnessing her interventions, I initially cringed in my seat at what seemed to indicate a rather bad failure of inclusion. What did we, especially we on the governance committee, do wrong that caused this person to feel so unheard? During the debrief the next day, however, it became clear that this person had personal issues, perhaps even mental health issues. During the plenary sessions she had made disturbing statements about her past, claiming that her kids had been euthanized without her consent. None of the coaches or facilitators had been able to engage with her. One of the facilitators described her as "a wall." The three citizens present at our meeting confirmed that judgment.

Perhaps not everyone can be helped or fully included in even the most inclusive processes. Perhaps there are larger background issues, from mental illness to extreme desocialization to life events, and larger political contexts—of systemic inequalities, among others—that cannot be fixed within the confines of a deliberative assembly. It was in itself a victory that this person stayed until the very end of a long, intense nine-week process and felt comfortable enough to speak up, even against the process.

The next day, at the Élysée Palace, I noticed her, dressed to the nines, sitting in the second row in a grand and gloriously gilded room to watch President Macron receive the citizens' report. She was also one of the first people to go and shake his hand during the meet and greet. The fact that she felt safe enough to protest so loudly and publicly during the last day of the convention was, in some way, proof of the convention's success. Despite her undeniable feeling of exclusion, she was able to make herself heard, and did not hesitate to do so.

The Forgotten Butterfly

Another intervention, however, proved more worrying still. It was voiced by Mathéo from Guadeloupe, who, as recounted in the previous chapter, had just the day before expressed his pride in and gratitude for being a part of the process. Addressing the larger public beyond the convention, though (this session was televised), his tone was a bit different.

He now clearly wanted to send a message to the people in overseas territories who were probably watching him on the internet: "I want to put in a word for my parish. . . . Often one forgets that Guadeloupe . . . and Martinique are part of France. That's probably why yesterday the little butterfly of Guadeloupe was forgotten on the drawings [by the graphic artists]." The man went on to invite the larger public watching the streaming of that session to visit Guadeloupe, which, he said, "is not Las Vegas but isn't the third world either." He concluded, "Come visit, because we need your money."

Everybody burst into applause and laughter at the last invitation, even though there was a real bite to the message. When he mentioned that the butterfly-shaped territory of Guadeloupe, in the French part of the Caribbean, had been forgotten by the graphic designers, he obviously took it as a symptom of a larger problem in the relationship between metropolitan France and the overseas territories. When he said that Guadeloupe was not the third world, he took aim at the prejudices of white metropolitan

French people. When he said, "We need your money," he meant the money of richer French people, referring to the problematic gap in wealth between metropolitan France and its overseas territories, which further tracks a number of other socioeconomic inequalities. When the facilitators summarized his remarks, they predictably did not dwell on any of this. They also failed to mention the comment about the forgotten butterfly.

Not properly representing the butterfly of Guadeloupe is a problem when it comes to the topic of the end of life, since people who live in overseas territories tend to be much more religious and against assisted suicide.[11] But as one of the main minority leaders testified, the minority point of view against assisted suicide had been properly represented, perhaps in fact overrepresented, in the convention.

The more serious problem in forgetting the butterfly, instead, is that it symbolically marginalized people who already found themselves at the geographic periphery of France and who are also part of the ethnic or racial minority of France as a whole (mainland plus overseas territories). Forgetting the butterfly meant they were made to feel unrepresented and invisible and were indeed literally erased from the map drawn by the graphic designers. The graphic designers, like the members of the governance committee, were all white metropolitans. Among the experts involved in organizing the convention, only a couple of facilitators were people of color.

This oversight may not be catastrophic on its own, but it highlights a deeper issue. Random selection or stratified sampling can bring the shy into the room, but that alone is not enough. Citizens' assemblies, no matter how carefully designed, remain reflections of the imperfect societies they represent. They inevitably mirror the biases, blind spots, and inequalities of the outside world.

Once inside, the shy risk being erased or silenced by the same systemic prejudices these assemblies aim to transcend. Creating truly inclusive spaces requires more than good intentions and good design—it demands an ongoing commitment to addressing inequality. The challenge is great, but so is the opportunity. By striving to empower every voice, assemblies can model the welcoming democracy that Chesterton once envisioned.

NINE

How to Be a Jolly Hostess

Make It Worth People's Time ▪
Make People Feel Welcome, Valued, and Well Taken Care Of ▪
Trust First and by Default ▪ Be Trustworthy ▪
Sharing (Power) Is Caring ▪ Make It Fun!

Let's circle back to the metaphor we started with: democracy as a jolly hostess. A jolly hostess is a hospitable, warm, welcoming, and entertaining figure. In this chapter and the next, we're stepping into the shoes of an institutional designer to lay down a set of guiding principles for improving real-world democracies and making them more aligned with this vision. What follows in this chapter are the six behavioral rules of a jolly hostess, drawn from my own experience in observing and designing successful democratic processes. Along the way, I'll also spend some time explaining why current governance committees in properly designed citizens' assemblies aren't as powerful as they might seem, although future implementations should move toward full autonomy of the citizens.

Make It Worth People's Time

The first rule is to make whatever you ask citizens to do worth their time. That means, first and foremost, not wasting it. Citizens' time is too often taken for granted when it is in fact something precious and to be treasured. There is no point in convening a citizens' assembly (or a referendum, for that matter) if its recommendations will only be ignored. At the very least, there should be a credible commitment up front to seriously consider the conclusions of the citizens' assembly—and, ideally, a clear and convincing explanation afterward of how the commissioning body (whether parliament, the government, or another group) plans to respond to them.

Making an activity worth citizens' time typically also means compensating citizens for the hours they will spend in demanding activities over days, weeks, and often months. The money is, technically, not to pay them for the task but to compensate them at least partially for the opportunity costs of the time you are taking away from them. This is why it is now an international best-practice standard to pay participants in citizens' assemblies. And it goes without saying that all related expenses should also be covered, preferably up front, including transportation, hotel nights, meals, and, of course, childcare.

Note that here the devil is in the details. Reimbursing people for their expenses is not the same as paying for them up front. Ideally, participants should not have to disburse a dime or incur the costs (including wasted time!) of dealing with a cumbersome administration. Even when it comes to childcare, a generous, no-questions-asked approach such as a cash transfer is preferable to the requirements of submitting receipts for services rendered. This is something that was brought home to me when I casually chatted with the first few women who arrived at the Convention on the End of Life in December 2022, on the first day of the first session.

I asked the first three women I met, who sat together in the café area of the CESE, if they had needed to use childcare to be able to come. To my surprise, the women all said that they were not planning to ask for childcare reimbursement, even though they were aware of the option, because their solutions did not involve hiring official babysitters for the occasion. Instead, their solution consisted of exchanging favors with other women (relatives or neighbors). The CESE's policy of reimbursement just did not work for them. Yet those women still incurred a cost because they would eventually have to repay with their own time and energy the favor done to them by their family and neighbors. And yet the CESE would not recognize that cost as one it could reimburse. Therefore, it would be much simpler to give everyone who asks a lump sum for childcare per child.

Finally, respecting people's time may also mean being attentive to the schedule of activities, both the time at which activities take place and their duration. Nicole Curato is the researcher we already encountered at the end of chapter 7, who was put in charge of evaluating the first Global Assembly on Climate, one hundred people randomly selected from around the globe and convened in the fall of 2021 for the purpose of an online deliberation about climate justice.

Curato's team generally gave a positive evaluation of the global assembly, but they highlighted a key flaw: The three-hour online deliberation sessions were scheduled at night, based on the mistaken assumption that evenings are universally more convenient. While this worked for participants in the West, it caused significant problems elsewhere. In the Global South, for instance, nighttime sessions cut into much-needed sleep for workers who had to rise early. Parents with young children also struggled, especially in homes without proper insulation or separate spaces, disrupting their children's sleep.

More concerning were the safety issues noted by Curato's team, particularly for women in violent areas with curfews. One woman had to leave her restaurant job, travel twelve kilometers by motorbike-taxi to meet her community host and translator, participate in the three-hour session, then return to work for her night shift. Beyond these logistical hardships, many women faced social stigma for traveling at night, even when supported by their families.

Curato and her team concluded that while these stories highlight the courage of participants, they also underscore a deeper lesson: We must carefully examine the assumptions embedded in our designs—especially the idea that everyone has full control over their "free" time.[1]

Make People Feel Welcome, Valued, and Well Taken Care Of

Democracy should make its citizens feel welcome, valued, and well taken care of. Institutions and events that citizens are asked to join should be conceived in that spirit. Note that this requirement has much larger socioeconomic implications—such as ensuring that no one is destitute to the point of not being able to make use of their political voice. The question of the kind of economic reforms (a basic universal income? a job guarantee?) that this would take go beyond the scope and ambitions of this book.

Focusing on political design, however, a good example is the Belgian mixed parliamentary commissions, which bring together two-thirds ordinary citizens and one-third parliamentarians. These "invited spaces," as they are sometimes called because they require a selection process and a guest list, are also "inviting." In Brussels, the letters of invitation to participate in parliamentary commissions go out in French, English, Dutch, Spanish, and Arabic. They are made available in audio versions and in more languages on the official website. Additionally, invited people can show up with a "buddy" (the term of art) to help translate for them if needed, just as nice hostesses let guests bring friends if that makes them more comfortable or if it is a condition of their coming. The buddy is treated the same as everyone else, being paid the same compensation for their time taking part in the deliberations.[2]

The physical building in which activities are conducted matters too. It needs to be central rather than peripheral to power structures and open and inviting rather than coldly impersonal. The Iéna Palace in Paris presented both advantages and challenges in that respect. On the positive side, it couldn't have been more central, sitting right next to the Eiffel Tower and with a gorgeous view of it from multiple angles. When the citizens arrived, they necessarily felt special to be invited into such a building, in the heart of France, in the middle of Paris. Additionally, the citizens were given passes, which gave them access to a special door that allowed them to skip the security controls. It was a clear signal that they belonged here and were trusted. In stark contrast, consider how the Icelandic government housed the twenty-five members of its 2010 constitutional assembly, tasked with rewriting the nation's social contract after the 2008 crisis. They were placed in a drab, prefabricated building on the outskirts of Reykjavik, in a nondescript room that seemed to signal their insignificance. The message couldn't have been clearer: *What you're doing doesn't really matter, and we won't take it seriously in the end.* And that's exactly what happened. The architecture itself seemed to foreshadow the assembly's fate—the writing was, quite literally, on the wall. Unlike earlier, more successful conventions, this one was undermined by its own design and setting.

However, not everything was ideal in the French example. Setting the meeting in Paris, at the center of the metropole, was a way to reinforce the feeling of being peripheral experienced by people from the provinces and, even more so, by the inhabitants of overseas territories. The Iéna Palace is also an imposing brutalist building made of concrete and hard surfaces, whose acoustics are so terrible that every time meetings were held in its central room—the hypostyle room, famous for its many columns—people complained they couldn't hear one another and that the sounds were deafening.[3]

Once people are on site, words, and words of welcome in particular, also matter. Words that signal fear and distrust matter even more and are to be avoided at any cost. On that front, here is an example of what *not* to do.

As the first weekend of the Climate Convention came to an end, one of the copresidents of the governance committee addressed the citizens. After predictable self-congratulating statements about how well everything went, she expressed relief: "It's really scary to bring over a random group of people like this. We didn't know what you would be like." Though she may have intended this as a lighthearted joke, no one laughed. Instead, we all cringed in our seats. Several of the citizens that I talked to afterward said they had resented the assumption behind that unfortunate comment. This person had inadvertently betrayed her fear that "randomly selected people" would be crazy, dangerous, and impossible to control. Obviously, greetings that express trust are much preferable.

There are many ways to make people feel welcome. One is by meeting people where they are in terms of their cognitive styles and ways of processing information. Citizens' assemblies tend to be run by nerdy people and academics who like to read reports and footnotes. But not everyone likes to read, or can. So, one has to think of creative ways to incorporate people who think and learn differently, such as using visual aids, games, or even art as a way to communicate and learn.

People should also feel taken care of, which is another way to signal that they are valued. Being well taken care of is a relative notion, of course. Different societies will have different standards. But at minimum it means catering to the citizens' basic needs while they engage in any civic activity of some duration: decent housing, good nutritious food throughout the day accommodating a range of diets, and refreshments, as well as time for bathroom, cigarette, breastfeeding, and other breaks.[4]

Taking care of people may also require providing psychological support for those who may need it. A number of participants in the French Citizens' Convention for Climate struggled psychologically throughout the process because of the enormous responsibility they felt and the intense work pace of the sessions. One woman, a young artist, even left the process as a result of her distress. Additionally, after returning to the normalcy of their lives and losing the intensity and solidarity of the convention, a couple of citizens reportedly fell into depression in its aftermath.

On the subject of end-of-life issues, the organizers fully expected people to struggle emotionally. In anticipation of this problem, the CESE planned for psychologists—we called them "coaches"—to be on site from day one. They wore a lanyard of the same color as that of the members of the facilitation team, so as not to stigmatize those who wanted to talk to them. People could choose to ask for help without fear that fellow assembly members would look down on them. In many cases, however, the initiative came from the animation team members, who spotted people having difficulties and kindly guided them toward a professional suited to help.

Our worst fear going into the sessions was that discussions on assisted suicide might trigger a participant to harm themselves. One incident during the second weekend set off alarms. A panel of health care professionals—nurses and doctors—was invited to speak, and they unanimously opposed assisted suicide. The real trouble came later, when one of the doctors said during a smaller working group, "If you want to kill yourself, go look for methods on the internet." That afternoon, shaken citizens voiced their concerns during office hours. A thirty-five-year-old man said he felt shocked and emotionally manipulated. A thirty-year-old warned ominously, "You have to be careful. There will be an incident." We didn't press him on what he meant—was he implying someone might attack the doctor or act on the suggestion?—but the comment rattled us, and we quietly monitored him for a while. Thankfully, no such incident occurred. Despite moments of high emotion, the convention was, in the end, remarkably positive—marked by intensity, but also by an unexpected sense of joy.

Not all topics may require professional psychological support or large investment in care work on the part of the organizers, however. As I documented before, members of citizens' assemblies are usually amazing at taking care of one another.

Trust First and By Default

Some party throwers distrust their guests. Leave shoes at the door, bring only white wine, leave your kids or pets behind . . . All these rules are meant to minimize the trouble for the organizers, and, to be fair, they can make sense in some contexts and for some people. But they can also come across as controlling and distrustful. Guests are treated as immature and careless people, who will dirty the house and spill, stain, or break things. Such expectations in turn may negatively shape people's behavior, from leading them to stay home to preventing them from sharing their true selves at the party. And the rules definitely will not make them feel comfortable or "at home."

Trust is something people in power need to model first if there is any chance to induce it in other people and create a virtuous feedback loop. Institution designers and organizers of democratic processes must therefore use trust as a guideline for all their decisions.

While I was on the governance committee of the Convention on the End of Life, we occasionally disagreed among ourselves about the best course of action to take. Some members were driven by fear of a loss of control and distrust of the actors involved, be it the citizens themselves ("They are going to say dumb things"), the organizers and facilitators ("They are going to make mistakes"), or the media we let into the assembly ("They're going to betray us"). In one very early stage, some even wanted to create a punishing system of expulsion for those who missed one or more meetings without proper excuses, anticipating unprofessional behavior and planning for general unreliability.[5]

Luckily, a majority of us on the governance committee were adamant that we needed to base every decision on trust in the common sense and reliability of most actors, especially the randomly selected ones. This strategy paid off: 184 out of the 185 participants stuck with the process till the end, and very few missed entire sessions. In the end, planning for expulsion turned out to be pointless.

The trust we placed in the citizens was repaid to us in kind. When we messed up, as we did on several occasions, the first instinct of the citizens was not to assume ill intentions on our part. Instead, they assumed lack of time and preparation, bad luck, or the unavoidable surprises of a partly unpredictable process, and offered their help in fixing problems.

Early on, the governance committee chose to hold votes throughout the process, rather than just at the end as was done in the first climate convention and many other citizens' assemblies. Voting is often seen as a fallback to deliberation or a source of division, which explains why the first convention's organizers, wary of failure and eager for clear outcomes, avoided it.

In reality, however, majority rule isn't a fallback but a necessary complement to deliberation. Few discussions naturally end in consensus, and voting helps capture existing differences. Interestingly, researchers from the first convention found that most participants supported using more voting procedures in future assemblies, reflecting a clear desire among citizens to reclaim control over how decisions are made.

During the second French citizens' convention, we decided to make it clear we were not seeking a consensus, and we introduced votes early and used them frequently throughout. As it turns out, an added benefit of socializing citizens to voting early on is that we could then also ask them to vote on decisions themselves when we weren't sure of the best course of action to guide the assembly. Asking them to vote early and often helped us pave the way for the sharing of power with citizens in the governance of the assembly. This decision to empower citizens was based on trust.

Our trust was oriented not just toward the citizens, but toward other important if less-central actors of the convention. We decided early on that we would let researchers and various observers access all spaces of the convention, including the meetings of the governance committee. That was a conscious departure from the first convention, which had kept the researchers at arms' length from the citizens and closed the meetings of the governance committee to absolutely everyone else.[6] Instead, our governance committee made the decision to trust that researchers would behave appropriately toward citizens, guided internally by their professionalism and social-scientific norms of impartiality. We also trusted that they would not use anything we said during our meetings against us in the press or elsewhere, which they indeed did not.[7]

Trust needs to be curated, however, and here being pedagogical and transparent about the procedures and actors involved really helped. We gave the researchers an opportunity to introduce themselves and their research topic to the citizens during the first session so that they would not be puzzled by the presence of so many people taking notes around them. During the first convention, we researchers had not been introduced at all, and for a long time the citizens were rightly distrustful of and annoyed at us, confusing us with journalists.

We also decided to trust the press on the whole, despite the catastrophic predictions by some on the governance committee, partly based on the negative treatment by the media of the previous convention. We gave them access to the plenary meetings and even some of the working groups, except when citizens explicitly told us they wanted to be left alone.

Correlation is not causation, of course, but unlike what happened with the first convention, the media proved remarkably benevolent in its coverage, even Catholic reporters who were opposed to the very idea of assisted suicide. There were some predictable exceptions on the right-wing side of the political spectrum, but on the whole, journalists never questioned the democratic nature of the process or the sincerity and competence of the citizens and the governance committee, and in the end they judged the exercise a success.

One of those exceptions is worth mentioning, though, because it both confirms the necessity of the principle of trust and allows me to say something about what to do in case of an actual breach of said trust by citizens or other actors. Trusting citizens (or researchers, or journalists) does not mean that you will never be betrayed or disappointed. During the Convention on the End of Life, one newspaper came out with an extremely negative story reporting on how citizens felt manipulated by the governance committee. To be fair, we kind of brought the suspicion of manipulation on ourselves by messing up several votes in a row. The journalist had some objective reasons to worry.

When the article came out, at noon on a Saturday, we were naturally extremely concerned and decided to put it up immediately for discussion in the plenary meeting at 2:00 p.m. that same day. I credit the chair of our governance committee for handling this announcement particularly brilliantly, saying to the group that it was "better to lance the abscess right away." The content of the article upset the citizens, including some who had been interviewed and whose words had been taken out of context or made to mean the opposite of what they said. The vast majority were angry at those among themselves whom they thought had leaked the story.

A group of about ten to fifteen citizens started to turn very apologetic, indicating that they had indeed drafted a letter of grievances addressed to the governance committee, the purpose of which was to complain about insufficient sharing of power and advocate for more citizen leadership. But they had never meant to either complain about manipulation or leak this letter to the press. They were very contrite. A lot of confusion ensued, as no one could figure out who had leaked the letter. But in the end, the group suspected of guilt apologized to the others, and everyone started to take responsibility for figuring out a way forward.

Weeks later, during the last weekend, we finally came to understand that those who took the blame that day were not at fault at all. Instead, a secret group of seven truly disgruntled citizens vehemently opposed to assisted suicide had plotted to derail the convention by planting that negative story in the news media. They had met in Deauville, on the coast of Normandy, at the house of one of the participants over one weekend and contacted a conservative journalist whom they knew would publish the story. The journalist then used quotes from citizens' interviews that they had conducted to make them sound like they supported views they did not. This had nothing to do with the letter from the other disgruntled group, who (rightfully) were trying to gain more influence over the process.

What is the lesson there? It is not clear to me that being less trustful and preventing journalists from accessing citizens or observing their deliberations, or being witness to our multiple governance mistakes, would have done more good or prevented this particular cabal from forming in the first place. By being open we took the risk of being criticized and having a tiny minority derail the process. But by trusting the citizens, we got the convention to regulate itself. As to the press, the accusations of manipulation would probably have been worse had we kept things away from them.

Still, the rogue actions of the seven were a breach of trust. Had we known in time, we might have felt compelled to intervene—but in this case, ignorance worked in our favor, as the plot fizzled out on its own. In the end, the crisis prompted a valuable reassessment of how the governance committee could better involve citizens in decision-making. It also showed how citizens could push for more influence without fracturing the convention, ultimately strengthening their unity and deepening their sense of shared purpose.

This is a story with a happy ending. But among the other experiences of citizen participation run at a smaller scale by the CESE, I know of at least one case (the citizens' jury on vaccination during COVID-19) when things got really ugly. (I know only because I was on the evaluation team for that process, as these negative cases do not tend to be advertised widely.) In that case, some participants bullied others into voting their way, through constant WhatsApp messaging as well as in-person intimidation tactics. Alerted by some of the victims, the CESE ultimately had to convene an ad hoc ethics committee that addressed the issue and threatened to expel offenders from the group, after which the bullies promptly corrected their behavior. Breaches of trust are inevitable and must be dealt with swiftly. But equally important is offering a second chance—trust begets trust. The citizens trusted us because we trusted them first and throughout.

Be Trustworthy

A jolly hostess is trustworthy. She does not cancel the party at the last minute, she does not spread gossip about her guests, and she apologizes when something goes wrong due to her own mistakes. (I realize the metaphor is getting strained here, but it still helps to keep in mind the accountability that democratic designers should build in spaces and institutions.)

Our strategy during the Convention on the End of Life was not just to trust the citizens but to prove to them that we were trustworthy. To do so, we first tried to establish accountability mechanisms throughout so that the citizens could have direct access to voice their complaints, grievances, or demands. Every Sunday afternoon, four citizens (two men and two women) were chosen at random from among the entire pool of 184 people to join our debrief sessions, which involved the governance committee, members of the president's cabinet, and the facilitation team. In this setting, they could give us feedback on what went wrong and what went right and express any concerns they had. They also witnessed us do the same thing openly; occasionally we had to deal with some rather serious business among ourselves. This was not as inclusive a design as I would have hoped myself—I thought those citizens should have been a part of every meeting of the governance committee—but it was something.

To earn trust, we made a point of owning our mistakes. Voting procedures, in particular, were a recurring source of trouble—a running joke among citizens who dubbed it the "curse of voting" after repeated issues from session 3 through the end. One notable mistake occurred when the governance committee framed a vote so narrowly that citizens were forced to choose between options they didn't support. Later, a service provider mishandled vote weighting, producing meaningless averages and a distorted view of the group's preferences. During the final weekend, we introduced a new selection method—liquid democracy, or candidate-less elections—which requires people to choose anyone they want as their representatives, even if they haven't expressed an interest in the function (they can always opt out when presented with the position). The problem is that the assembly was so large that, even at that point, people did not always know one another's names. In order to do this well, we should have provided the citizens with a "facebook" including everyone. Instead it caused a lot of frustration.

Any of these mishaps could have sparked rebellion or rejection of our authority, jeopardizing the entire process. But they didn't— and I believe that's because we owned our mistakes, apologized, and held ourselves accountable.

To strengthen accountability, we introduced additional mechanisms beyond the presence of those four citizens at our Sunday debrief meetings. One key initiative was informal office hours. It was through these office hours that minorities first expressed that they didn't feel heard or included. Combined with similar feedback from a citizen during session 4's debrief, this led us to introduce opinion groups in session 5—a move that proved vital to the convention's success.

In the second half of the process, we added another layer of accountability: a subcommittee tasked with reading and responding to emails, letters, and suggestions from the suggestion box. This helped us gauge the group's mood and provided a chance to answer questions that couldn't always be addressed publicly in plenary sessions.

The members of the governance committee also began attending the piloting committee meetings on Friday nights before each session—critical moments when last-minute implementation decisions were made. In hindsight, many early issues, such as the first plenary vote snafu, might have been avoided had we been present from the start. Ultimately though, our time and effort in these meetings played a crucial role in maintaining trust and ensuring the process stayed on track.

Finally, we made ourselves as available as possible. The governance committee had its own break room, in a part of the CESE that was inaccessible to citizens (something I'm not sure I would recommend). We sometimes ate and held some informal meetings there. But many of us were visible and available during breaks, lunches, and dinners. Many of us also had regular one-on-one and group conversations with the citizens, who got to know, appreciate, and trust us. This kind of access staved off potential sources of anger and frustration.

Sharing (Power) Is Caring

A good hostess is not a control freak who micromanages the fun of her guests. She will encourage initiative, improvisation, and shared leadership of the party. A democratic setting is one in which power is distributed widely and equally. In the context of citizens' assemblies, that means institutionalizing citizen leadership and representation until the day we can remove the current scaffolding of external governance structure and give full autonomy to these assemblies.

David Farrell and Jane Suiter, the academics behind the pioneering Irish citizens' assemblies, emphasize the importance of citizen leadership, which they see as an essential supplement to the official governance structure of the assembly (called the "secretariat" in the Irish assemblies) and the experts who provide information and counsel to the citizens. Their recommendation is to establish "a small steering group elected from among the members" in order "to represent the interests of the wider membership, meet with the secretariat and the expert advisory group, react to the proposed agenda for each meeting, and make their own suggestions on how best to proceed."[8] They give the example of how, through their elected representatives, the members of the Irish citizens' assembly on abortion were able to request and receive an extra weekend to discuss the issue.

Farrell and Suiter make it explicit that citizen leadership requires a form of citizen representation at the level at which the decisions are made. Interestingly, and to my mind problematically, they embrace electoral representation, even though it is far from the most obvious solution in the context of an assembly based on the principle of random selection. Nonetheless, citizen representation of some kind is a good idea if one wants the conveners to be able to act as more than an indistinct mass whose will is hard to understand and articulate.

In the first French citizens' convention, I observed how the sharing of power and the emergence of citizen leadership and representation occurred over the course of the nine-month process. During the Convention on the End of Life, as a member of the governance committee I was able to witness firsthand that the sharing of power was the result of both conscious decisions by our committee and the pressure of citizens asking for more leadership.

Citizen leadership emerged from the very start. During my first lunch on the opening day, I sat across from a citizen who pulled out a book on assisted dying—one not listed in the informational brochure we'd provided. He already seemed remarkably well informed and told me he had spent months preparing for the convention, reaching out to the book's author and meeting with doctors involved in end-of-life care to better understand their concerns.

Later, when our governance committee failed to arrange visits to palliative care units, a leader of the anti–assisted suicide group, who worked with people with disabilities, took the initiative herself. Over several weekends, she organized visits to hospitals in and around Paris for at least forty convention members, allowing them to engage directly with care staff. These visits often stretched late into the night, as citizens stayed to listen and learn. Additionally, citizens secured attestations from the CESE to visit similar facilities in their regions between sessions. By the end of the convention, about 70 percent of the participants had visited palliative care units.

Our first formal step to institutionalize citizen leadership came when we invited four randomly selected citizens (two men and two women) to join our Sunday afternoon debrief meetings after each session. While participation was optional, few declined. Once involved, the citizens quickly began asking for more input in decision-making.

During the second weekend, frustrations flared when the piloting committee made a key decision without consulting us. We had asked the animation team to organize a speed-dating session with experts in the hypostyle room, modeled after a successful approach used for the climate convention. Instead, the team organized a scripted, top-down discussion with a few care workers in the plenary room—far less engaging and spontaneous than what we had envisioned. When questioned, the piloting committee's representative explained, "It was too cold to use the hypostyle room, so we did something else."

The members of the governance committee, myself included, were livid, and tensions ran high during the debrief. The four citizens present observed the heated discussion. At one point, one of the women spoke up: "Why not make us co-responsible for these decisions? If you can't agree or aren't sure, ask us. We'll decide if we want to wear sweaters and coats to make the hypostyle room work."

The governance committee, however, did not embrace the citizen demand for co-responsibility with great enthusiasm. Some of its members saw this demand as a threat to our authority. They thought it was enough for the citizens to be included in the debrief sessions, even though they must have been aware that nothing was decided during these sessions and the citizens had very little time or opportunity to speak. During one meeting, I asked that we vote on the principle of having citizen representatives attend every single one of our governance meetings, not just the Sunday debrief meetings. Including citizens in the meetings of the governance board had been the practice of the Citizens' Convention for Climate, and I couldn't see any reason not to follow in their footsteps, especially after citizens had explicitly asked us for co-responsibility. To my dismay, however, the vote among the eleven members present that day resulted in four votes for and six votes against, with one abstention (from the chair of the committee, who had made it clear, however, that she opposed the idea too). The citizens would not be included in the governance meetings going forward.

But despite institutional resistance to formalizing co-responsibility through a system of citizen representation on the governance committee, the principle eventually imposed itself in other ways.

Co-responsibility became particularly striking during the ninth and final weekend, when the governance committee concluded that we needed to let the citizens decide themselves how to choose who should speak to the media on their behalf; who should write the two-page "manifesto" intended for the general public; who should address the nation on TV during the final Sunday; and who should present the final report to President Macron at the Elysée on the following Monday. By that point, clearly, we had reached some de facto level of co-responsibility. In fact, we had reached a level at which it was clear we were allowing citizen representation—without the name.

The convention naturally evolved toward both citizen leadership and citizen representation under the pressure of the citizens themselves, and as a result of the fact that we on the governance committee were encountering more and more momentous questions that we couldn't figure out alone. Still, I think the main lesson for organizers of future assemblies or institution designers of similar processes is that you shouldn't wait until the very end, or until you are forced, to share power and institute citizen representation. Sharing power is caring. Do it right away, or as early as possible. It is better to front-load those principles of citizen empowerment, leadership, representation, and co-responsibility rather than being forced to implement them under pressure, as you will have to do anyway in due course.

The Convention on the End of Life went from hyper-centralized, with power concentrated in the hands of the governance committee members, especially the CESE members, and no real citizen representation, to a much more shared and decentralized form of co-responsibility with the citizens. This was in large part the result of the growing confidence and empowerment of the citizens themselves.

The ultimate proof of trust, of course, would be to let these assemblies run themselves. While we have yet to figure out the exact way to do this well, there is no doubt that this is what the citizens are both asking for and capable of. Most important, in my view, this is what politics without politicians, both of the revolutionary and reformist kind, requires.

Make It Fun!

A last guiding principle, at the most general level, is obvious yet often forgotten: Have fun, and make it fun. Politicians make us believe politics is serious and boring (and it is, but mostly because we are excluded!). It is serious, but it need not be boring. It can be, in action, incredibly joyous and fun. One of the greatest surprises of observing these assemblies is the centrality of emotions, especially joyful emotions, in them.

Emotions turn out to play a crucial role in the success of any form of joint endeavor and collective deliberation, even when the primary goal of such activities seems informational, argument oriented, and rather cerebral. I already talked about the kind of emotions—a form of civic friendship, even love—that I think needs to underpin any successful joint project.

But the emotion organizers can most actively encourage is joy. If we want to make our politics more joyful, we need to have more fun in and with it. Fun is the necessary counterpart to intense work. If you work hard, you must play hard, right? Well, the citizens I have observed and accompanied certainly worked really, really hard. They needed to let off steam at various points. They did so somewhat during the lunch breaks and more so over drinks at the hotel bar at night. They did so during the events that we organized for them and all the unobserved events—dinners and parties—that they organized themselves outside the walls of the convention.

The first gathering we organized at the convention was a party held at the Iéna Palace on the first weekend to watch the soccer match between France and Morocco. The match saw France qualify for the semifinal of the World Cup, with Morocco holding their own in defeat—a perfect outcome, given the multicultural makeup of the French population and, therefore, our micro-sample. There are a lot of descendants of North Africans in France, so citizens were very proud of Morocco too.

The last event was a party on the Saturday night of the ninth and last weekend. The evening was a concert by a band recommended by one of the governance committee members. People danced from 7:00 p.m. to 1:00 a.m., nonstop. There was a joie de vivre that I would have never expected from a convention on the end of life. As one of the elderly ladies in the convention commented, with humor, on the last day, "I got pretty stressed with the subject, given my age. But I woke up with a real hunger for life." She noted, to collective laughter, the paradox of their group showing "such an extraordinary vitality on a subject that is, after all, rather morbid."

Joy further erases the barriers between people that the use of random selection was a first attempt at leveling. In my observation, social distinctions, still somewhat present during the day, vanished during those few hours of pure fun. Even the president of the CESE (and quite a few of us on the governance committee and the animation team) ended up dancing with citizens to songs ranging from ABBA to Rammstein to Clara Luciani. It was truly moving (and a bit surreal). One thing we concluded during the debrief on the following day was that we should have had a party like that much earlier, perhaps halfway through the process.

The friendship and camaraderie of the group came in part from such moments. It also manifested throughout in small but sweet gestures between the citizens and between them and the governance committee. People were exchanging treats and wines from their home regions. We on the governance committee were given strawberries and local sweets and cookies. Our chair was given flowers, a printed copy of a historic newspaper article, and cards and letters, including a poem written by a citizen who never spoke.

Does all of this mean democracy has to be "jolly" at all times? Probably not. Democracy also needs to be able to handle times of scarcity and even war, as the world keeps reminding us. But if we want its institutions to have enduring legitimacy and retain the support of the population even in tough times, it needs to have a more inviting face and attitude than the ones we're familiar with. These six rules may serve as a guide for institutional designers, ensuring that democracy remains not just resilient in times of crisis, but also compelling and worthy of the public's trust in the long run.

Designing for All

Accessibility ▪ The Guest List ▪ "Homeyness" ▪
Amplifying Weak Signals ▪ Coping with Hurt People Who Hurt People ▪
Protecting the Vulnerable

B eing an attentive, jolly hostess is a demanding task. Living by the six principles delineated in the last chapter is an important step toward including the shy, who may have less time, less self-esteem and confidence, less trust in the system, less of a sense of agency and efficacy, and fewer opportunities for joy than most people. But even being a perfect hostess would probably not be enough to bring all the shy people out. To do this fully, we also need to rethink the very design of our institutions at the systems level, ensuring—procedurally, architecturally, and intentionally—that they foster accessibility, inclusion, and a sense of homeyness.

This chapter shifts from behavioral to design principles, while also confronting the thorny question of how to deal with hurt people who hurt others—and where to draw the line between interpretive charity and protecting the vulnerable.

Accessibility

The first thing to do in order to make democracy more inclusive is facilitate access to the site of political participation, whether physical or virtual. I remember visiting the European Parliament in Strasbourg in 2013 with my mother and my first daughter, then an infant, who was in a stroller. I was supposed to deliver a talk there and was wearing a dress and heels. The main entrance, unfortunately, featured a long flight of steps with no ramp in sight, so my mom and I had to carry the stroller up. I later learned that there was an accessible entrance, but it was located at the far side of the building and poorly signposted. The design clearly wasn't welcoming to people with disabilities or to those with young children.

Making a site accessible means more than making it physically accessible. You also need to make it easy to navigate. That may require clear indications of where things can be found (restrooms, cafeteria, breastfeeding space, etc.) and accommodating for language differences and communication barriers. But it also means making the environment conducive to the activities and conversations you want to see take place. For deliberation in small groups, the standard practice is to use small round tables, which symbolize equality of status and allow for multidirectional conversations. When the table is too big or too long, by contrast, people will not necessarily feel equally included or be able to address everyone equally.

Online accessibility is an issue that will be more and more important as we move toward ever more digitized lives and forms of interaction. It is crucial to help older generations and poorer people, as well as technophobes of all ages and backgrounds, successfully plug in. Making digital tablets available and offering technical support, as the CESE did during both the Convention for Climate and the Convention on the End of Life, is a good beginning. During the 2019 Great National Debate, the government also paid for students with tablets to stand in train stations and reach out to the homeless people who frequent them so they, too, could provide their thoughts about the four themes of the national deliberation. Using platforms, apps, and visualization designs that are sufficiently intuitive for most people is a must.

There are, however, people who may refuse to engage in digitally enabled processes, including those who fear surveillance. It might not always be possible to find solutions to accommodate an absolute refusal to engage digitally in situations where participation is purely digital. But hybrid settings, albeit complicated to manage and perhaps never fully satisfactory, are now very common and can offer a solution.

The Guest List

Designing for inclusiveness starts with thinking about who is going to show up. For what are called "open spaces," such as participatory budgeting processes, where anyone who wants can join and participation is entirely based on self-selection, you need to be attentive to who is likely to participate and establish clear expectations around the norms of that space. These norms include equality, inclusiveness, respect, and what I propose to call "interpretative" charity, that is, charity in the way one interprets an interlocutor's statement. Interpretative charity assumes good rather than bad intentions and aims to clarify the meaning rather than rush to dismiss it as unintelligible. Interpretative charity starts from the view that there is no dumb idea and that everyone deserves to be heard.

For what are called, by contrast, "invited spaces," such as citizens' assemblies, a lot of the inclusiveness has to do with how the guest list is constituted, as I discussed in chapter 8. Ideally, the take-up rate would be high, and the sample would be as statistically representative as possible. Statistical techniques such as stratified random sampling help here, but sometimes reaching out to underrepresented communities that can't be connected with through the usual methods will be necessary.

Having a diversity of people on a governance committee and facilitation teams that participants can identify or feel at ease with is also a great way to facilitate inclusion. This starts from the composition of the committees in charge of organizing the democratic space. The Global Assembly had no one from the Global South on their board, which came back to haunt them later in the implementation phase, when the hired hands, most of them in and from the Global South, pushed back against impractical and insensitive guidelines and designs that did not take into account the real needs of people from developing countries. Similarly, if you're going to organize a citizens' assembly on homelessness, your governance committee and animation team would preferably not be all from middle-class backgrounds, and probably not all homeowners either. The decisions made would be too much at risk of being inadequate, tone-deaf, or plain wrong at various key points.

Teams' behavior also needs to model the democratic norms that organizers are trying to cultivate in the citizens, such as respect for others and interpretative charity. Casting the right people in the right role is thus crucial.

Inclusion also means being attentive to and accommodating, as much as possible, the needs of various minorities. A good hostess will include some vegetarian and nonalcoholic options, even if only to accommodate the needs of one person. Offering these options is not only fair to the people who depart from majority preferences, but it also crucially frees other people who may be more conformist to, say, tone down their alcohol or meat consumption without having to fight social norms themselves. Accommodating minorities' preferences is thus not caving to the tyranny of the minority (which would be the case if the only options were exclusively vegan and nonalcoholic). It is, rather, opening up a space for different preferences to be respected and for new preferences to emerge.

"Homeyness"

Generally speaking, the deliberative environment should put the participants at ease and reflect the promise that participatory sites are theirs and that they belong there, as opposed to being invited as only temporary guests.

Recall that ordinary citizens are not used to occupying and moving about buildings that were historically designed for socioeconomic elites to invoke pomp and grandeur. I remember the look and demeanor of the first people who arrived at the Iéna Palace. They looked small and intimidated. They spoke softly. A few months later, of course, they came back as if they owned the place, joked with the staff, and were a lot louder inside the building. But the first weekends, when the participants wondered whether they belonged there, were in some respect wasted time. There has to be a way to signal from the beginning that citizens do belong in democratic spaces and are in fact most welcome. One way to make a place inviting in that sense is to apply the principles of Danish design.

Bernardo Zacka, a professor of political science at MIT, studies the ways architecture and interior design mediate encounters between the citizens and the state. He looked at the architectural evolution of public unemployment offices in three countries—the UK, the United States, and Denmark—and found that they embody different values. He contrasts what he calls the "homeyness" of Danish architecture, which borrows design elements from the home and coffee shops, with the cold, dehumanizing design of British unemployment centers, which are inspired by supermarkets and banks, and the impersonal design of American unemployment centers, which are inspired by the generic spaces of office architecture.

Zacka gives as an example the waiting area of Silkeborg Youth Center, with its inviting swivel armchairs, plush rugs, stacks of modular wooden boxes with colorful cushions, and even a foosball table. Or the shared foyer of the Aars Job Center and City Hall, with its small round tables, such that the counselor and the unemployed person can sit next to each other as two people working together on a common solution to a problem rather than being separated by a desk, in a configuration that places the job seeker in a position of supplicant, patient, or problem to be solved. Additionally, the Danes planned for office doors to be transparent but partially frosted, to balance counselor safety and visitor privacy. The doors allow for enough privacy and sound insulation that, as Zacka points out, people can cry and raise their voices (as many recently fired people will) without causing a public scene. By contrast, the fully exposed and undivided space of American and British unemployment centers triggers punishing interventions for people who fall apart, such as having guards humiliatingly escort them out of the building. That is because any emotional reaction in the British and American open spaces attracts attention, calling for an immediate resolution, whereas the semitransparent doors in the Danish design protect the privacy of individuals, saving or at least postponing the need for more forceful interventions.

Zacka's analysis of these contrasted architectural designs reveals that societies have different views of the unemployed and how the state should treat them. Zacka thus contrasts the view that the unemployed are leeches on the body politic and need to be made to feel worthless with the view that the unemployed are worthy individuals who need help finding a new path in life.[1]

The "homeyness" principle of Danish design is well described by one counselor: "If I were to invite you to come to my home, I would clean, buy flowers, and light some candles, and I would make a good dinner, so it smells nice. I want you to feel welcome. Maybe some of the way we meet our family and our friends, we transform that a little into how we meet our citizens." Ideally, we'd be able to build entirely new environments guided by the principle of homeyness. Such a principle opens up the possibilities of designing welcoming public buildings, but also urban spaces, architecture, and landscaping that are more inviting than those we are familiar with and also more conducive to healthier and happier lives. While, in practice, we have to live with existing legacies, and it is probably more environmentally sound and cost-effective to repurpose old buildings and cities than to build entirely new, better-designed ones, it is worth considering how to make these existing spaces more inclusive and welcoming.

Amplifying Weak Signals

One way to empower the shy and make sure they are seen and heard is by paying attention to, and amplifying, the weak signals they send. Proper facilitation is usually capable of doing that well. An important role of facilitators is not just to rein in outspoken people, but also to spot wallflowers. A blush, a timidly raised hand instantly retracted, a question in a Zoom chat from someone who never speaks in plenary meetings . . . these are some of the ways shy people signal that they would like to enter the conversation despite not feeling confident enough to go all the way in. Chairs and facilitators need to be trained to spot these weak signals and amplify them.

What happens when you ignore weak signals? Let me share a firsthand example from the Great National Debate. In January 2019, I attended one of the local meetings in a Paris suburb. About twenty-five citizens gathered, and without facilitators, an older gentleman quickly assumed the role of chair, with unspoken approval from the group. His chairing style, however, was blatantly biased: He primarily called on other men.

As an observer, I noticed a younger woman repeatedly raising her hand but consistently being overlooked. After about half an hour, I couldn't take it anymore. Though hesitant about intervening, I decided to prioritize my duty as a citizen over my neutrality as a researcher. I interrupted, pointing out the oversight as tactfully as possible. The older gentleman turned to the woman and, absurdly, said, "Oh, I'm sorry, but you need to be more visible." The young woman's cheeks flushed from the sudden attention, but she met my gaze with a look of recognition. She voiced her point, and from that moment on, participated more confidently in the discussion.

To avoid having to rely on outside interventions, however, one solution is to have the meeting chaired by someone who is typically underrepresented in that kind of function—someone who will know from experience what it is to be unseen and passed over. Having two chairs, one male and one female, for example, as the Citizens' Convention for Climate did, is another option, even though it may come at some cost to efficiency. Additionally, it is even better if professional facilitators can be present, who are trained to spot shy or typically overlooked people and bring them into the conversation. It is also better if the facilitators themselves are sufficiently diverse to know from experience the types of signals that different subgroups send out. Again, this is not to say that only women will be able to spot the blushing woman who does not dare to speak, or that only Black people can spot the self-effacing person of color and bring them in. Many white men can do those things, too, of course, and very often do. It's just that some of them can't or won't, not out of ill will or indifference but literally because the experience of invisibility is foreign to them.

Another particularly smart institutional principle to empower the most vulnerable among the shy is that of having what the German sociologist Nicole Doerr calls "political translators" on location.[2] Political translators fulfill the purpose of translating between different linguistic groups. But, in addition, they also understand and can explain to the organizers and dominant groups the cognitive and emotional burden that certain groups suffer from because of systemic inequalities, historic injustices, and marginalization. They can explain misunderstandings that stem from cultural differences rather than linguistic mistakes. Political translators help redress imbalances between people who tend to dominate and all other participants. What this suggests is that political translators may need to be present even in monolingual contexts.

There might be circumstances, however, where no budget is available for either facilitators or political translators, and you cannot count on the intervention of outside observers. In such circumstances, the organizers need to empower people so they can remind everyone of the norms. In Ireland, organizers had the norms listed on a piece of paper in the middle of the table so that anyone who felt talked over or saw someone taking too much airtime at the expense of others could appeal to the norms in a way that saved them from having to seem partial or unfair.

Coping with Hurt People Who Hurt People

Empowering the shy, especially the weak and more vulnerable among them, may require protecting them from prejudice and even creating "safe spaces" for them. Here is where we run into a possible conflict: on the one hand is interpretative charity, according to which every idea deserves a generous hearing; on the other hand is the principle that some people should be protected from damaging or triggering views.

There is no easy answer to that dilemma, but my experience is that in the highly curated setting of deliberative spaces, the shy feel safer than in regular public spaces, and there is room for exploring uncomfortable zones of disagreement among different groups in a spirit of respect and trust.

There should, of course, be a limit to what can be said: incitement to violence, hatred, and unadulterated racism, sexism, and homophobia are off limits, in any setting. In the movie *12 Angry Men*, which nicely models the strengths and challenges of deliberation, everyone gets to say what they want to say, but only up to a point. The group initially tolerates one of the jurors' not-so-subtle racist dog whistles, when he complains about "*those* people" and how "*they* can't be trusted." But as the offenses become gradually more explicit and form more of a systemic pattern—as the juror goes from saying things that could be interpreted as racist to establishing that he is an unreformable racist to the core—every other juror ends up turning their back on him, de facto denying him the right to be heard and excluding him from the deliberation. (He remains silent for the rest of the proceedings, and the film suggests, perhaps problematically, that he redeems himself *partly* by ultimately voting "not guilty.")

That said, more ambiguous statements or off-the-cuff remarks or jokes that may come off as racist, sexist, or otherwise offensive need to be treated with some sensitivity, according to the principle of interpretative charity. Not everybody comes from the same background, has grown up in the same culture, is equally aware or capable of nuance, or has a full understanding of what diverse audiences may hear in what they say. A remark that might sound shocking or provocative in one community may be entirely ordinary in another.

That does not make all such statements okay, of course. But immediate stigmatization and angry denunciation will only make the person clam up, with no chance of their coming to realize that their views are ultimately hurtful or a result of ignorance, and with no chance of learning, growing, and possibly making amends. In turn, by forcing the person to toe a strict politically correct line, we risk ignoring important issues and information that may lie beneath what is taken to be a problematic statement or surface provocation. Crucially, we may also lose the contributions of the person on other topics, as they feel ostracized and refuse to engage further.

I never witnessed improper statements or conversations in the context of the citizens' assemblies I observed or even in the context of the crowdsourced legislative process in Finland that I helped design (and my Finnish coauthor, who was monitoring the online exchanges in her native language, said she had to remove only a handful of borderline comments from the platform). I was, by contrast, struck by the number of racist and xenophobic comments on the French governmental platform of the Great National Debate set up in January 2019, which was just a high-tech version of a suggestion box and was not facilitated in any way. When people are behind a keyboard with no sense of having an actual human being on the other side who can judge them, they become uglier versions of themselves.

But in deliberative face-to-face or even minimally facilitated online contexts, the problem is nowhere as serious. If anything, what has struck me in the context of deliberative assemblies is how sensitive to personal boundaries and possible misunderstandings people are, sometimes to the point of self-censorship, which is its own kind of problem. This suggests that we can probably afford to be more rather than less tolerant of the occasional departure from such careful behaviors, as they are likely to be the exception rather than the norm.

To use again the example from Jane Suiter and David Farrell's reports on the Irish Convention on the Constitution, the man who stood up at the end of the weekend devoted to marriage equality to express his endorsement of it had not been entirely silent on the subject before. In fact, he had been confrontational throughout the convention, expressing derogatory judgments about homosexuals. If he had been met with contempt and judgment right away, rather than patience and tolerance, he might not have been able to change his mind.

It is possible that people need to get a certain amount of venom out of their system before they can come to more reasonable conclusions. Preventing angry outbursts from happening or penalizing them too much, too soon might thus be counterproductive. In the same way that Danish design allows people to cry and shout in relative privacy in unemployment offices without being immediately escorted out, there has to be a way for collectives to tolerate some amount of unpleasantness and discomfort, especially if that is the cathartic path to change for at least some people. Hurt people hurt people, and statistically, there will be a lot of hurt people in any human group. We can't expel them all.

And of course, the people on the other side of that anger (the Danish employee accused of being part of an unjust system while having to console the unemployed, the gay person having to endure bigoted statements from the homophobic person coming to terms with their prejudices) are doing emotional labor that is hard and taxing. That, too, should be acknowledged. But going into these deliberative spaces, most of us should be prepared for taking on at least part of that emotional labor. Those of us who can do more to alleviate the burdens on others should do so. We know who we are.

I mentioned in a previous chapter the behavior of Omar, who took on the burden of fighting for the more shy and vulnerable people in the assembly, talking back to experts and putting them in their place when he felt they were overstepping their boundaries, even at the risk of becoming a bully himself. Everyone in that scenario was taking on part of the burden.

Omar took on the burden of the shy, and the shy in turn tolerated a certain amount of explosive behavior on his part as the price to pay for his dedication to the group. In the end, Omar's anger turned to tears and, hopefully, some amount of personal healing. Of course, not all deliberative processes will have this cathartic, healing effect, and you cannot let all angry statements go unchecked. In general, it is the role of facilitators to calm things down and bring people back to a respectful and measured behavior.

What about more problematic behavior still, including aggressively homophobic, racist, or otherwise discriminatory statements? I would say it depends. Obvious cases can be addressed straightforwardly, through firm interventions of the facilitators and possible reprimands from the governance committee members, with the possibility of exclusion for the most egregious cases. But these cases are likely to be extremely rare in a truly deliberative context (in part because people smartly self-censor). So, the problems will come from much more ambiguous attitudes and statements, which are harder to call out.

We want to find the right balance between protecting the usual victims of discrimination from hurtful comments and behaviors, and maximizing the space for self-expression. If we accept that we are all in this together, we need to find a way to listen to statements that may come out the wrong way or reflect ignorance more than prejudice, but still reflect prejudice.

Think of your parents, uncles, and other relatives who say politically incorrect and sometimes downright offensive things at

Thanksgiving dinner. What to do about them? Do we stop talking to them? Do we lecture them? They are family, after all. The question is not whether to keep the peace at all costs—some lines should never be crossed—but how to get our points across and allow for the possibility of mutual education. The same applies to the extremely polarized debate between Democrats and Republicans in the United States these days, whether on deficits, transgender issues, or immigration. We need to find a path back to a common deliberation, and this will take enormous effort on both sides.

Does this mean it will inevitably fall to the shy to shoulder some of the emotional and cognitive burdens of educating others? Unfortunately, I don't see how we can avoid that entirely. But that does not mean the burden needs to be heavy or the same for everyone. The question is, rather, can we make that burden as light as possible and reward people for taking it on?

For people at the intersection of multiple injustices, the burden should probably be zero. They should be free to opt out entirely of having to say something in reply to an inconsiderate statement. They should be protected by "political translators," to reuse Nicole Doerr's category, who are able to fight for them and explain to the dominant group why what was said was hurtful to them, or coaches who can help them process the emotional injury if they experience it. They should also be understood, though probably not commended, if they reply with anger or walk out of the room.

But in a randomly selected group, there will be a diversity of profiles. Few people will be at the intersection of every injustice. So those who can afford it should take it upon themselves to speak up. It is, I would argue, their moral duty.

Protecting the Vulnerable

Let me share two more stories from my own life. When I was young, in the rather paternalistic environment of French society, I never dared to say anything back to any older man (well, except my father, with whom I have butted heads my whole life). I was socialized to defer to their judgment, to never criticize, to deflect but never oppose or contradict directly.

When I moved to the United States, my confidence slowly improved, but even twelve years after arrival I still let an obnoxious older guy ignore me during a workshop at Stanford University. At that point, I was a young assistant professor, three years into the tenure track at Yale, my first book just about to be published. We were given one hour by the organizers to separate into groups, identify a big collective problem, and solve it (if that sounds like a typical, absurdly overambitious Silicon Valley thing to do, don't worry—it was).

The first step was to go around the table (about twelve people) and collectively identify a topic. At my table, my recollection is that I was the only woman. Some ideas were floated by the first two people to my left, but then the oldest gentleman (he looked about eighty to me) spoke with great assertiveness to dismiss them and said we should tackle the problem of the filibuster, which was then causing the paralysis of Congress and its incapacity to increase the debt ceiling. The next person to speak, a Nobel Prize winner in physics, I recall, thought it was a great idea and started developing some thoughts about it.

After those two high-status people had spoken, the group clearly assumed we had decided on the topic. I mustered the courage to raise my hand and say something like, "I think we're not done going around the table. Maybe we could hear some other ideas?" At which point the older man turned to me and said, pointing at the cookie and coffee I had brought for myself from the display in the lobby, "Oh, you only brought cookies for yourself?" And that was it. He proceeded to ignore me, and the conversation moved on.

I leaned back in my chair, stunned. My blood was boiling, my cheeks were burning. I had a sinking feeling of injustice, humiliation, and powerlessness. But the saddest thing is that the first and main thought that went through my mind was the following: I'm *so* rude. I should have brought cookies for everyone. It took a while for that thought to give way to a more rational one: This is America, and everyone is responsible for their own damn cookie and coffee. And why on earth should the one young woman in the group be responsible for bringing treats to the table? I still couldn't move. My brain was going into overdrive while everyone else was engrossed in the conversation.

I considered getting up and leaving. I saw myself slamming the door on the way out. But I also realized it would make zero difference. Instead, I got up and went to the bathroom. I came back determined to at least stay at the table—to "lean in," as Sheryl Sandberg would later put it—no matter how pointless in terms of my actual influence. On the way back, a middle-aged man from my table stopped me and said, "I'm so sorry for what just happened back there. When I see you, I think of my daughter. It made me feel bad." I forgot the rest of what he said, because all I could think was: Why didn't you say something then? I just needed one person to stand up for me, or by me. Instead, I smiled, thanked him for his concern, and went back to the room.

Now picture me ten years later, a tenured full professor, a recognized scholar, a mother of two, and a proud American citizen. I found myself appointed to an academic committee in France, which included a mix of people, including several women and a high-status older gentleman, whom I had been recommended to ingratiate myself to. At one point, two media specialists, both women, gave a presentation to our group about how to manage the communication aspect of our work. The high-status gentleman did not like the proposal and proceeded to tear it down. That was fine, until he felt the need to add the phrase: "You are naïve, you're just little girls."

In French, the word he used was *gamines*—a term that can be affectionate, like something you'd say about toddlers playing in the park. But here it was meant to diminish and belittle, reducing these women to childish innocents out of their depth. My blood pressure immediately rose. When my turn came to speak, I said, "Look, Gaston [not his real name], I'm going to play the grandstanding American here. You cannot call these two grown-up women '*gamines*.' They may look young to you, but they are professionals." I was barely done saying this when he interrupted me: "Oh, in my mouth '*gamine*' is a term of endearment." I replied, "You know it's not going to be perceived that way. And if I may say so, they are of a generation that understands the media much better than we do. If I were them, I would reply to you, 'Okay boomer.'" At that point, he was not listening to me any longer but blustering about until he finally said, "Okay, I'm sorry, I take that back."

Later, the two media specialists got a chance to reply to him and did so in the light-touch, French female way: "We have spent hours and hours thinking about this and considering all options. We are not naïve. If anything, we are in a business where you have to be paranoid all the time." Later one of them came to me and thanked me explicitly for stepping in.

Why am I telling this story? Not to shame Gaston, who shall remain anonymous. Nor because I want to look like a hero, because it took very little courage on my part to do what I did. Given my position as an outsider to the French system at that point, even if I had alienated Gaston forever, it would have had zero repercussions on my professional or personal life. If anything, I instantly knew it would make me look good and potentially earn me the respect of the rest of the group and the gratitude of the media specialists, which it did. More problematically, as you can probably tell from the "boomer" comment, there was even a little schadenfreude motivating my behavior. I can't help but think this smackdown was my long-delayed revenge on the eighty-year-old American blowhard from that Stanford workshop. Yet I don't think revenge is an acceptable motivation here, and so my attitude was far from exemplary.

Instead, I recount all this because I want to show how those of us who can afford it should intervene on behalf of those who can't. At Stanford, it would have taken just one voice among the other men to buttress my legitimate demand to complete the round of suggestions on the topic to be considered. Maybe other people would have then piled on, with the same request. Whatever we had decided on in the end, the process would have been a lot more inclusive and democratic for it. On that more recent committee, I had to intervene because I could, and because if I hadn't, I'm not sure anyone else would have. And why risk it? I suspect for many of the other members of that meeting, the comment did not even register as a problem and they thought I was overreacting.[3]

The other lesson is that we cannot waste occasions for prejudiced persons to learn. People who think or say prejudiced things, and perhaps *are* fundamentally prejudiced, can be transformed in a deliberative context. I'm not convinced my Stanford boor could have been changed, but I think Gaston was. More important, even when prejudiced individuals won't budge, it's still important to set expectations for the audience around them.

Of course, for change to happen, it takes a certain context, certain egalitarian norms, and a certain way of packaging the message. Citizens' assemblies are one of those rare contexts, where social distinctions are not supposed to matter and, at the very least, are made as invisible as possible for a while. A teacher can talk to a banker, who can talk to a butcher, who can talk to a nurse, who can talk to an astrologer. (I confess I did not believe "astrologer" was an actual profession until I met one of those in the Convention on the End of Life.) A seventeen-year-old can talk to an eighty-two-year-old. People of all backgrounds, colors, and religions can bond and exchange views. This creates enormous potential for learning and evolving.

Am I sending mixed messages here? On the one hand, I insist we should use the principle of interpretative charity so that we give one another a chance to learn and progress. On the other hand, I'm asking each of us to take it upon ourselves to stand up for injustice in deliberative contexts and play the role of champions for the most vulnerable, calling out bad behavior when we see it. I realize there is a fine line here, and it might not be possible to get it right on every occasion. But I do think we can at the same time try to stay maximally open and generous in our interpretations of what is being said or how it's being said, and gently call out people (all the while curbing the schadenfreude or desire to humiliate) when they cross a line. It is actually a key part of democratic deliberation to practice this difficult art and to develop the maturity to handle situations of conflict in a respectful way.

ELEVEN

The Future of Democracy, and How to Get There Fast

Some ideas are so stupid that only intellectuals believe them.

GEORGE ORWELL

It is out of the question that sortition replace elections.

PRESIDENT OF THE FRENCH NATIONAL ASSEMBLY

Revolutions always happen when reasonable people haven't been crazy enough before.

THOMAS BERNHARD

First, They Ignore You . . . ▪ The Objection About Legitimacy ▪
The Objection About Agency ▪ Too Extremist or Insufficiently Radical? ▪
What About Leadership? ▪ What About the Economy? ▪
Getting from Here to There ▪ Academics, Activists,
and Even Politicians ▪ To Earth!

There are many different ideas about what politics without politicians should look like. As I said in the first chapter, I distinguish between reformist and radical agendas. In the reformist agenda, the one that starts from where we are, politics without politicians consists in carving out spaces in the existing system for ordinary citizens to make influential decisions at all levels of a polity. My work on French citizens' assemblies with the CESE, and more recently on student citizens' assemblies in both France and the United States, falls into this category. There is a lot of room for ingenuity and innovation in that reformist space that, in my view, would do a lot of good while stopping short of changing things at a fundamental or constitutional level.

At the more radical level, which would involve constitutional changes, the biggest split is between people who envision a pure form of politics without politicians and those—more numerous—who favor a hybrid one, keeping elected politicians in key positions. The Rutgers University philosopher Alexander Guerrero, the author of *Lottocracy*, advocates for a system doing away with elections and any form of mass voting entirely, replacing them with a myriad of single-purpose lot-based deliberative assemblies.[1] In this vision, we get rid of politicians as we know them, but we also constrain citizens' agency. They can directly shape policies and laws only as members of minipublics, not through voting in elections for representatives or even in referenda.

Among the advocates of a hybrid system, the political scientist John Gastil and the late sociologist Erik Olin Wright favor a hybrid form of democracy, in which a single citizens' assembly serves as a veto point for the work of a classic elected chamber.[2] Their proposal arguably gets us the best of both worlds: agency (through the act of electing the members of the assembly) and citizen equality (through the random selection process to the second chamber). The problem is that these authors do not really explain how to avoid paralysis in a system that creates an additional source of veto and pits two types of legitimacy—that of politicians and that of ordinary citizens—against each other.

As for me, at the theoretical level, I tend to favor a third vision centering a large agenda-setting chamber based on lot—a lotto-cratic parliament of sorts. This setup would be combined with lower-level assemblies also based on lot and frequent referenda. These referenda would include multiple questions and bear on both the package of policies and laws put forward by the assembly and specific laws of particular importance. My favored system thus does away with politicians entirely and replaces them with ordinary citizens chosen by lot, as in the ancient Athenian model. Legislators are no longer elected but, instead, are appointed through civic lotteries and rotated frequently, perhaps every two years or so at the national level, more frequently at lower levels. This system brings to the sites of agenda-setting and lawmaking people from all walks of life who would never have dreamt of running for elections and would not have stood a chance to win them if they had.

Additionally, this system includes elements of direct democracy, which are crucial both because direct democracy expands every citizen's ability to influence political outcomes and because they form an important accountability mechanism on the decisions of the lot-based legislature. Direct democracy crucially empowers the masses by allowing them to decide on issues, or bundles of issues, without any intermediary. Popular votes can be triggered in a top-down fashion by the decision of the lot-based assembly or some other established body to submit some proposal or bundle of proposals to a vote. They can also be triggered bottom-up, by so-called citizens' initiatives, whereby a fraction of the citizenry, if they care enough about an issue and manage to convince enough people to sign on to their proposal, can put to a referendum a law, a constitutional amendment, or a call for a repeal of an existing law or the recall of political personnel.

In this model—which I called "open democracy" in a prior book—I favor a single chamber over multiple single-issue bodies or bicameral systems, because a central body can weigh trade-offs across political domains and avoid the gridlock and minority vetoes that often cripple divided structures.

Am I certain which model is superior in the abstract? Not at all. In fact, I have remaining questions, including about how conflict would be structured and resolved if parties were no longer the primary vehicle for groups seeking power. But do parties need the ability to win power in order to form and organize conflicts? Or could they redefine their role—mobilizing voters for referenda, presenting testimony to minipublics, and advocating for the interests they represent? While parties might no longer serve as a breeding ground for politicians, they could still play a vital role in generating ideas and fostering civic engagement. Similarly, just because citizens' assemblies are primarily sites of common good–oriented deliberation does not mean some amount of conflict resolution cannot happen within them as well. While these questions and others are unresolved, they are what makes my job as a political theorist exciting. And I think more people should take them seriously and try to answer them.

First, They Ignore You . . .

I'm used to the ideas presented in this book provoking strong reactions. I remember giving a talk in January 2017 at the headquarters of the *Mercurio*, a conservative Chilean newspaper, in

Santiago. The paper had invited me during a yearly conference called Congreso Futuro, where I gave a TED Talk–like presentation on my then in-progress book *Open Democracy*. In the smaller setting of the newspaper venue, I was given a similar opportunity to present my views but with the added possibility to interact with the audience—the newspaper's employees and readers, and the general public. At the end of the talk, one older man raised his hand and asked a very hostile "question," the gist of it being that I was a fool for wanting to hand over the reins of power to the ignorant masses. I politely replied something to the effect that it did not seem to me that the current elites were doing such a great job in Chile, given the palpable frustration in the population at the time. And indeed two years later Chile would erupt into massive protests and violent riots, followed by two failed attempts at rewriting the constitution. The man stood up and left the room.

Another time, in March 2022, I was paired with an elected politician from the center-right French Republican party at a public event at the Dutch embassy in Paris. In my talk, building on the Icelandic and French examples, I defended the concept of citizen legislators, with the clear implication that such citizen legislators might even be capable of replacing elected ones. When his turn came to talk, the politician went ballistic, going on a rant about the fact that, and I quote, "*ordinary citizens do not belong in parliaments.*" It was a splendid demonstration of the elitism and, frankly, arrogance of some members of the political class, which earned me many smiles in the room and whispered thank-yous during the cocktail hour afterward.

Beyond these angry reactions, I'm also used to the more friendly but skeptical frown or cocked eyebrow, motivated by perfectly reasonable concerns. "Have you really thought this through?" So let me guide the still-skeptical reader through several of the objections I have overcome myself over the years and have not yet addressed directly or indirectly in the book.

The Objection About Legitimacy

Perhaps the most common, if not the most powerful, objection to politics without politicians is that ordinary citizens put in charge of making decisions for the rest of us have no "legitimacy," that is, the right to decide. This objection typically comes from elected officials who feel threatened by the competition of ordinary citizens. It is implicit in some of the reactions I just described. But it manifested most spectacularly in an address to the French Citizens' Convention on the End of Life issue by the president of the French National Assembly.

During the first weekend of the convention, various officials, including the prime minister, the president of the CESE, and the president of the governance committee of the convention, made it clear that citizens' recommendations would not be taken up "unfiltered" by the legislative or executive branches. This time around, citizens could not expect to have a direct influence on policymaking.

The repeated evasions sent a clear signal: The assembly's authority wasn't taken seriously. One young citizen finally said what many were thinking. Addressing the president of the National Assembly, he asked, "You say you trust us, but you keep reminding us we have no power—less than the previous climate assembly. What are we supposed to make of that?" Rather than offer reassurance, the president bristled. Ostensibly there to show respect, she used the moment to reassert hierarchy. In a long and defensive reply, stripped of its platitudes, she said: "Sortition will never replace election. That's not my idea of democracy, now or ever. You're not representative of the French people—you haven't been elected. You have no legitimacy to decide."

Later, she doubled down: "You are representative of French society because you come from different parts of it, but you do not represent society."

And finally: "It's better that way. It's less of a burden for you. Good for you to know that others will decide after you."

The citizens reacted to this diatribe rather respectfully. There were no loud protests and some in the audience even clapped. But a man in the audience pointed out that if the National Assembly failed to take the Convention's proposals seriously, its own legitimacy, already under attack, would likely plummet further. Sitting in the front row, however, I felt the blow. I left the building and walked for hours through Paris, sure that I'd resign the next day. What was the point of wasting public money and trust (not to mention my own unpaid time) if this assembly was a charade? Were we empowering citizens to shape democracy, or staging another Potemkin process to appease public anger? It felt like participation-washing—wrapped in paternalism. (In the end, I didn't resign. I figured I was more useful inside, and as a researcher, there were still things of value to study.)

But this attack on the legitimacy of the convention deserves an answer. As I have shown in previous chapters, many people can act as political representatives of other people—that is, speak and act on their behalf. The fact that citizens' assemblies are also representative in a descriptive sense (they look like the larger public) does not prevent them from being representative in that second sense as well. In fact, it is because they look like the rest of the people that citizens' assemblies are good political representatives in my view, and indeed better ones than elected assemblies. So, the president of the National Assembly was plain wrong on that front.

Now, the more interesting question is: Who has more legitimacy to speak and act on behalf of the people—elected officials, or the people drawn by lot? Legitimacy is a difficult and contested concept. I'm not talking about sociological legitimacy—how much support an institution enjoys at any point in time. I'm not even talking about legal legitimacy—the right to decide, as it is spelled out in the constitution or the law. I'm talking about normative legitimacy: what morally deserves our support. For two centuries, we've treated elections as the main, if not the only, source of such legitimacy. But history shows legitimacy is not fixed. It once came from God, or bloodlines, or arcane knowledge. That changed with the Enlightenment, which brought the idea of popular consent. But in practice, consent translates into majority rule, and that means elected officials often rule without the consent of large minorities. As a result, elections transfer only partial legitimacy. And like the kings of yesteryear who lost their normative legitimacy to elected parliaments, nowadays the normative legitimacy of elected parliaments is in crisis too.

So we are allowed to ask anew: What *should* legitimacy—and specifically democratic legitimacy—mean and require in the twenty-first century?

The president of the National Assembly had no interest in that discussion. Her view of legitimacy was past-oriented and narrowly legalist—rooted in law, not democratic renewal. She missed the opportunity to explore the deeper question: Who should decide in a democracy? And what kind of legitimacy should we aspire to now?

A more honest answer is that electoral and sortition-based bodies embody different, sometimes competing, sometimes complementary, forms of legitimacy: one rooted in consent via the vote, the other in equality via the draw. We should be having more conversations—open, public, political—about how these forms can coexist, reinforce, or challenge one another. Our current systems are creaking, and the next phase of democratic life may depend on getting this right.

Note that, when exposed to the reality of citizens' assemblies, ordinary citizens in the larger public quickly rally behind the idea that such assemblies could be legitimate, at least for the purpose of making proposals on behalf of the larger public. Recall that by June 2020—less than a year after France launched its first citizens' convention—70 percent of the population had heard of it, and 60 percent among them believed it had the legitimacy to propose policies on behalf of the public. By February 2021, 55 percent of the French thought governments should be required to implement the recommendations of citizens' assemblies, while only 15 percent opposed the idea. Across Europe, the popularity of these assemblies has only grown in recent years. The public may not be ready to grant them full legislative power just yet, but that may be just a matter of time—once the proof piles up that they can deliver.

The Objection About Agency

Another objection is that sortition assemblies, if they were to be the end-all of a new form of government, would de facto exclude most people and deprive them of agency. Even if we recognize the limited value and causal influence of any individual vote in any mass election, it's another ball game altogether to move to a system where citizens can participate only if they have won a lottery of some kind. This loss of agency—both at the individual level of the voter and at the collective level of "the people"—is one of the worries behind political philosophers Cristina Lafont and Nadia Urbinati's critique of schemes that seek to give any form of actual power to lot-based bodies. For them, popular sovereignty manifests first and foremost in the act of voting in elections, without which there is no democracy to speak of. As a result, they can advocate only an advisory role for citizens' assemblies.

I take this objection seriously, and this is why I am not a pure "lottocrat," unlike, say, Alexander Guerrero. I do reserve a central space for voting, not in elections but in referenda, in my vision of politics without politicians. That said, it is questionable whether individual agency is so limited, even in a purely lottocratic system. Assuming, as both Guerrero and I do, that we should multiply empowered citizens' assemblies and similar minipublics at every level of the polity, and even rethink the governance of many other organizations on their model (including hospitals, companies, and schools), people would inevitably gain a lot more agency in this system, over the course of their lifetimes, than most people can ever dream of achieving by voting every four years.

Of course, it would still be only *individual* agency. What would be lost in a pure lottocracy such as Guerrero envisions is a form of collective power, when all citizens come together to vote and make a decision, as in an election or a referendum. This form of collective agency is key to the idea of "people's power," and therefore to the idea of democracy. It is also an important accountability mechanism in case the members of the lot-based bodies go mad or are corrupted, which cannot be completely ruled out.

This is why, like Lafont and Urbinati, I believe in the necessity to supplement representative institutions (whether elected or randomly selected) with direct democracy mechanisms such as referenda.

The need for agency is also why, in my model of open democracy, I plan for a greater availability to citizens of extensive participatory rights, such as citizens' initiatives and rights of referral, through which any individual or group of individuals, provided they manage to gather enough signatures, would be able to put certain proposals onto the agenda of the government or directly to a vote in a referendum. They would also be able to recall certain laws and policies through referendum. The frequency of popular votes would likely be higher than it is currently in most existing systems, though likely not as high as it is in Switzerland. Because Switzerland does not have citizens' assemblies and still relies on skewed electoral representation, the countervailing mechanisms of direct democracy are needed more often than would presumably be the case in a politics centering the deliberations of ordinary citizens.

Note, finally, that agency would likely take new forms and be available to groups beyond the usual suspects. As members of lot-based assemblies would be going home between sessions, their family, relatives, friends, and neighbors—some too shy to engage in the form of political activism that the confident seek out—would ask questions and share information, as they did during the French conventions. More distant groups might also organize to access these local representatives, but the point is that the shy might actually have a shot at being heard for a change. That, too, is a form of agency that could spread evenly and deeply into society via lot-based representatives.

Too Extremist or Insufficiently Radical?

Even among those who are open-minded about the possibility of doing democracy differently, there often remains a general worry about the type of citizens who would show up in the lot-based assembly, with two opposite types of concerns: that citizens would be too radical (if self-selection is too pronounced); or that citizens would be too attached to the status quo (if the deliberative sample is truly representative).

The first worry can and should be addressed as we improve the sampling methods and increase the take-up rate. But even using current recruitment methods, the members of citizen assemblies have not shown themselves to be partisan or extremist. While citizens' recommendations were in favor of liberalizing the law on abortion in Ireland, this is in relation to a constitutional baseline that criminalized it quite harshly, by Western standards. Conversely, in South Korea, a large deliberative poll of 471 randomly selected South Koreans asked to debate nuclear energy policy chose to continue the construction and exploitation of two nuclear plants—a choice viewed as conservative—despite the progressive president's desire to shut them down permanently. Citizen assembly members do not aim to posture or score points in partisan ways, but to solve problems for their fellow citizens.

What about the opposite worry, which is that citizen assemblies will represent the preexisting consensus in a country and be unable to formulate the radical proposals that the times may demand, for example on climate policy, and that a visionary leader or a differently selected assembly might?

A lot-based assembly will, by design, reflect the broader consensus of the larger polity. For example, on end-of-life issues, the second French convention aligned with public sentiment, supporting a more permissive legal framework. However, there are instances where simply mirroring public consensus is, in itself, a radical act—particularly when political elites wish to block progress. This was evident in Ireland, where assemblies helped push forward transformative change on marriage equality and abortion despite elite resistance. In some cases, such assemblies help reveal the possibility of a consensus that no one was really aware of. Who knew that the French would be so supportive of a global housing renovation plan?

Should citizens' assemblies be expected to fulfill the role of visionary leadership as well? I am not sure. Their role is basic democratic representation, which we need more of. Randomly selected citizens' assemblies produce ideas and proposals that are more aligned with the preferences of the larger population and draw on a more diverse pool of views and information than those of elected assemblies. As a result, their proposals are likely to be better and more likely to be accepted by the public than those of elected assemblies. The standard of success for deliberative democrats is not whether citizens' assemblies can generate outstanding new policies that no one had thought of before. It's whether they can produce laws and policies that are better and more legitimate than those produced by elected politicians.

What About Leadership?

But surely, a democracy needs visionary leaders? In politics without politicians, who would fulfill that function if not elected politicians?

First, note that contra the president of the French National

Assembly's claim that power would be too much of a burden for them, ordinary citizens want more responsibility, not less. But it is true that they aren't power-hungry in the way politicians too often are. Most want power not for themselves but for the assembly they are a part of, and beyond that for the larger public they hope to serve. A few might get a taste for politics, sure. But the vast majority return to private life—more confident and more engaged, but not seeking office. They don't want to rule again and again and again, as some of our life-politicians do. They just want to do their duty and pass the responsibility to others.

That does not mean, however, that there would not be natural leaders emerging from the group of ordinary citizens. In a lot-based democracy, however, they would come to the fore and be elevated by their peers, often in more organic ways than the highly constrained competition between elites through which our current leaders emerge, or rather, are anointed by party elites.

What about the executive function specifically? How should the president of the United States or France be chosen in politics without politicians? Surely not by lot? Indeed, lot, at least used on the basis of universal inclusion (all members of the polity being candidates), would not be appropriate to select for a one-person position endowed with such extraordinary power. But maybe the solution is in part to rethink and humble the executive function in these presidential regimes. In theory, the executive branch exists to "execute" the laws, not to make policy or law itself. It's a strange and rather undemocratic historical development, and perhaps a mistake on the part of constitutional designers, that we have let presidents become so powerful, and indeed so much more powerful than parliaments.

Instead of electing a powerful political figure through universal suffrage, which produces monarch-like figures with dangerously

inflated egos, which in turn fosters unhealthy cults of person-
ality in the larger population, we could find inspiration in the
never-applied French constitution of 1793, which considered a
twenty-four-member executive board, or in the current Swiss
model of an executive council of seven. In Switzerland, the seven-
member collegial body is elected by the Federal Assembly (the bicameral parliament). No one really knows the names of these
officials, or cares, in a healthy, depersonalized way of defining the
function. We could imagine something a bit similar for a lot-based
democracy: for example, a multimember collegial body randomly
selected from, or otherwise chosen by, the lot-based legislature,
with one of them rotating every year as the official figurehead of
the government for the purpose of representation on the foreign
stage. The point is, we should be thinking creatively while we still
have the luxury to do so.

What About the Economy?

Last but not least, some readers might worry that the solution proposed in this book will do little to address the elephant in the
room: capitalism, or rather the crony version that seems to have
crept up in the United States and elsewhere. If elected officials are
already captured by economic powers and interests in the current
system, what guarantees that changing the selection method will
do anything to address the problem? While sortition has some anticorruption virtues, it alone cannot stem the flood of money in
politics and the enormous power of international corporations to
shape policies and laws to their liking.

It is true that in this book I have more or less taken for granted
the background economic conditions of existing democracies—a

variety of market-based capitalism. This is partly because there is only so much one book can accomplish. But it is also because I believe that politics can tame economics up to a point (even given the constraints of an open economy) and that a more democratic politics could considerably improve the current situation.

That said, I also happen to believe that it is both desirable and necessary to engage with economic questions as well. My work with the sociologist Isabelle Ferreras and the #DemocratizingWork group (a group of female scholars interested in exploring the tensions between democracy and capitalism and how to solve them) is an effort in that direction.[3] We explore in particular the various ways employees should be given proper democratic representation and voice inside large companies. More recently, I have explored with the economists Oliver Hart and Luigi Zingales the ways lot could be used to empower people who own shares in the stock market, including everyone who has a 401(k) plan, in a way that takes them seriously as human bearers of ethical values, not just rational seekers of financial value. We propose using so-called investor assemblies (citizens' assemblies of shareholders) to inform the decision-making of wealth fund managers when it comes to difficult ethical trade-offs between financial return and, say, climate mitigation, women's rights, or economic patriotism.[4] All of these, however, are arguments for other books.

Getting from Here to There

Even if we've addressed these and other objections, the question remains: How do we move from today's suboptimal, dysfunctional political system, dominated by politicians, to a system where they play little or no central role?

It seems impossible to answer this question in the abstract, as if one could map out an ideal path to an imagined other place. The late Maurice Pope had to resort to the dystopian scenario of a nuclear catastrophe wiping out all of humanity save for a handful of researchers in Antarctica to be able to imagine how we could re-create human societies in the image of lot-based democracies.[5]

Hopefully, the ultimate path would involve a less-dramatic form of orderly constitutional process in a time of peace. This process could model itself after, say, the constitutional Icelandic process of 2010–2013, combined with elements of the French Great National Debate and the best examples of citizens' assemblies. My recommendation would be, at any rate, to select the constitutional assembly itself by lot rather than through elections, for all the reasons already adduced in this book.

How would this work in the United States? And who would have an interest in transitioning from the current system to a different one? It is hard to imagine the United States escaping from the constraints of its gilded "frame" at the federal level—a constitution made intentionally difficult to amend by the Founding Fathers. It requires a two-thirds majority in both the House of Representatives and in the Senate, followed by ratification from three-fourths of the state legislatures or state conventions. In the current hyper-polarized context, the prospect of such a consensus at the federal level is slim.

But change might happen at the state level, where experimentation with one-off citizens' assemblies is already happening.[6] Long-term, the institutionalization of permanent sortition-based bodies at the state level in the United States is not unthinkable. Technically, both Republican and Democratic voters would have an interest in moving to random selection of sorts. Republicans because random selection ensures proportional representation in the assembly and they would be guaranteed a substantial presence despite their de facto minority status in terms of registered voters at the federal level, by contrast with the winner-take-all system under which both parties currently operate. Democratic voters should embrace it, too, if only in the name of the inclusion that they champion.

But at the moment, the prospects of institutionalization in the United States are still far off, as they are in most other countries, so let me turn instead to the more immediate lessons that one can derive from the relative successes, and some of the failures, of democratic innovations over the last forty years.

One lesson is that the possibility of radical change should be approached with an attitude of open-minded pragmatism, humility, and readiness to experiment rather than ideological and theoretical purity. This has been a lesson for me, who came at some of these experiments from the perspective of a theorist.

An example here is the 2012–2014 Irish Convention on the Constitution, whose hybrid design mixed two-thirds randomly selected citizens and one-third traditional politicians. On paper this sounds like a bad idea, mixing principles of legitimacy (elections versus sortition) without either good theoretical reasons or empirical evidence to go by. Yet in practice, this hybridization seemed to have built trust between two distinct constituencies (ordinary citizens and elected officials) and paved the way for a purely randomly selected assembly in 2016. By then politicians understood and trusted the potential of such an assembly, having seen it operate from within to great success just a few years earlier. The same mixture of politicians and ordinary citizens (one third to two thirds) also seems to work well in the context of Belgian deliberative commissions.[7] Whatever works!

By contrast, in France, one mistake was probably not to create more interactions with Parliament earlier in the process, even though these contacts would have risked jeopardizing the independence of the conventions. One successful aspect of the French design, however, was the relative flexibility of the conventions made possible by the creation of governance committees in charge of maneuvering the intrinsic uncertainties of such processes as well as constantly evolving circumstances (such as the pandemic, social movements, etc.). Recognizing our limited knowledge about the optimal design and procedures of democratic innovations calls for adaptability, flexibility, and a readiness to revise theory based on practice. This open-minded, pragmatic approach is essential because no two countries are the same—reform strategies must be tailored to fit local cultures and circumstances.

Another lesson is that change happens mostly during or just after crises. The 2008 financial crisis was the opportunity needed to introduce democratic innovations both in Ireland and Iceland, as it sufficiently unsettled existing elites and faith in their competence to allow for a more experimental mindset. The Yellow Vests protests in France similarly triggered a chain reaction that led to the Great National Debate and ensuing citizens' conventions. Crises are what open the Overton window and unsettle power players to the point where they are willing to try, or at least appear to try, something new. In that fleeting moment of disruption and uncertainty, there is opportunity and potential for change.

Academics, Activists, and Even Politicians

At critical moments, having ready-to-go ideas is essential—and that's where academics play a crucial role. Milton Friedman famously noted in the 1982 preface to *Capitalism and Freedom* that the "basic function" of academics is "to develop alternatives to existing policies, to keep them alive and available until the politically impossible becomes politically inevitable." While politics without politicians isn't inevitable yet, it has become increasingly viable in recent years, thanks in part to the work of academics and activists. In Ireland, the political scientists David Farrell and Jane Suiter patiently engaged parliamentarians, first securing a small pilot, which eventually led to the hybrid model of the country's first citizens' assembly, and then turning citizens' assemblies into an almost routine feature of the Irish system. In Belgium, the historian and writer David Van Reybrouck championed democratic innovations like the G1000 and Ost-Belgium's permanent citizens' assembly. Magali Plovie drove the creation of Brussels's deliberative commissions, which bring together parliamentarians and randomly selected citizens. Meanwhile, James Fishkin from Stanford has successfully persuaded governments and even a corporation like Meta to run deliberative polls worldwide.

Activists have been equally pivotal. In Canada, Iceland, Ireland, and Belgium, reforms often began with years of activist pressure for new political approaches. When crises emerged, these activists were ready with concrete proposals, offering policymakers an easy solution. Iceland and France offer prime examples.

In Iceland, the National Forum of 2010—launched by the government as the first step in rewriting the constitution—was directly modeled after the 2009 National Forum, an initiative led by a group of Icelandic entrepreneurs called the Anthill. Believing in collective intelligence, they organized a forum in response to the financial crisis, which was so well received that parliament adopted the same design for the constitutional process.

In France, the origins of the Citizens' Convention for Climate vary by account. Reportedly, Van Reybrouck gave his book to President Emmanuel Macron just before the Yellow Vests movement erupted. Around the same time, the activist and documentary maker Cyril Dion, together with the actress Marion Cotillard, met with Macron following the Great National Debate and pitched the idea of a national citizens' assembly on climate.

These examples show that when thoughtful proposals meet the right moment, real change is possible. Academics and activists must keep refining ideas, ensuring they're ready to seize the next opportunity for a more participatory future.

Of course, politicians are needed, too—an irony that is not lost on me. Politics without politicians can start without them, certainly, but short of a revolution, reforms and changes will have to happen through them and with their help.

Ireland's extraordinary success in passing two major reforms (marriage equality and the decriminalization of abortion) is no doubt largely due to the politicians being on board with the process and trustful of it from day one. By contrast, one of the reasons Iceland failed to pass its constitutional reform, ultimately, is that the main protagonist, the Icelandic Constitutional Council, failed to measure how much it depended on the goodwill and support of existing political actors. Its refusal to compromise alienated part of the political class, which then sought to sink the process at every turn. Somewhere in the middle we find the case of the French conventions, which started with a bang but, because they threatened existing legislative institutions, are looking more and more like they will go out with a whimper.

Visionary politicians with sufficient influence need to put their political capital behind democratic innovations, less they remain academic and impactless exercises. President Macron's much-publicized visit to the climate convention in January 2020 marked the moment when this assembly went from obscure focus group to political actor on the national stage. In Ireland, enough parliamentarians similarly had to embrace the premise of a citizens' assembly for the original pilot put forward by academics to be turned into an actual political assembly whose recommendations were morally if not legally constraining. Even deliberative polls have the potential of making an impact if political authorities incorporate them as a governance method and commit to taking seriously their recommendations.

Of course, there is a risk here, that of participation-washing and co-opting by established elites, especially as using citizens' assemblies is initially a good way for a government to regain some legitimacy. It is striking, for example, that the country where citizens' assemblies have been the most sucessful—Ireland—is at the moment one of the least likely to evolve toward the more radical form of politics without politicians, because it has been so successful at implementing the reformist version! Irish citizens are indeed among the European citizens least interested in replacing politicians with randomly selected representatives, perhaps precisely because the Irish citizens' assemblies have succeeded in restoring a form of trust between ordinary citizens and politicians.[8]

The key actors for change, however, are ultimately ordinary citizens themselves, the anonymous, regular people, many of whom fall into the category of those I called "the shy" throughout this book. Their support is key to the success of democratic innovations; without it, even good ideas are bound to wither. Activists and academics played a role in bringing about the French conventions, but so did the thousands of French citizens who participated in the regional citizens' assemblies of the Great National Debate. Their deliberations converged on the idea that new democratic forms of governance were needed to address climate and environmental issues. Their views shaped the decision by President Macron to convene the Citizens' Convention for Climate as much as academics' and activists' pressure.[9]

Some citizens possess unique leverage—and a few choose to use it in remarkable ways. Take Marlene Engelhorn, an Austrian heiress who inherited twenty-five million euros. Believing she neither needed nor deserved such wealth and unable to persuade the Austrian government to tax it (no wealth or inheritance tax exists in Austria), she took matters into her own hands. Aware that she might lack the moral authority to determine how best to use the money, she entrusted its distribution to a citizen jury of fifty randomly selected Austrians. Inspired by what she had read about citizen juries (including, I'll gladly admit, some of my own work), she thought: Why not apply this democratic principle herself? This kind of selflessness is rare and perhaps not to be counted on, but it speaks to a deeper truth: Institutionalizing real democracy demands more than figuring out the right political design; it depends on and calls on those with privilege, wealth, and influence to voluntarily share power. Real change begins when those who can afford it lead by example.

To Earth!

My main bet, however, is not even on today's generations of passionate citizens who believe in change, because we, and I include myself here, are still too caught up in old paradigms, too cynical, and our powers of imagination are already too ossified. My bet, instead, is on the younger generations.

Over the last ten years I've regularly taught a class called Reinventing Democracy to undergraduate students at Yale University. They always strike me as the more open-minded of my interlocutors, even though they often start out being extremely deferential toward existing institutions, especially those of the United States (though that deference has strikingly nose-dived since 2016). Toward the end of the class, which we spend reading classics of contemporary democratic theory, I encourage the students to imagine what an ideal democratic system, in their view, should look like.

One year, I asked my students to write up a constitution for a new colony of humans on planet Mars. The idea for this assignment was to free them of their preconceptions about what a good form of government looks like so as to be able to imagine a completely new constitutional design for a new planet, based on the best political theory and social science available today. As it turns out, the group of nine students who chose to work together on this assignment produced a stunningly good and original thirty-page document, which, while clearly indebted to some of my ideas and ideas by the authors we read during the class, also went far beyond them.

I was so proud of their work that I celebrated it on Twitter, and their constitution for Mars ended up being covered in a *Financial Times* article.[10] Shortly after publication, a group of Washington outer-space lawyers contacted me and asked for a meeting with the students, which took place shortly after. The lawyers were impressed, including by the fact that we had ignored all preexisting legal constraints. (To be fair, I'm not a legal scholar, so it did not occur to me to make the students read existing treatises on space law.) The students more than held their own in this conversation, often making more informed and better points than these seasoned professionals (I'll admit I'm probably a bit biased here).

While this experiment focused on constitutional rules for a new society on Mars, the point was, really, to get things right for Earth, where we've been muddling through attempts at democracy for thousands of years now and have yet to get it right. Later cohorts of students developed ideas on the constitutional process that would lead to the writing of a new constitution for the United States. Another group spent time thinking about architecture, envisioning, for example, a circle-shaped parliament with transparent glass walls built on a farm with animals, in the middle of nature. Their idea was to reconnect the natural world with political institutions, which are too often nested in hyper-urban environments. The latest cohort of students I taught, in 2024, sought to create a students' assembly at Yale University to debate issues of relevance to the student community, with the hope of helping shape university policies. They held this assembly, on the topic of institutional neutrality, in March 2025, as I was completing this manuscript.

What struck me the most in every single one of the projects conducted by these students was not so much the end result, but rather the way they interacted with one another, applying the values and principles they had learned about in class and calling on one another to live by those principles. They made all their decisions democratically, they made sure to listen to the least vocal people in the group, they rotated chairing and representation duties, and they ensured at every step that even as leaders naturally emerged, those never came to dominate the discussion and turn into power-hogging figures.

Understanding what democracy means in practice should start earlier than college—in high school, for example. Instead of electing class delegates, they could be chosen by lot, as demonstrated by the sortition advocate Adam Cronkright's 2009 experiment in Bogotá, Colombia. In this trial, students who wouldn't have run for election were randomly selected and given the opportunity to step up. Not only did these lottocratic representatives prove capable, but the issues they addressed went far beyond the typical concerns of an elected council. Rather than focusing on popularity-boosting events, they tackled real needs. They opened a school library where none existed, secured a computer donation from the ministry of education, and established a student ID system that allowed peers to access half-price bus fares—something previously impossible due to the lack of school-issued IDs. While they also organized fun activities like soccer tournaments and poetry competitions, their work had a far broader impact than that of their elected predecessors.[11]

One could imagine introducing democratic principles as early as kindergarten, using games and collaborative tasks assigned by lot. This approach would likely resonate with schools in the United States and elsewhere that aim to empower all children equally, fostering autonomy rather than dividing them into leaders and followers, as is still too often the case.

Democracy, as it stands, has long been defined by elections, parties, and elites. But it's time for a Copernican revolution—one that places ordinary citizens back at the center of the democratic universe. If this vision of politics resonates with you, there is much work ahead. We need to reimagine democracy not as a system confined to the ballot box, but as a daily practice—a way of living, thinking, and engaging with others and with the world.

The most critical step toward a politics with fewer politicians and more active citizens is to empower new generations to experience democracy as something they *do*, not something they *watch*. Teaching people to live democratically—deliberating, sharing power, caring for one another—and modeling that way of life at home, in the office, and in our daily encounters is how democracy not only survives but, ultimately, thrives.

Acknowledgments

In somewhat random order, as befits a central theme of this book, I want to thank, first, the members of the two French citizens' conventions, respectively "the 150" and "the 184," for the transforming experience of joining them on their civic journey and letting me observe, document, and even somewhat shape it. I hope they will recognize their experience in my description and analyses, even as I had to change their names (save a few exceptions) for publication. I thank the French CESE (Economic, Social, and Environmental Council) and its president, Thierry Beaudet, for the honor and opportunity of observing the first citizens' convention and serving on the governance committee of the second one.

I thank my friends and younger colleagues Claudia Chwalisz, Antonin Lacelle-Webster, Lex Paulson, Théophile Pénigaud de Mourgues, Andrew Sorota, and Miguel von Fedak for a fun, Calvados-fueled and (no doubt partly as a result) intellectually scintillating three-hour workshop on the first version of the manuscript, which they made me realize needed more work and drastic trimming. Théophile, a postdoctoral research associate at Yale, in particular, helped me sharpen some key ideas in chapter 6.

I thank my friend Vladimir Borovnica for feedback on the early chapters. I thank Shao Ming, Pierre-Etienne Vandamme, and Victor Wu for close reading of and helpful feedback on later versions. I thank Hugh Pope for encouraging me to bring more of my personal voice forward in this book and curbing my academic instincts.

I thank the University of Michigan for giving me an opportunity to develop the ideas contained in chapter 7 ("The Power of Love") for their Tanner Lecture on Human Values. I thank my Yale colleagues Bryan Garsten, Giulia Oskian, Lucia Rubinelli, and Steven Smith, as well as the graduate students, lecturers, and postdoctoral associates attending the Yale political theory workshop, for excellent feedback on the first draft of that chapter.

I thank Luigi Zingales and Oliver Hart, two admired colleagues in economics with whom I started developing a different though related project on what we call "investor assemblies" halfway through the writing process. They both generously took the time to read the manuscript at a crucial juncture. Luigi made me realize the book was missing a key chapter (which became "The Case for Lot"), and Oliver pointed out some important holes in my vision for democracy, including on the question of democratic leadership. Despite my best efforts, I could not plug them all.

I thank the University of Chicago for a fabulous conference on sortition in January 2025, at which I introduced some of the newer ideas in the chapter "The Case for Lot." Exchanges with fellow sortitionists Alex Guerrero and Camilla Vergara helped bring out more clearly the anticorruption argument in favor of lot. Debating our common critics Nadia Urbinati and Cristina Lafont helped me anticipate likely objections and misunderstandings. I'm grateful to all of them.

I thank José L. Martí for organizing a symposium on the book manuscript in June 2025 at Pompeu Fabra University in Barcelona, Spain, as well as the participants in this symposium, who gave me a last chance to improve the book: Chiara Destri, Roberto Gargarella, David Lefkowitz, Felipe Rey, and Pierre-Etienne Vandamme.

I thank my brilliant undergraduate student Thalsa Thiziri-Mekaouche for inspired research and editorial assistance as I was nearing the finish line.

I thank Joshua Cohen for putting me in touch with the amazing Margo Beth Fleming at Brockman when the idea for this book was still just a thought. I thank Margo herself for believing in this project to begin with, enthusiastically supporting it throughout, and even coming to check on me in New Haven when I was getting stuck for too long after a few very unproductive months. At Penguin Random House, I thank Noah Schwartzberg and his team for extremely thorough editorial advice and making me feel special during the whole process (what a difference from academic publishing!). I also thank Greg Villepique for turning my prose into proper English through patient and generous copyediting.

I thank Nathan Heller at *The New Yorker* for the title of the book, which is cribbed from an article of his on my earlier work. Nathan really nailed the main concept behind my ideas with this title, and as much as I tried, I just couldn't find a better one.

Last but not least, I thank my husband, Darko Jelaca, and my daughters, Émilie and Sophie, for everything else that truly matters.

Notes

Chapter One: Fixing a Broken System

1. According to Gallup, which began tracking Congress's approval rating in 1975, the all-time high was 84 percent, in October 2001. Since then, it's hovered below 50 percent and was last recorded at 15 percent in November 2023. Gallup Organization, "Congress and the Public," news.gallup.com /poll/1600/congress-public.aspx.

2. Richard Wike, Laura Silver, Shannon Schumacher, and Aidan Connaughton, "Many in U.S., Western Europe Say Their Political System Needs Major Reform," Pew Research Center, March 31, 2021, pewresearch.org /global/2021/03/31/many-in-us-western-europe-say-their-political-system -needs-major-reform.

3. "Americans' Dismal Views of the Nation's Politics," Pew Research Center, September 19, 2023, pewresearch.org/politics/2023/09/19/americans-dismal -views-of-the-nations-politics.

4. We'll spend time analyzing such results in chapter 3.

5. Garett Jones, *10% Less Democracy: Why You Should Trust Elites a Little More and the Masses a Little Less* (Stanford University Press, 2020).

6. Two other famous quotes of his also involve democracy but are less relevant for my purposes, comparing democracy to falling in love and blowing one's nose, or calling tradition "the democracy of the dead."

7. His children, who retrieved a copy long after Maurice Pope himself thought it lost, sent it to me to see if I would endorse it and help get it published, which I enthusiastically did.

8. "En quoi les français ont-ils confiance aujourd'hui?" The Center for Political Research at Sciences Po (CEVIPOF), February 2024, sciencespo.fr/cevipof /sites/sciencespo.fr.cevipof/files/BConf_V15_Extraction1_modif.pdf.

9. Kofi Annan, "The Crisis of Democracy," keynote speech, 2017 Athens Democracy Forum, Athens, Greece, September 13, 2017, kofiannanfoundation .org/publication/athens-democracy-forum.

10. "Innovative Public Participation and New Democratic Institutions: Catching the Deliberative Wave," OECD, 2024, oecd.org/en/publications/innovative -citizen-participation-and-new-democratic-institutions_339306da-en.html.

11. "What Is Deliberative Polling®?," Deliberative Democracy Lab, Stanford University, 2016, deliberation.stanford.edu/what-deliberative-pollingr#Case Studies.

12. "The Ostbelgien Model: A Long-Term Citizens' Council Combined with Short-Term Citizens' Assemblies," International Observatory on Participatory Democracy (OIDP), oidp.net/en/practice.php?id=1237.

13. "Permanent Climate Assembly in Brussels," Bürguerrat, February 4, 2024, buergerrat.de/en/news/permanent-climate-assembly-in-brussels.

14. For an account of the process, see this Substack article at DemocracyNext, whose founder, Claudia Chwalisz, was one of the assembly's designers: "How a Permanent Citizens' Assembly in Paris Passed a Bill into Law," Democracy-Next, July 25, 2024, demnext.substack.com/p/how-a-permanent-citizens -assembly. For direct access to the bill (in French) taking up the twenty measures proposed by the citizens and voted on by the Paris city council, see "2024 DDCT 141—Délibération de l'Assemblée citoyenne relative à la prévention et à l'accompagnement des personnes en situation de rue," a06-v7.apps.paris.fr /a06/jsp/site/plugins/odjcp/DoDownload.jsp?id_entite=62292&id_type _entite=6.

15. Emmeline Cooper, Remco van der Stoep, and Rob Bauer, "Deelnemersdia-loog Report," Pensioenfonds Detailhandel, 2024, pensioenfondsdetailhandel .nl/content/publications/Deelnemersdialoog-English.pdf.

16. Gwladys Fouche, "How Should Norway Spend its Cash? Solve Global Problems, Says Citizen Panel," Reuters, May 13, 2025, reuters.com/sustainability /boards-policy-regulation/how-should-norway-spend-its-cash-solve-global -problems-says-citizen-panel-2025-05-13.

Chapter Two: The Problem with Politicians

1. Una Hajdari, "Serbia Protests: How Much Trouble Is Aleksandar Vučić In?," *Politico*, March 17, 2025, politico.eu/article/serbia-protests-president -aleksander-vucic-corruption-belgrade-country-europe.

2. Valur Grettisson, "From Iceland—36 Bankers, 96 Years in Jail," The Reykjavik Grapevine, February 7, 2018, grapevine.is/news/2018/02/07/36-bankers -96-years-in-jail.

3. Susan Cain, *Quiet: The Power of Introverts in a World That Can't Stop Talking* (Crown, 2012).

4. Despite my own personal ambivalence toward identity politics, and despite the general backlash against it at the current political moment, I will regularly refer to and remark on people's gender, age, and also skin color and ethnic origins in the book (for example, when I identify and quote a participant). This is because it would be foolish to think that these categories do not exist and importantly shape our interactions. And in the context of the citizens' assemblies I have observed, I think it is important to be able to identify certain dynamics that even random selection and deliberation cannot fully neutralize. Conversely, when random selection and deliberation do good things for some category or other of "the shy," we want to be able to notice it and talk about it in explicit terms.

5. This is no doubt even more true on the right than on the left. Even former Speaker of the House Kevin McCarthy publicly stated, "When you look at the Democrats, they actually look like America. When I look at my party, we look like the most restrictive country club in America." Ariel Messman-Rucker, "Watch Kevin McCarthy Take Down His Own Party While Praising Democrats in New Viral Video," Yahoo! News, December 8, 2023, yahoo.com/news/watch-kevin-mccarthy-down-own-140521574.html.

6. You can see it for yourself here: "Grand Débat d'Emmanuel Macron avec les maires de Normandie," January 15, 2019, Élysée, www.youtube.com/watch?v=gx68VBfKOoY.

7. The French parliament might now be inching closer to 40 percent women, thanks to various parity laws that have made it progressively easier for women to access electoral politics at the national level since the year 2000. Since it's illegal to track race in France, however, no such quotas have been put in place for minorities, and the parliament is still overwhelmingly white, even as France is a multicultural and multiracial country with over 30 percent first-, second-, or third-generation immigrants, mostly from North Africa.

8. The truth is that they were not that ordinary. They were, in fact, much more educated and urban than the average Icelander. They were also not that diverse in absolute terms, of course—being all white and Christian. But then again, this is Iceland. The diversity point is relative.

9. Jennifer L. Lawless and Richard Logan Fox, *It Still Takes a Candidate: Why Women Don't Run for Office* (Cambridge University Press, 2012).

10. Brian Klaas, *Corruptible: Who Gets Power and How It Changes Us* (Scribner, 2021).

11. Rory Stewart, "The Livestock Ring," *How Not to Be a Politician: A Memoir* (Penguin Press, 2023), 31.

12. A solution put forward by Julia Cagé, for example, advocates quotas for the working class. See Julia Cagé and Patrick Camiller, *The Price of Democracy: How Money Shapes Politics and What to Do About It* (Harvard University Press, 2020).

13. Josefina Erikson and Cecilia Josefsson, "Does Higher Education Matter for MPs in Their Parliamentary Work? Evidence from the Swedish Parliament," Representation 55, no. 1 (January 2, 2019): 65–80, doi.org/10.1080 /00344893.2019.1581077.

14. Terry Bouricius, "My Path," Democracy Creative, June 3, 2023, democra cycreative.substack.com/p/my-path.

15. Bernard Manin, *The Principles of Representative Government* (Cambridge University Press, 1997), 1.

16. Manin, *The Principles of Representative Government*, 9.

17. Manin, *The Principles of Representative Government*, 134.

18. Manin, *The Principles of Representative Government*, 149.

19. Manin, *The Principles of Representative Government*, 149.

20. See Hélène Landemore, "Is Representative Democracy Really Democratic?," Books & Ideas, March 2008, booksandideas.net/is-representative-democracy -really-democratic.

Chapter Three: Democracy by Coincidence

1. Bernard Manin, *The Principles of Representative Government* (Cambridge University Press, 1997), 178.

2. Larry Bartels, *Unequal Democracy: The Political Economy of the New Gilded Age* (Princeton University Press, 2009).

3. Martin Gilens and Benjamin I. Page, "Testing Theories of American Politics: Elites, Interest Groups, and Average Citizens," *Perspectives on Politics* 12, no. 3 (2014): 564–81, doi.org/10.1017/S1537592714001595.

4. Omar S. Bashir, "Testing Inferences About American Politics: A Review of the 'Oligarchy' Result," *Research & Politic* 2, no. 4 (2015), doi.org/10 .1177/2053168015608896; J. Alexander Branham, Stuart N. Soroka, and Christopher Wlezien, "When Do the Rich Win?," *Political Science Quarterly* 132, no.1 (2017): 43–62, doi.org/10.1002/polq.12577; Peter K. Enns, "Relative Policy Support and Coincidental Representation," *Perspectives on Politics* 13, no. 4 (2015): 1053–64, doi.org/10.1017/S1537592715002315; Peter K. Enns and Christopher Wlezien, eds., *Who Gets Represented?* (Russell Sage Foundation, 2011), jstor.org/stable/10.7758/9781610447225;

Stuart Soroka and Christopher Wlezien, "On the Limits to Inequality in Representation," *Political Science and Politics*, April 2008: 319–27; Christopher R. Ellis and Joseph Daniel Ura, "United We Divide?: Education, Income, and Heterogeneity in Mass Partisan Polarization," SSRN, November 6, 2008, doi.org/10.2139/ssrn.1302856.

5. Jarron Bowman, "Do the Affluent Override Average Americans? Measuring Policy Disagreement and Unequal Influence," *Social Science Quarterly* 101 (2020): 1018–37, doi.org/10/1111/ssqu.12791.

6. Based on two combined studies that report respectively 59 percent congruence of ten high-profile issues across the fifty states and 48 percent congruence for thirty-nine policies across the fifty states.

7. Lea Elsässer, Svenja Hense, and Armin Schäfer, "Not Just Money: Unequal Responsiveness in Egalitarian Democracies," *Journal of European Public Policy* 28, no. 12 (2020): 1890–1908, doi.org/10.1080/13501763.2020.1801804.

8. M. A. Elkjær, "What Drives Unequal Policy Responsiveness? Assessing the Role of Informational Asymmetries in Economic Policy-Making," *Comparative Political Studies* 53, no. 14 (2020), 2213–45, doi.org/10.1177/0010414020912282.

9. Wouter Schakel, "Unequal Policy Responsiveness in the Netherlands," *Socio-Economic Review* 19, no. 1. (2021), doi.org/10.1093/ser/mwz018; Wouter Schakel and Daphne van Der, "Degrees of Influence: Educational Inequality in Policy Representation," *European Journal of Political Research* 60, no. 2 (2020): 418–37, doi.org/10.1111/1475-6765.12405.

10. Ruben B. Mathisen, "Affluence and Influence in a Social Democracy," *American Political Science Review* 117, no. 2 (2023): 751–58, doi.org/10.1017/S0003055422000739.

11. Eric Guntermann and Mikael Persson, "Issue Voting and Government Responsiveness to Policy Preferences," *Political Behavior* 45, no. 2 (2021): 561–84, doi.org/10/1007/s11109-021-09716-8; Mikael Persson, "From Opinions to Policies: Examining the Links Between Citizens, Representatives, and Policy Change," *Electoral Studies* 74 (2021), doi.org/10.1016/j.electstud.2021.102413.

12. Noam Lupu and Alejandro Tirado Castro, "Unequal Policy Responsiveness in Spain," *Socio-Economic Review* 21, no. 3 (2023), doi.org/10.1093/ser/mwac040.

13. Zoe Lefkofridi and Nathalie Giger, "Democracy or Oligarchy? Unequal

Representation of Income Groups in European Institutions," *Politics and Governance* 8, no. 1 (2020), doi.org/10.17645/pag.v8i1.2526.

14. Mikael Persson and Anders Sundell, "The Rich Have a Slight Edge: Evidence from Comparative Data on Income-Based Inequality in Policy Congruence," *British Journal of Political Science* 54, no. 2 (2024): 514–25, doi.org/10.1017/S0007123423000066.

15. Richard Wike, Laura Silver, Shannon Schumacher, and Aidan Connaughton, "Many in U.S., Western Europe Say Their Political System Needs Major Reform," Pew Research Center, March 31, 2021, pewresearch.org/global/2021/03/31/many-in-us-western-europe-say-their-political-system-needs-major-reform.

16. Kay Lehman Schlozman, Henry E. Brady, and Sidney Verba, *Unequal and Unrepresented: Political Inequality and the People's Voice in the New Gilded Age* (Princeton University Press, 2018), 161.

17. Steven W. Webster, *American Rage: How Anger Shapes Our Politics* (Cambridge University Press, 2020).

18. Other scholars, like the French political theorist Yves Sintomer, have sought to provide more refined explanations for the disappearance of lot in the eighteenth century, pointing out other factors in the history of ideas, such as the Enlightenment constellation of choice, rationality, and autonomy, which centered human decision and made lot—which on the face of it is the absence of choice, rationality, and autonomy—appear archaic and backward. Maxime Mellina, one of Sintomer's students, wrote a fascinating dissertation on the disappearance of lot in Switzerland in the nineteenth century: *Le Sort ou la Raison: persistance et disparition du tirage au sort en Suisse (1798–1831)*. He recounts how Napoléon Bonaparte himself came to talk to the Swiss and tried to convince them not to give up on traditional anticorruption mechanisms they still used at the time, including lot, in their faddish attempt at copying the French constitutional model. And yet a couple of decades later lot was no longer in use.

19. See Ian Hacking, *The Taming of Chance* (Cambridge University Press, 1990).

Chapter Four: Citizen Politics, Old and New

1. Thucydides, "Pericles' Funeral Oration," trans. Richard Hooker, Human Rights Library, University of Minnesota, hrlibrary.umn.edu/education/thucydides.html.

2. This is, I recognize, only one of many possible interpretations of the fourth-

century reforms, and it's worth acknowledging that democratic Athens often serves more as a Rorschach test for one's pre-held political views than an objective source of evidence. Scholars attached to electoral democracies and suspicious of sortition will claim, for example, that the *nomothetai* were extensions of the assembly rather than bodies that supplanted them, while others still interpret them as existing in a checks-and-balances relationship. My reading that the *nomothetai* supplanted, or at least gained legislative oversight over, the assembly is closer to how Manin (1997) interpreted the change.

3. Paulin Ismard, *Democracy's Slaves: A Political History of Ancient Greece* (Harvard University Press, 2017).

4. Rachel Griffith, "Archaeologies of the Greek Past: Obol," Brown University, brown.edu/Departments/Joukowsky_Institute/courses/greekpast/4792.html.

5. See Jon Elster, "Accountability in Athenian Politics," in Adam Przeworski, Susan C. Stokes, and Bernard Manin, eds., *Democracy, Accountability, and Representation* (Cambridge University Press, 1999), 253–78.

6. Josiah Ober, *Democracy and Knowledge: Innovation and Learning in Classical Athens* (Princeton University Press, 2009).

7. Josiah Ober, *Mass and Elite in Democratic Athens: Rhetoric, Ideology, and the Power of the People* (Princeton University Press, 2009), 123.

8. Ober, *Mass and Elite in Democratic Athens*, 123.

9. Ober, *Democracy and Knowledge*, 123.

10. Joseph Bailly, "Pericles' Funeral Oration" (Thucydides, 2.35–46, para. XL[2]), University of Vermont, Accessed July 16, 2025, uvm.edu/~jbailly/courses/clas158/etexts/funeralOrationText.html.

11. Yves Sintomer, *The Government of Chance* (Cambridge University Press, 2023), 126–35.

12. In other regions of the world, though, one can find similar political practices of judgment by peers that go back even further, certainly predating the Greeks.

13. Jeffrey Abramson, *We, the Jury: The Jury System and the Ideal of Democracy* (Harvard University Press, 1994), 61–68.

14. He himself was inspired by the thinking of his mentor, the Yale political scientist Robert Dahl, who had coined the term "mini-populus" to refer to a representative sample of the public that could be seen as a better locus of decision-making for politics.

15. Deliberative polling is sometimes deemed less political or less concerned with empowering citizens than citizens' assemblies. Yet it is crucial to mention them because even though they are and remain conceptualized as an improved form of polling—one meant to help politicians make more informed decisions about the preferences of their constituents rather than compete with them in a political role—they have sometimes evolved toward a more expressly political role.

Chapter Five: The Case for Lot

1. "EBJ in Practice," Election by Jury, electionbyjury.org/learn-more/ebj-in -practice. Special thanks to Terrill Bouricius for this information.

2. Gwyneth K. Shaw, "Saving the Civil Jury System: New Report Offers Ways to Revive an 'Essential Bulwark of Justice,'" UC Berkeley Law, October 4, 2021, law.berkeley.edu/article/saving-jury-system-civil-justice-research -initiative.

3. Tiago Peixoto and Paolo Spada, "Reflections on the Representativeness of Citizens' Assemblies and Similar Innovations," DemocracySpot, democra cyspot.net/2023/02.

4. Bailey Flanigan, Paul Gölz, Anupam Gupta, Brett Hennig, and Ariel D. Procaccia, "Fair Algorithms for Selecting Citizens' Assemblies," *Nature* 596 (2021): 548–52, doi.org/10.1038/s41586-021-03788-6.

5. Gerdus Benadè, Paul Gölz, and Ariel D. Procaccia, "No Stratification Without Representation," ACM Conference on Economics and Computation (EC '19), Phoenix, June 24–28, 2019, doi.org/10.1145/3328526.332 9578.

6. Flanigan, Gölz, Gupta, Hennig, and Procaccia, "Fair Algorithms for Selecting Citizens' Assemblies," 548–52.

7. See, respectively, Sam Bagg, "Sortition as Anti-Corruption: Popular Oversight Against Elite Capture," *American Journal of Political Science* (2022): 93–105, onlinelibrary.wiley.com/doi/pdf/10.1111/ajps.12704; and Camilla Vergara, *Systemic Corruption: Constitutional Ideas for an Anti-Oligarchic Republic* (Princeton University Press, 2022).

8. For example, you will find that the longer you keep rolling a die, the closer the statistical frequency with which each face appears comes to one out of six, which is the "true" value of this probability for an idealized die (a mathematical model of it).

9. See Scott E. Page, *The Difference: How the Power of Diversity Creates Better Groups, Firms, Schools, and Societies* (Princeton University Press, 2008), and my own book *Democratic Reason: Politics, Collective Intelligence, and the Rule of the Many* (Princeton University Press, 2013).

10. Aristotle, *Politics*, book 3, section 1281b. There is some uncertainty whether Aristotle had in mind mere aggregation of judgments, as in voting, or an actual discursive exchange of arguments, as in deliberation. Both voting and deliberation play different and complementary roles in the way democracies produce collective intelligence.

11. I draw here on a wonderful essay written by the Yale undergraduate student Thalsa-Thiziri Mekaouche for my 2025 spring seminar on deliberative democracy.

12. John Zhuang Liu, "Juries, Public Trust in the Judiciary, and Judicial Performance: Evidence from Cross-Country Data," February 20, 2018, dx.doi .org/10.2139/ssrn.3127261. Special thanks to Luigi Zingales for this reference and the next.

13. Stefan Voigt, "The Effects of Lay Participation in Courts: A Cross-Country Analysis," *European Journal of Political Economy* 25, no. 3 (2009): 327–39.

14. Marco R. Steenbergen, André Bächtiger, Markus Spörndli, and Jürg Steiner, "Measuring Political Deliberation: A Discourse Quality Index," *Comparative European Politics* 1 (2003): 21–48, doi.org/10/1057/palgrave.cep.6110002; André Bächtiger and Dominik Hangartner, "When Deliberative Theory Meets Empirical Political Science: Theoretical and Methodological Challenges in Political Deliberation," *Political Studies* 58, no. 4 (2010): 609–29, doi.org/10.1111/j/1467. Other routes include the index of intersubjective consistency (Simon Niemeyer and John S. Dryzek, "The Ends of Deliberation: Meta-Consensus and Inter-subjective Rationality as Ideal Outcomes," *Swiss Political Science Review* 13 [2007]: 497–526, doi.org/10/1002/j.1662-6370.2007.tb00087.x); the index of "cognitive complexity" (Dominik Wyss, Simon Beste, and André Bächtiger, "A Decline in the Quality of Debate?: The Evolution of Cognitive Complexity in Swiss Parliamentary Debates on Immigration [1968–2014]," *Swiss Political Science Review* 21, no. 4 [2015]: 636–53, doi.org/10/1111/spsr.12179), or the measurement of adequate support for given conclusions (Henrik Friberg-Fernros and Johan Karlsson Schaffer, "Assessing the Epistemic Quality of Democratic Decision-Making in Terms of Adequate Support for Conclusions," *Social Epistemology* 31, no. 3 [2017]: 251–65, doi.org/10.1080/02691728.2017.1317866).

15. See, for example, Hélène Landemore, "When Public Participation Matters: The 2010–2013 Icelandic Constitutional Process," *International Journal of Constitutional Law* 18, no. 1 (2020): 179–205, doi.org/10.1093/icon/mo aa004.

16. For the full analysis see chapter 7, "Let the People In! Lessons from a Modern Viking Saga," in Hélène Landemore, *Open Democracy: Reinventing Popular Rule for the Twenty-First Century* (Princeton University Press, 2022).

17. For the detailed analysis, see Hélène Landemore, "Inclusive Constitution Making and Religious Rights: Lessons from the Icelandic Experiment," *The Journal of Politics* 79, no. 3 (July 2017): 762–79, doi.org/10.1086 /690300.

18. "Opinion on the Draft New Constitution of Iceland Adopted by the Venice Commission at Its 94th Plenary Session," Venice Commission of the Council of Europe, March 8–9, 2013, remark 27, 6: coe.int/en/web/venice -commission/-/CDL-AD(2013)010-e.

19. "Opinion on the Draft New Constitution of Iceland Adopted by the Venice Commission at Its 94th Plenary Session," remark 55, 11.

20. Zachary Elkins, Tom Ginsburg, and James Melton, *The Endurance of National Constitutions* (Cambridge University Press, 2009), 2.

21. Article 128 of the Venice Commission's report states: "The Venice Commission welcomes the clear intention that underlines the above-mentioned provisions, namely, to enhance citizens' opportunities to influence legislation and more generally the decision-making on issues of key interest of the public. It finds this aim entirely legitimate and understandable in the specific socio-economic and political context of Iceland, and recalls that, this is also a part of a certain tradition of direct participation that exists in Iceland." "Opinion on the Draft New Constitution of Iceland Adopted by the Venice Commission at Its 94th Plenary Session," remark 23, 5.

22. That is what Jason Brennan argues against me in our joint book *Debating Democracy*. Jason Brennan and Hélène Landemore, *Debating Democracy: Do We Need More or Less?* (Oxford University Press, 2021).

23. Julia Abelson, Pierre-Gerlier Forest, John Eyles, Patricia Smith, Elisabeth Martin, and François-Pierre Gauvin, "Deliberations About Deliberative Methods: Issues in the Design and Evaluation of Public Participation Processes," *Social Science & Medicine* 57, no. 2 (2003): 239–51, doi.org/10

.1016/s0277-9536(02)00343-x; Kristin L. Carman, Pam Dardess, Maureen Maurer, Shoshanna Sofaer, Karen Adams, Christine Bechtel, and Jennifer Sweeney, "Patient and Family Engagement: A Framework for Understanding the Elements and Developing Interventions and Policies," *Health Affairs* 32, no. 2 (2013): 223–31, healthaffairs.org/doi/full/10.1377/hlthaff.2012 .1133; Katherine R. Knobloch, John Gastil, Justin Reedy, and Katherine Cramer Walsh, "Did They Deliberate? Applying an Evaluative Model of Democratic Deliberation to the Oregon Citizens' Initiative Review," *Journal of Applied Communication Research* 41, no. 2 (2013): 105–25, doi.org /10.1080/00909882.2012.760746; Robert C. Luskin, James S. Fishkin, and Roger Jowell, "Considered Opinions: Deliberative Polling in Britain," *British Journal of Political Science* 32, no. 3 (2002): 455–87, jstor.org/stable /4092249.

24. Kristin L. Carman, Coretta Mallery, Maureen Maurer, Grace Wang, Steve Garfinkel, Manshu Yang, et al., "Effectiveness of Public Deliberation Methods for Gathering Input on Issues in Healthcare: Results from a Randomized Trial," *Social Science & Medicine* 133 (2015): 11–20, doi.org/10 .1016/j.socscimed.2015.03.024.

25. Sean J. Westwood, "The Role of Persuasion in Deliberative Opinion Change," *Political Communication* 32, no. 4 (2015): 509–28, doi.org/10 .1080/10584609.2015.1017628; Marlène Gerber, André Bächtiger, Susumu Shikano, Simon Reber, and Samuel Rohr, "Deliberative Abilities and Influence in a Transnational Deliberative Poll (EuroPolis)," *British Journal of Political Science* 48, no. 4 (2018): 1093–1118, doi.org/10.1017/S0007123 416000144; Kevin M. Esterling, Archon Fung, and Taeku Lee, "When Deliberation Produces Persuasion Rather than Polarization: Measuring and Modeling Small Group Dynamics in a Field Experiment," *British Journal of Political Science* 51, no. 2 (2021): 666–84, doi.org/10.1017/S000712341 9000243.

26. Min Reuchamps, Julien Vrydagh, and Yanina Welp, *De Gruyter Handbook of Citizens' Assemblies* (De Gruyter, 2023), doi.org/10.1515/9783110758269.

27. Ramon Van der Does and Vincent Jacquet, "Small-Scale Deliberation and Mass Democracy: A Systematic Review of the Spillover Effects of Deliberative Minipublics," *Political Studies* 71, no. 1 (2021): 218–37.

28. James Fishkin, Valentin Bolotnyy, Joshua Lerner, Alice Siu, and Norman Bradburn, "Can Deliberation Have Lasting Effects?," *American Political Science Review* 118, no. 4 (2024): 2000–2020.

29. James Fishkin, *Democracy When the People Are Thinking: Revitalizing Our Politics Through Public Deliberation* (Oxford University Press, 2018).

Chapter Six: Another French Revolution?

1. "Ce qui sortira de cette convention, je m'y engage, sera soumis sans filtre soit au vote du parlement soit à référendum soit à application réglementaire directe." Élysée, "Press Conference Given at the End of the Great National Debate," April 25, 2019, www.elysee.fr/emmanuel-macron/2019/04/25/conference-de-presse-grand-debat-national.

2. Recall as a comparison point that the 2004 British Columbia assembly convened 160 citizens, and the 2016 Irish one 99.

3. This striking result was published for the first time in March 2023 by a reputable statistical institute, causing the debate about immigration in France to reach a new fever pitch: See Agence France Presse, "En France, une personne sur dix est immigrée selon l'insee," *Le Point*, March 30, 2023, lepoint.fr/societe/en-france-un-tiers-de-la-population-est-issu-de-l-immigration-30-03-2023-2514312_23.php#11.

4. For the Bosnian example, see "Citizens' Assembly of Mostar," mostargradimo.ba/en/home; for Colombia, see "Bogotá Itinerant Citizen Assembly," participate.oidp.net/processes/award2023/f/277/proposals/3170?page=2; for Lebanon, see "A Pilot Citizens' Assembly on Electricity and Energy Justice in Hamra, Lebanon," discovery.ucl.ac.uk/id/eprint/10129878/7/Shehabi_CA_Hamra_WP_JUNE21_v2.pdf.

5. Mark E. Warren, "Citizen Representatives," in *Designing Deliberative Democracy: The British Columbia Citizens' Assembly*, eds. Mark E. Warren and Hilary Pearse (Cambridge University Press, 2008), 50–69.

6. Hélène Landemore, *Open Democracy: Reinventing Popular Rule for the Twenty-First Century* (Princeton University Press, 2022), 55.

7. Gaspard D'Alleins, Nicholas Gaspard, Boeuf, Nicholas, and Léa Dang, Léa. "Convention pour le climat: Seules 10% des propositions ont été reprises par le gouvernement," *Reporterre, Le Média de L'écologie*, March 31, 2021, https://reporterre.net/Convention-pour-le-climat-seules-10-des-propositions-ont-ete-reprises-par-le-gouvernement.

8. Éric Buge, "Did the Citizens' Convention on Climate Work Like a Parliamentary Assembly?," *Participations* 34, no. 3 (2022): 205–35, doi.org/10.3917/parti.0340205.

9. Ministère de la Transition Écologique, "Suivi de la Convention citoyenne pour le climat: Les mesures pour le climat," République Française, accessed July 16, 2025, www.ecologie.gouv.fr/suivi-convention-citoyenne-climat/les-mesures-pour-le-climat.

10. "L'appel de 1,000 scientifiques: 'Face à la crise écologique, la rébellion est nécessaire,'" *Le Monde*, February 20, 2020, lemonde.fr/idees/article/2020/02/20/l-appel-de-1-000-scientifiques-face-a-la-crise-ecologique-la-rebellion-est-necessaire_6030145_3232.html.

11. "Sondage: Des Gaulois pas si réfractaires à l'action climatique," Réseau Action Climat, June 26, 2020, reseauactionclimat.org/sondage-des-gaulois-pas-si-refractaires-a-laction-climatique.

12. "Les Mesures de La Convention Citoyenne Séduisent Les Français . . . à l'Exception Notable Des 110 Km/H," *Odoxa*, June 25, 2020, odoxa.fr/sondage/mesures-de-convention-citoyenne-seduisent-francais-a-lexception-notable-110-km-h.

13. Mathieu Saujot, Nicolas Berghmans, Andréa Rüdinger, Sébastien Treyer, Michel Colombier, Laura Brimont, and Yann Briand, "Convention Citoyenne sur le Climat: 149 mesures pour une nouvelle vision de la transition," IDDRI, December 2020, iddri.org/fr/publications-et-evenements/etude/convention-citoyenne-sur-le-climat-149-mesures-pour-une-nouvelle.

14. This phrase, sometimes credited to Winston Churchill, was in fact first coined by George William Russell, the editor of an Irish paper, in 1910.

15. Hélène Landemore and Théophile Pénigaud, "Citizen Legislators: Experts on Tap and Citizens on Top in the French Citizens' Convention for Climate" (working manuscript).

16. See Louis-Gaëtan Giraudet and Hélène Guillemot, "Rôle des experts et des citoyens dans la fabrication des mesures: Le groupe 'se loger,'" in Dimitri Courant and Bernard Reber, eds., *Démocratie délibérative et transition écologique: La Convention citoyenne pour le climat* (ISTE, 2024).

17. "Macron annonce une réduction 'de moitié' des membres du CESE," *Le Monde*, January 30, 2018, lemonde.fr/politique/article/2018/01/30/macron-annonce-une-reduction-de-moitie-des-membres-du-conseil-economique-social-et-environnemental_5249386_823448.html.

18. See Naruna Kaplan de Macedo, dir., *Convention Citoyenne: Démocratie en Construction*, Les Films d'Ici (2020), film-documentaire.fr/4DACTION/w_fiche_film/61781_1.

19. Dimitri Courant and Simon Baeckelandt, "Impartialité délibérative et légiti-mité des influences," in Courant and Reber, eds., *Démocratie délibérative et transition écologique*, 201–32.

20. Collectif citoyen, *La Grande Désillusion: Vécus de la Convention Citoy-enne sur le Climat* (Atlande, 2023).

21. This figure is, interestingly, even higher in Italy (71 percent), Germany (65 percent), and the United Kingdom (62 percent). "Baromètre de la con-fiance en politique—Vague 12," The Center for Political Research at Sci-ences Po (CEVIPOF), February 2021, 132–33, https://www.sciencespo.fr /cevipof/sites/sciencespo.fr.cevipof/files/OpinionWay%20pour%20le %20CEVIPOF-Barome%cc%80tre%20de%20la%20confiance%20 en%20politique%20-%20vague12%20-%20Rapport%20international %20(1).pdf.

Chapter Seven: The Power of Love

1. This was not environmentally responsible at all, as the participants in the Citizens' Convention for Climate had lovingly already made me feel guilty about, which is partly why I attended only five of the nine weekends of this new convention in person and stayed for two weekends at a time when it was possible. I should also say that being a member of the governance com-mittee was an unpaid responsibility, though my traveling costs (economy), hotels, and meals were paid for by the convention, along with those of the other thirteen governance committee members.

2. This story was recounted to me by the two women in question when they came to the office hours of the governance committee during the second session of the Convention on the End of Life.

3. For instance, the first plenary vote in the third session was widely consid-ered "catastrophic," and the CESE employee who had taken it upon herself to organize it without the consent of the governance committee ended up removed from her position. Later, we had to deal with an attempt to sabo-tage the convention from within. There were social movements or orga-nized groups that made it difficult for people to attend the sessions.

4. Bastian Berbner, "The Other Guy and Me," True Story Award, 2019, truestoryaward.org/story/51.

5. Nicole Curato and Septrin Calamba, "Deliberative Forums in Fragile Con-texts: Challenges from the Field," *Politics*, June 2024, doi.org/10.1177 /02633957241259090.

6. Jürg Steiner, Maria Clara Jaramillo, Rousiley C. M. Maia, and Simona

Mameli, *Deliberation Across Deeply Divided Societies: Transformative Moments* (Cambridge University Press, 2017).

Chapter Eight: Bringing the Shy People Out

1. Alice Siu, "Deliberation and the Challenge of Inequality," *Daedalus* 146, no. 3 (2017): 119–28, doi.org/10.1162/DAED_a_00451.

2. Jane Mansbridge, "Deliberative Polling as the Gold Standard," *The Good Society* 19, no. 1 (2010): 55–62, doi.org/10.5325/goodsociety.19.1.0055.

3. "'Race' Out, Gender Equality In as France Updates Constitution," France 24, June 28, 2018, france24.com/en/20180628-race-out-gender-equality-france -updates-constitution.

4. And, as if the story could not get any more French, this was revealed by Hollande's disgruntled ex-lover after he left her for the woman he was cheating on her with while he was still in office: "'Sans dents': Valérie Trierweiler dévoile un SMS de François Hollande," *Le Parisien*, October 12, 2016, leparisien.fr/laparisienne/people/sans-dents-valerie-trierweiler-devoile -un-sms-de-francois-hollande-12-10-2016-6197907.php.

5. See the brilliant analysis of observer Hugh Pope: "Not a Big Reader? No Problem: How Graphic Artists Facilitate Deliberative Democracy," DemocracyNext, March 7, 2023, demnext.substack.com/p/not-a-big-reader -no-problem-how-graphic.

6. *Rapport de la Convention sur la fin de vie*, CESE, April 2023, convention citoyennesurlafindevie.lecese.fr/sites/cfv/files/CCFV_Rapportfinal.pdf.

7. For accuracy, I just want to note that the actual number was 76 percent.

8. I want to commend my undergraduate student Miguel Von Vedak for unearthing these important findings in his research on the French Citizens' Convention on the End of Life.

9. These comments were publicly made during the conference Governing Citizens' Assemblies, held at Yale University on February 28, 2024.

10. Christiane Rafidinarivo, "Le tirage au sort fait-il justice épistémique? Le cas des citoyens ultramarins de la Convention citoyenne pour le climat," in Grégoire Molinatti, Christiane Rafidinarivo, and Bernard Idelson, eds., *Démocratisation de la démocratie: mouvements sociaux, institutionnalisations citoyennes et mobilisations numériques* (Presses Universitaires Indianocéaniques, 2023), 177–220.

11. Léa Warrin, "'Abandonnés dans les mains du Seigneur': en outre-mer, coutumes et religion au cœur du débat sur la fin de vie," *Le Figaro*, August 9, 2023,

lefigaro.fr/actualite-france/abandonnes-dans-les-mains-du-seigneur
-en-outre-mer-coutumes-et-religion-au-coeur-du-debat-sur-la-fin-de-vie
-20230809.

Chapter Nine: How to Be a Jolly Hostess

1. See Nicole Curato et al., "Global Assembly on the Climate and Ecological Crisis Evaluation Report," University of Canberra, June 2023: https://researchprofiles.canberra.edu.au/en/publications/global-assembly-on-the-climate-and-ecological-crisis-evaluation-r.

2. This inclusiveness by association presents some trade-offs, of course, one being that the representativeness of the sample is certainly affected, as is the principle of political equality. But based on the principle of trust further delineated later in the chapter, we should assume that the option of bringing a friend will be used by only the few people who actually need it, thus not distorting the random sample and political equality beyond reason.

3. In that particular case, a possible (admittedly costly) solution would have been to install wood panels or curtains and rugs so that people could hear one another better. Movable partitions were introduced to create more intimate settings for small group meetings, but that hardly took care of the acoustic problem. Another problem with such grand and dated public buildings is their poor insulation. We had to give up meeting in the hypostyle room in January and February not just because of the acoustics but because people were getting sick from sitting for hours on end with icy drafts coming through the large single-pane windows. Somehow the view of the Eiffel Tower did not suffice to keep people warm and cozy.

4. You'd think this goes without saying, but the Citizens' Convention for Climate was quite inhumane in the amount of work it required of participants, who complained of feeling pressed like lemons. The second convention paced things more appropriately, by starting at later times, finishing earlier, and planning for longer lunch and coffee breaks—to the point that some people ended up asking for shorter breaks to get more work done. There are no scientific rules, of course, and that is why it is imperative to adjust the schedule and timing to the expressed needs of the citizens (see the point about co-responsibility and sharing power later in the chapter).

5. The first version of the charter as drafted by CESE bureaucrats was thus schoolmarmish and threatening, treating citizens like schoolchildren. A

similar distrust was manifested by some CESE Cerberus toward a hapless documentary maker from the Czech Republic, who was locked up for forty-five minutes in a nearby office because she had dared to ask if she could film the first hours of the convention.

6. One journalist who was working on a book was allowed to take notes, but with the explicit agreement that she couldn't voice an opinion or report on anything that was happening at those meetings until way after the convention was over. I'm not aware that she ended up publishing anything.

7. In fact, the researchers proved quite crucial to our own progress and learning curve. It was Chloé Santoro, then a PhD student, who pointed out the problem with wrongly weighted votes in session 8. Those who observed the governance committee's meetings were also eager to share their opinions in a helpful but nonjudgmental way. It seemed to me that even as they strove for objectivity, researchers also became invested, as citizens, in the success of the overall process.

8. David M. Farrell and Jane Suiter, *Reimagining Democracy: Lessons in Deliberative Democracy from the Irish Front Line* (Cornell University Press, 2019), 46.

Chapter Ten: Designing for All

1. Of course, one reading of that evidence is that neoliberalism is much more efficient when it takes the appearance of a boho coffee shop, easing individuals' painful transitions between various economic positions, but doing nothing to empower them as more than cogs in the capitalist system. In that sense, the American and British designs, in all their ugliness and cold-as-fish reality, are simply more honest. But from a less-cynical perspective, the analysis also shows that design matters and should be used, in authentic democracies, to improve the nature of our civic interactions, considering and being forgiving of the emotional vulnerability of each of us.

2. Nicole Doerr, *Political Translation: How Social Movement Democracies Survive* (Cambridge University Press, 2018).

3. Yet I'm sure I did the right thing. The best proof of it is that Gaston, who had rather ignored me until then, started to treat me much more nicely when we saw each other next. It's as if I had earned his respect. That said, I also remember how impossible it is to fight back when you are not on the level of such people. On that committee, I was his peer, and he could hear and process criticism only from a peer. From anyone else, he would have perceived the comment as rude and a challenge to his authority

(perhaps how the eighty-year-old interpreted my question in the earlier incident).

Chapter Eleven: The Future of Democracy, and How to Get There Fast

1. Alexander Guerrero, *Lottocracy: Democracy Without Elections* (Oxford University Press, 2024).

2. John Gastil and Erik Olin Wright, *Legislature by Lot: Transformative Designs for Deliberative Governance* (Verso, 2019).

3. Isabelle Ferreras, Julie Battilana, and Dominique Méda, *Democratize Work: The Case for Reorganizing the Economy* (University of Chicago Press, 2022).

4. Luigi Zingales, Oliver Hart, and Hélène E. Landemore, "How to Implement Shareholder Democracy," George J. Stigler Center for the Study of the Economy & the State Working Paper No. 350, December 2, 2024, papers .ssrn.com/sol3/papers.cfm?abstract_id=5039736.

5. Maurice Pope, "A Democratic Utopia," *The Keys to Democracy: Sortition as a New Model for Citizen Power* (Imprint Academic, 2023).

6. "Launching a First-of-Its-Kind Civic Assembly in Deschutes County, Oregon, USA," DemocracyNext, July 11, 2024, demnext.substack.com/p/launching -a-first-of-its-kind-civic.

7. Min Reuchamps, "Belgium's Experiment in Permanent Forms of Deliberative Democracy," ConstitutionNet, January 17, 2020, constitutionnet.org /news/belgiums-experiment-permanent-forms-deliberative-democracy.

8. See comparative graph on page 315 of David Talukder and Jean-Benoit Pilet, "Citizens' Support for Citizens' Assemblies," in Min Reuchamps, Julien Vrydagh, and Yanina Welp, eds., *De Gruyter Handbook of Citizens' Assemblies* (De Gruyter, 2023), https://library.oapen.org/bitstream/handle /20.500.12657/63773/9783110758269.pdf?sequence=1.

9. But to get people enthused about political reforms, they need to speak to their needs and vital interests. The 2004 British Columbia Citizens' Assembly did not manage to keep its momentum going around a much-needed electoral reform probably because the topic was too technical and not all that inspiring—or rather, mostly vital and inspiring to political parties themselves, which prodded their electorate to vote in the parties' interests. Neither did the Icelandic movement for a new constitution, once it became clear that the moment of crisis had passed and nothing existential was at stake in replacing an old but functional document with a new one, even if it was

probably better on the whole. By contrast, the Irish citizens' assemblies and the French citizens' conventions touched on issues at the heart of social debates in both countries at the time: fundamental rights (marriage and abortion) in the Irish case, climate justice and end-of-life issues in the French one.

10. John Thornhill, "Designing Democracy on Mars Can Improve How It Works on Earth," *Financial Times*, May 27, 2021, ft.com/content/f0d95e10 -ca83-47f4-9c06-3eab19261ab4.

11. Malcolm Gladwell discussed this experiment on his podcast. Malcolm Gladwell, host, "The Powerball Revolution," *Revisionist History*, season 5, episode 3, February 7, 2020, pushkin.fm/podcasts/revisionist-history/the -powerball-revolution.

Index